Yes We Have No

Yes We Have No

ADVENTURES IN THE OTHER ENGLAND

NIK COHN

ALFRED A. KNOPF

NEW YORK ■ 1999

THIS IS A BORZOI BOOK
PUBLISHED BY ALFRED A. KNOPF, INC.

Copyright © 1999 by Nik Cohn
All rights reserved under International and Pan-American
Copyright Conventions. Published in the United States by
Alfred A. Knopf, Inc., New York, and published in Canada
by Random House of Canada Limited, Toronto. Distributed
by Random House, Inc., New York.

www.randomhouse.com

Originally published in Great Britain by
Secker & Warburg, London.

Knopf, Borzoi Books, and the colophon are registered
trademarks of Random House, Inc.

Some of the material in this book appeared, in different
form, in the *Weekend Guardian* magazine, *The Sunday Times*
(London), and the *Evening Standard* magazine.

Library of Congress Cataloging-in-Publication Data
Cohn, Nik.
Yes we have no : adventures in the other England /
Nik Cohn. — 1st American ed.
p.   cm.
"Originally published in Great Britain by Secker & Warburg,
London"—T.p. verso.
ISBN 0-394-56870-2 (alk. paper)
1. England—Social life and customs—20th century.
2. Popular culture—England—History—20th century.
3. Subculture—England—History—20th century.   I. Title.
DA589.4.C64   1999
306'.0942'09049—dc21   99-15607   CIP

Manufactured in the United States of America
First American Edition

306. 0942
C

For Lucy Cohn and for Mary C

For many years I've owned a house in north-east Hertfordshire. The village it belongs to has some thirty homes, the whole parish perhaps a hundred. For me, it has been the land that time forgot.

The sense of displacement begins with its physical setting. To get there from London, you catch a train to Stevenage, drive past miles of little brick boxes in rows, through a dormitory town, along a nondescript country road with dusty hedges and a reek of petrol fumes, and up a narrow lane. Another couple of miles, and the lane starts to rise. A long, steep hill, and you turn a blind corner. Around the corner lies Brigadoon.

Parish church, village green, thatched cottages, wishing-well, duck-pond, lych-gate, pub—not an element is missing. The feeling of unreality, of having blundered onto a movie set, is so strong that many people, the first time I take them there, tend to burst out laughing, like the victims of a magician's trick.

I was twenty-three when I moved there. I had just written a book on Rock & Roll, which gave me my first solid lump of money, and I plunked it all down, every penny, on a seventeenth-century cottage. Three cottages joined together, in fact, without proper heating, riddled with damp and worm, but mine, all mine.

There was an apple orchard out back, and a rotating summerhouse, and an evil old sofa on the porch, with broken springs and spilling guts, too disreputable to be allowed indoors. The morning I took possession, I dumped my bags on the lawn and hit that sofa in a running belly-flop. I had found my safe house.

It was a bolthole I badly needed. I'd been living in England since the age of fifteen, but it still seemed a foreign country to me, a place where I didn't fit, and could never be fully at ease.

On the surface, this didn't make sense—I was London-born, my father was English, I had an English voice and English roots. As a child, growing up in Northern Ireland, I never doubted that England was where I truly belonged. Derry, the town of my raising, seemed no more than a detour. At night, my father used to walk me along by its docks and weave elaborate schemes of escape. He spoke of his own childhood; of his school in Norfolk, of long country walks in winter, of English villages and parish churches, English rituals, English manners. His memories were not all happy; far from it. But there was an inwardness about his voice, a sense of displacement that I took for yearning, and this yearning became my own.

The England I imagined then was a sanctuary. But that was not the country I found when I actually moved there, in my mid-teens. Instead of welcoming me home with brass bands, its handshake was cold and distant. Not that you could blame it, exactly. I was riotous and disordered, all surface arrogance and inner dreads. What I craved, above all things, was response. And England gave me none. Just looked me up, looked me down, and sniffed.

The indifference enraged me. There was a massive assurance about England then, at the start of the sixties. The war might be over, but its afterglow remained. People still believed that honest British sweat and guts would always get the best of foreign wiles; still believed, by and large, in their own divine right. *Look Back in Anger* and the Angries were isolated sandstorms. Away from Soho and a few other bohemian outposts, there was a world of Horlicks and tea cosies, *Dixon of Dock Green,* Gilbert Harding and bowling greens; a nation of sensible shoes.

Certain key words—sportsmanship, decency, tolerance, manners—kept recurring, to be pulled out and paraded whenever the subject of Englishness cropped up.

The English Way of Life—that was the magic phrase. But there was no need for bragging; not then. One of my first employers, a travel agent with a ginger moustache and a militaristic strut, who wished to be addressed as major, liked to say: "An Englishman never claims to be best. Merely knowing it suffices."

The smugness was suffocating. When I went into the world, a young romantic abroad, I sought out rebels and misfits. My mentors were mostly fringe dwellers: Rockers, Beats, market people, all-in wrestlers, gays and a few criminals. Compulsive storytellers, all of them; mythologisers like myself. When I started to write, at seventeen, my central theme was buried beauty.

Then something odd happened—the rebels and misfits became fashionable. Dick Rowe, the man who turned down the Beatles at Decca records, inadvertently opened the floodgates for uppity young pups of all persuasions. Suddenly, employers started falling over themselves to sign up new blood. Better to get landed with a tribe of no-talent bums, whole regiments of degenerates and freaks, than let the next John Lennon or Joe Orton go by unclaimed.

I was one of those who reaped the harvest. My first attempt at a novel was published without delay; magazines and TV shows lined up for interviews. I appeared in a book called *The Young Meteors,* and wore the shades to prove it. Still, I knew I was only fashion. The Sunday supplements might rave on about Swinging London but all that meant, as I knew from my royalty statements, was half a dozen clubs and trattorias, maybe five thousand souls all told. A splashy party, fun while it lasted, but wicked for longevity. Within five years, it had chewed me up and spat me out.

That was when I came to this village. A friend had mentioned the place, thinking it might make a suitable hideout, so I took a day off from killing myself and headed up the A1. Turned the blind corner at the top of the hill, and fell into my childhood vision—the lost world my father had drawn for me, walking the Derry docks all those nights.

Nothing could touch me here, I felt. And nothing ever did. In the whole spinning world, it seemed, the village alone kept still. It was a geographical freak of sorts, barely an hour from the West End, yet locked in its own universe, entirely untouched by events outside. Houses stood till they fell down, and were rarely replaced when they did; humans, likewise. Bert Oakley, the old man who trimmed my hedge, recalled going up to Barnet as a boy, to help with the harvesting. Many in the village thought of this as globe-trotting.

The one divergence from complete timelessness was the fact that the squire, Edward Carter, no longer lived in the Jacobean manor house. Unwise in his investments, he'd been forced to sell up and now lived with his two sisters in a wooden, chalet-style bungalow, a few yards from the gates of the lands he had once owned. He was still the dominant figure in the parish, gently mocked but also profoundly loved, with his rheumy eye and soup-strainer moustache, his pink gins, and his tropical sun-hat, but his family home had passed to incomers. A succession of new owners came and went; a banker, a stockbroker, a captain of industry. None of them were much seen about the village, and they remained shadowy in my mind.

Somewhere around 1990, though, I began to notice a new face in the pub—a strapping young woman, loud and flashy, with a rich hippie's taste in kaftans and ethnic jewellery. She was the newest daughter of the manor, I was told. Her father was never at home, so she had the place to herself. Just her, and her infant child, and her boyfriend, who wrote jingles for TV commercials.

I'll call the woman Susan, the boyfriend Jude. In time, we were introduced and had a drink in the beer garden. It was a midsummer evening, one of those dusks when the light never dies. Susan talked and laughed freely, but Jude, sour and sallow, seemed to be brooding. His narrow mouth was set in a pre-packaged Rock & Roll sneer, which hardened and tightened when anyone spoke to him. I asked him what jingles he'd written. "Fairy Snow," Jude muttered. He made it sound like Beethoven's Ninth.

When he took himself off to the Gents, Susan ticked me off for being too direct. I must understand that Jude was an artist; his music was his life. "He was born on a housing estate. Somewhere in Sheffield, you know," she told me, sounding faintly awestruck, as if South Yorks was the Dzanga-Sangha rainforest. Everything he'd achieved had been won by bitter struggle and sometimes this made him brittle, quick to take offence. "He lives on his nerves," she explained.

Perhaps that's why he wouldn't meet my eyes. Or anyone else's, come to that. Edward Carter, the squire, passed by and wished us a good evening, but Jude only grunted. When Susan invited me back to the manor for a glass of wine, he looked disgusted. His pint was still full. "Tell the landlord I'm taking this home," he commanded, as I went to return my own glass. "Tell him yourself," I replied. Words that caused Susan to draw in her breath and stare at me with tragic eyes, a fifteen-stone Bambi in batik and turquoise bracelets.

I had never been to the manor before, merely glimpsed its far turrets through the trees, from the footpaths that ringed the estate. We passed through the gate, down a long drive lined with chestnut trees and sycamores, and emerged into a wide space of barbered lawn. Peacocks strolled on the grass, tail-feathers ablaze in the dying light. There was a moat.

Susan led me along a broad stone hall. The walls were covered with day-glo murals, all fairies and trolls and leering satyrs. "I painted them myself," she said. Then we were in the drawing-room, sipping Pouilly Fuissé. But Jude was no longer with us. At some point between the moat and the ice bucket, he had vanished upstairs to his studio. Soon a synthesiser began to thunder out dark organ chords above our heads; howling, storm-swept washes of sound. "I think you've upset him," Susan said.

She stared wretchedly through the French windows at the peacocks, then excused herself and lumbered off. For a few moments, the organ chords died away, only to surge up again, more tortured than ever. Beneath the Walpurgisnacht thrashings, I recognised the theme from an advert for some Italian sports car: a twisting cliff road, sparkling blue waters far below, and a leggy lovely at the wheel, her long blonde hair flying free. I drank my wine, and Susan crept back, stricken. "You'll have to leave," she said, regretful but firm, and showed me the door.

On my way back to the cottage, I passed Edward Carter. He was driving home from the pub in his ancient Ford, barely outspeeding a strolling pheasant. As we crossed, he doffed his sun-hat, and out of nowhere, for no conscious reason, I started humming "Yes We Have No Bananas."

For the last twenty years, I'd seen little of mainstream England. As a teenager, I had travelled it extensively; spent three years in Newcastle, explored Yorkshire and East Anglia, done time in Bristol and Brighton, on Merseyside, in the Midlands. That was in another age, though, and I'd been another person. It was only when the shifting tides began to creep into my backyard that I had any urge to go exploring again.

In the past, as I've said, the village had been immune. No matter how the world outside might flail and implode, cataclysm here still meant a dead horse, a slate roof blown off in a storm, a sour barrel of Abbot Ale.

In the nineties, though, time at last got to work. Most of the farmers I had known were now decrepit or dying. Their replacements didn't speak of farming, but agronomy. Strictly speaking, farmers no longer existed. These days they were "small businessmen in the rural community."

The pig man across the road from me, who ceremonially bathed and changed his clothes every Boxing Day without fail, gave way to a commercial builder, whose work was in Stevenage. The painted lady next door—

daughter of an Anglo-Irish colonel, pre-war starlet, and inveterate swigger of double whiskies for breakfast—died, and was replaced by a young blood from Essex with a Porsche. Edward Carter died, too. The pub was refurbished and began to concentrate on food. Welly boots were no longer allowed within its doors. Germans and Scandinavians appeared in the beer garden. The village street no longer smelled of pig.

Even my own cottage was not sacrosanct. My parents had moved in, and I became a guest. Wall-to-wall carpeting, central heating, a shower—the place was hard to recognise. Instead of the sofa on the back porch, there were now smart garden chairs. The grass was freshly mowed, the orchard jungle tamed. I felt a stranger there.

An essential balance had been shattered. My nature has always swung violently between two extremes—the need to combust, and the need for shelter, with virtually no middle ground. When I thought of England, I pictured the skull of Professor Brainstawm, the mad inventor in the old Heath Robinson books, with two scanty frizzes of hair—one my village and the safe world it stood for, the other the killing floors of excess—on either side of a massive bald pate, faintly clammy to the touch. Now the first had withered, and the second had lost its allure. I was flushed from cover.

So I went back to travelling.

I retraced the steps of my early journeys. Just for a few days, at first; then for weeks and months. I started in London and worked my way slowly outwards, and when I'd revisited everywhere I knew, I struck out into the uncharted. I kept meeting people who knew other people, who knew other people in turn, until I'd built up a network, ramshackle but labyrinthine, that extended all over the country. Then I went back to the beginning. Took one last, deep breath. And started all over again.

The impact was overwhelming. Instead of the country I thought I knew, as welcoming as a basinful of cold porridge, I found a new land, full of wonders.

Introduction

This wasn't at all what I'd expected. Before I set out on my wanderings, I'd waded through a stack of recommended verbiage—political treatises, economic surveys, bright young novels—and the consensus seemed to be that England was a wreck. It had not only lost its power, but its dignity, its honour, and all pretence to morality. The prevailing tone was summed up in a sub-headline to a Martin Amis short story: *Bad food, bad breath, bad sex, bad health, and really bad politics. It's England, innit?*

No less than sixty per cent of the populace, I read, were struggling for survival. A third of these had fallen off the cliff altogether, a third were barely managing to cling on, and the last third were on shifting ground. If *Granta* was to be believed, there wasn't much left to do but sprinkle the ashes. "Is this a nation, a way of life, saying farewell to itself?" its cover asked.

The brief answer was yes. The old England was indeed dead or dying. Stability was gone; so was the sense of certainty. Despite the bromides of Tony Blair and his Cool Britannia cheerleaders, this was now a land full of trouble, violent and dispossessed, in some places close to anarchy.

And against all that, there was what? Passion, energy, humour, rage. The scattered outsiders I'd found on my first travels, back in the sixties, had swelled into an army. Not being an economist, I couldn't put a firm percentage on their number, but they seemed a mighty power to me. A whole country within a country, many millions strong. The jobless, the homeless, the fucked. The vast masses banged up in tower blocks and housing estates. Miners and dockers and steelworkers who would never work again, and school-leavers who would never work at all. Caribbeans and Irish, Africans and East Europeans, and their children, British-born, who were the new English. Travellers and techno freaks, the Tribal Nation. Born-agains, bikers, fetishists, faith healers, visionaries, squatters, druggies, lunatics and street heroes. Many of them were lost, and many would never be found. But they were full of sap, even so; wild and bursting with the stuff. This other England, unlike the older model, was permanently on heat.

One night in Sheffield, I lay awake in a B&B listening to the karaoke coming from the bar, while trying to read an article in an old magazine I'd found by the bed. The article bemoaned England's state—the loss of standards, the worship of false idols. At the end, as such jeremiads often do, it quoted Yeats' "Second Coming": "The blood-dimmed tide is loosed . . . / And what rough beast, its hour come round at last, / Slouches towards Bethlehem to be born?"

A fair enough question, I thought. But why should I complain? The Rough Beasts have always been my band.

In a pub in Notting Hill, I met a man who said: "I don't call this the world any more, I call it the whirl, and you have to keep whirling with it, otherwise you fall off, then you're dead."

RIOTOUS
ASSEMBLY

I WAS SITTING in an English garden. It was a hot and sticky afternoon, one of the first sweaty days of summer. Robin had been showing me his stamp collection indoors, and afterwards there was tea on the lawn. Shortbread, cream cakes, home-baked scones. An old blind spaniel called Duffer sat at our feet, feebly snouting at a stick. "Poor old boy, he's past his sell-by date. Glue-factory time for Duffer," Robin said, and everyone laughed.

China tea with lemon and honey. The pinks and sweet williams were in full blossom, but the peonies were almost done for. At every breath of a breeze, another fat red petal detached itself, drifting down. "Gardens are such a heartbreak, don't you find?" Alice said. She was pale and delicate-looking, and she favoured wispy clothes that drooped. "Roses are the worst," she confided, drooping too. Then her two sons came home from school, strapping pink boys in cricket whites, ravening for chocolate éclairs. They talked about leg-breaks; and Spencer, the games' master, who had a prosthetic hand; and Potter, whose mother had died. "I wonder what it's like, having someone die," the oldest boy said. "Oh, don't," said Alice. "Not at tea."

Fed and full, we drowsed in striped deck chairs. Tits and finches pecked for worms, the neighbour's cat kept watch from the fence and Robin discoursed on his compost heap. "I'm a horseshit man myself, always have been," he said. "Manure," said Alice, and the spaniel rose up to relieve himself. His eyes were milk-white, and he blundered into his master's legs. "Poor old Duffer," said Robin. "Who's a dead dog, then?"

In the evening, I caught the train back to London. Passing through Hertfordshire, through fields full of rape and ripening grain, I started to read *The State We're In,* Will Hutton's book on contemporary Britain. "The British are accustomed to success," it began. "This is the world's oldest democracy. Britain built an empire, launched the Industrial Revolution and was on the winning side in the twentieth century's two world wars. The British believe that their civilisation is admired all over the world. A Briton does not boast openly, but is possessed of an inner faith that he or she is special."

When I arrived at King's Cross, the station was swarming with football fans. England was playing Scotland the next night, and the fans were celebrating in advance. Drinking, chanting, waving Union Jacks, they formed a solid wall.

I pass through them.

Euston Road is in flames. One whole section—Barclays Bank, McDonald's, the amusement arcade where teenage runaways gather, the Greek-Cypriot greasy spoon—has vanished completely, swallowed up by smoke, and the blaze is spreading fast. A series of flashes go off, one, two, three, racing down the street as if whipped by a gale-force wind. But what wind? The city air is heavy and still. That is odd. And so is something else. Each time a new flash explodes, the one behind it begins to gutter and die.

An image of surfing comes to my mind. As if the flames ride a wave, at one moment cresting high and wild, then swooping into a deep hollow, gone from sight, only to spring up redoubled.

What style of inferno is this? "Petrol poppers," I'm told. A skullhead, his face daubed red and white like a St. George's flag, says they're all the rage. Miniature incendiary devices, no larger than a ping-pong ball, you can buy them by the dozen.

This is the routine: you load up with PPs, then you and your mates steal a car and you head for the West End. Any spot will do, so long as it's crowded. A station, or a club, or a cinema queue; outside a football stadium is best of all. Once you've picked out your venue, you circle in traffic, jockeying for position, until you get yourself slotted, right up front at a red light. Then, first flash of amber, you take off. Put the pedal to the metal and keep it there, hard down, while your mates lean out the windows and let the poppers fly.

"Never fails to make an impression," the skullhead says. Old ladies out shopping and winos sleeping in doorways are especially susceptible. The only pity of it is, you can't stick around to admire your handiwork, you're already half a mile down the road, history, you never get to enjoy the full show.

The fire is dying as he speaks. Within a few seconds, all that remains of the blanketing smoke, the wild jets of flame, are a few black scars on the pavement.

Across the street, outside Barclay's Bank, a man in a plastic raincoat has taken a direct hit. He is still smouldering.

The only way to reach him, short of vaulting the iron barriers and charging blindly between the buses, is via the underpass. That means joining up with the football fans, who've formed a conga line and are shuffling towards Gray's Inn Road, singing "Three Lions on a Shirt" as they go. So we make our way, gut to arse, through the bowels of King's Cross and up again into the charred night air.

The man in the raincoat has been brought under control. A goodly stout woman in lace-up shoes is standing over him where he sprawls, beating at the smoke with a rolled-up *Evening Standard.* You'd think the man is a carpet, but he makes no objection. On the contrary, he relishes the attention. His face is upraised towards the blows and a shy smile gleams through the wild tangle of his hair and beard. "You're nice. You are a very nice lady," he says. Flakes of burned newspaper detach themselves from his coat, swirling upwards towards the street lamps. "You've got lovely teeth," he says.

Picking up his bottle of Turbo, he checks its level, then checks out his own person, fore and aft. "You've put me out," he judges, and hauls himself upright. When he shakes himself down, a last puff of smoke billows from the depths of his coat; it makes him look like an amateur magician. "I'm sweet," he says.

Round the corner on Caledonian Road, two bouncers block the door of the Flying Scotsman. A taxi pulls up and four Yorkshire businessmen pile out. "This here's the shit end of town, lads," announces their leader, a blazered, broken-nosed bravo built like a second-row rugby forward. "Follow me." So they do, and so do I.

Past the bouncers, we push down a narrow passage filled with women, leading to a small dark room filled with men. Mariah Carey's "Dreamlover" is playing and a girl on all-fours crawls nude across a narrow stage. Pasty-fleshed, pendulous, she sports a number of spangled stickers on her thighs and upper arms, but they fail to hide the bruises. "It doesn't get ranker than this," the second-row forward crows. "Pints all round, lads?"

A small section of the bar is opened to the pavement. Three stools are unoccupied, but on the fourth sits a man with a gold bracelet on one wrist.

The bracelet apart, he's dressed in standard Britwear—a white tracksuit with sky-blue hoops, a nose-stud and trainers—but their immaculate cleanness and the careless elegance with which he wears them sets him apart. The way he lounges, self-consciously languid, he might be posing for a fashion shoot: a street-sharp West Indian, somewhere in his late twenties, rangy and loose-limbed, with lazy eyes that miss nothing.

There is a definite presence about this man, a built-in sense of authority, verging on contempt. First, he looks me over, measuring, and then he looks across the street, at the football fans with their tattoos and Union Jacks, at the popper-scarred pavements, the last commuters scurrying towards Thameslink, the Trotskyite bookseller putting up his shutters, the elderly Italians outside Il Due di Coppi, the Aussies in their shorts and muscle shirts heading for the Craic House, the Africans and Arabs, the Turks, the Eastern Europeans: "Welcome to the republic," he says.

THE WEST INDIAN's name is Laurence, and our meeting is not accidental. I've heard about him in advance from an Irish street-poet who lives in Somers Town and wanders over to King's Cross when he feels the need for damage.

If I mean to spend time in the Cross, Laurence is the man to show me around. "He's a mottled bird," the poet tells me. "A bit of a philosopher, a bit of a hustler. A bit of a bastard at times. But he has some sound ideas."

Laurence himself seems happy to oblige. It has been a lost day for him, and he could do with the exercise.

He's been down at the magistrate's court in Gray's Inn Road. Nothing serious, just the usual police harassment, but he was kept waiting till mid-afternoon, and when his case was finally called, he was only in the dock half a minute. His file had been mislaid; the law wasn't ready to proceed. Now he'll have to go back in six weeks, and be given the same runaround all over again. The whole thing is a travesty. "A man can get old young," he says.

If he's raging, he holds it inside. It takes more than a rabble of flatfoots to ruffle his elegance, or the air of ironic detachment that he wears like a second skin. "No probs," he says. It sounds a well-worn motto.

The only way to cope is to turn the aggravation to your own advantage. "Madness," Laurence says, fiddling with his bracelet. "I'm mad, you're worse, the whole world's lost its marbles. The only thing is, how do you handle it?

Do you try to cover it up, or do you get behind it? Feed the craziness? Make it big and strong?"

I have only been with him a few minutes, but the theme—In Praise of Lunacy—is already familiar. As we lounge outside the Flying Scot, he points out a girl striding down the street in an England football shirt and boots. The whole of her face is tattooed with a spider's web. "Stark-staring," Laurence says. "I love her."

Is she a prostitute? "She has that distinction, yes." Not that he's in the business himself; not any more. Running girls is hard fucking work. Drug habits, sick punters and sicker cops. Not to mention rival pimps. "They take umbrage, and you take stitches." He draws back his shirt collar to display a jagged purple scar on his throat. "It's no tea party, believe me."

The Flying Scot is the first stop on his night's rounds. A girl who owes him money is supposed to meet him here, but she must have a customer or else she's too wasted to haul her arse out of bed. "People can be very disappointing at times, don't you find? They can really challenge your faith," Laurence says, though he doesn't act much surprised.

A pneumatic redhead with an overbite and a sulky cat's face sneaks up behind him, drapes her breasts around his shoulders like water wings, then disappears inside the pub. "Another nutter," he says serenely, and drains his glass. We move on to the betting shop on Pentonville Road, then a pub in Swinton Street. I ask Laurence how he earns his living. "Talent management," he replies, silky smooth. "I am a facilitator."

By now, I've begun to work out the pattern. Ask questions, and all you get is flimflam. So I try staring out the pub window. The streets are still swarming with football fans, dodging in and out of traffic, waving their Union Jacks. "I make things happen," Laurence says.

He was born and raised in Jamaica, in a village outside May Pen. His father, a chartered accountant, was already in England, and his mother was a semi-invalid, so Laurence and his three sisters were mostly brought up by their Aunt Callie. "A mighty woman, very God-fearing. Most of our neighbours were Coptics or Cuminas, heavy into the ancestor worship, but she was staunch Anglican. To her, England was still the mother country."

Aunt Callie's England was a country of wisdom and grace, ruled by a storybook queen. "She had all these souvenirs of coronations and royal weddings, ashtrays and old chipped teacups, going back to Edward the Seventh. Every day she sat in her kitchen, and when I got back from school, she'd let me sit in her lap. She had a goitre on her neck. I would have killed to touch it."

When his father sent tickets for his mother and sisters and him, and he was transplanted to Streatham, he was eight years old, and it felt like falling through a trapdoor.

What he remembers most clearly about that first winter day is the greyness. "Grey concrete, grey clothes, grey air." His father was a skinny little man with faded skin and a suit too big for his bones. "He looked grubby somehow, I didn't want him touching me." They sat in a room above a terrace street, making conversation. His mother kept bursting into tears. Embarrassed, Laurence went to look out of the bay window. "It was the middle of the day, and all I could see was the dark."

In the evening his father took him for a stroll down the High Street to fetch a takeaway curry. On their way back, they passed a pub and a bunch of skinheads came running out. "National Front—boots and braces, swastika tattoos." One of them barged into his father and the curry went flying. Laurence saw his father, this old feeble man, down on hands and knees, groping for his glasses. There was chicken and rice and chapatis all over the pavement and the skinheads were roaring away up the street, while music blasted inside the bright pub. "'Shake Me, Wake Me,' I still remember the tune." His father was making a choking noise, as if he'd got a bone stuck in his throat. Clumps of curry were stuck to his trousers and his suede shoes. "Poor bastard, I despised him."

This came as a shock to him. "Aunt Callie always taught us that my father had sacrificed his own happiness and gone off to make the family fortune, so we would never want." But there must be a mistake. How could this mess at his feet be that same shining hero? "To me, he was an impostor. From the moment the skinheads ran him over and he didn't strike them dead, I didn't have a dad."

The skinheads were the heroes here. "They blew me away." They had energy and power and style. They made noise in this muffled land, splashed colour on the greyness. "When we got home and the old man was explaining to my mother, he called them a gang of roaring boys. I thought, Right, roaring boys—I could use some of that myself."

Retelling the story now in the pub, he tests me for disbelief. "You think I'm embellishing, don't you? You can't picture a boy of eight being so sorted, so certain in himself." He's drinking brandy and lemonade; he draws a restless squiggle in the slop marks left by his glass. "I was born certain," he says.

Slippery, too. "Aunt Callie used to call it my slyness, but it's just common sense. You need to jive to thrive."

So he never betrayed his feelings. As far as his family knew, he was a dutiful, hard-working son, not a thought of rebellion in him. Education was his father's religion, and Laurence developed into an ace student. "I won prizes every year—physics, algebra, any problem with figures was child's play. When all the other lads in my year were out screwing anything with a pulse, I was locked up with my homework. I didn't even have a girlfriend, if you can believe that. I was a virgin at fifteen."

His sisters thought he was soft but that didn't bother him. "Well, I'm a Gemini, aren't I? There's two of me at all times." While everyone was distracted by his front— the scholar, the conformist, the passionate virgin—his other self was left free to ramble. "I could go where I wanted, do anything I fancied, and no one suspected. I was Jekyll and Hyde with a permanent tan."

He started roaming London. He went down to the West End, hung out in Leicester Square, sampled sex shows in Soho, got a blow job in a gay bar, tried his first pipe of crack. Wandering at random, he talked to anyone who would talk to him—junkies, alkies, street philosophers, preachers, punks—and they opened up horizons that he'd never imagined. "I jumped into another world."

This world he now calls the republic.

He describes it as an independent state, peopled by all those who live in England, but not by Englishness: "Anyone who's not in the Anglo Club."

"Outsiders, you mean?"

"Insiders."

Not that all republicans see eye to eye. "It's like any other state, full of haters. Half of them would like nothing better than to see me wiped out." Still, they do have one thing in common: the Anglo Club despises them all. At the first whiff of the republic, out comes The Look.

What look?

"Pie-eyed." That blank, veiled face, infinitely superior, that the Anglos put on whenever they sense attack or the presence of a intruder: "Saintly sufferance."

It was The Look that brought him close to his father, for the first and only time. To Laurence, his old man had always remained a shameful weakling, while his father, having found out Laurence's double life, had come to think him depraved. "A freak, a bad seed—the first time the police came for me, all my dad said was, 'What took you so long?'"

For years, they hardly spoke. Then his father got a cancer in his bowels and went into hospital to die. Laurence, who was using a lot of drugs at the time, kept making excuses not to visit him. When he finally showed up, bunch of grapes in hand, he could hardly see the man for the tubes. All that was left was this little parcel of bones, propped up like a ventriloquist's dummy, mumbling. The nurse, a beefy pink woman, was bending over him, trying to understand what he was saying, but it was no use, she couldn't make out a word. So Laurence had a go. He leant in close, put his ear against his father's mouth. "I remember how his breath smelled—mothballs and baked beans." At first he couldn't pick up the words, then suddenly he caught on. The old man was talking Jamaican patois, like a Rasta. After all these years of acting the fastidious accountant, trying to play the English game, he'd finally reverted. "He kept repeating one word—'Bamclaaat!'" So Laurence passed it on to the nurse. "My father says you're a bumclot," he informed her. But the nurse was not ruffled. Instead of flinching or yelling, she simply pursed her lips and called up The Look. "Just like children," it said.

If it wasn't for that nurse, he might have weakened, and followed his family's blueprint. Become an economist or a numbers-cruncher, a man with a calculator, a white wife, kids the colour of weak tea and a home in Hampstead Garden Suburb. "I had the brain for it, no probs." But not the stomach.

Having left school with nine O levels and three A levels, he put in a spell at the London School of Economics. He didn't last long there, though. "They had nothing to teach me. A bunch of wankers, with their heads stuck up their sphincters." He preferred to tutor himself, take his reading where he found it. History and politics, psychology. He enjoyed chess puzzles and travellers' tales. George Orwell was a favourite. So was Nietzsche. "Men of mind," Laurence says. "I like to stretch myself."

Dropping out of the LSE, he headed back to the streets. "I threw myself into the cement mixer. Got royally fucked up." Crack and smack, an ocean of booze. He chauffeured rock groups, appeared in a few porn films. Ran in fast company, and it landed him in jail. "Just a brief holiday, to help clear my mind." Then he spent a year in Amsterdam, eight months in Tangiers and got kicked out of both. "I was a provocative fucker, what else can I say?"

Now, here he is in King's Cross, still running the

streets, but smarter, a lot more focused. "Being a loser got tired. I didn't mind the grief, but the boredom really wore me down."

He has a master plan. "I want to tap the media, republican style." He and a partner have got their hands on an early Pamela Anderson film, never seen by the general public. Well, they can't actually prove it's Pamela Anderson, not as such, but it certainly resembles her, and the picture itself is dynamite. "Graphic action; it would get a eunuch hard." All they need is a little investment capital to sharpen the visual quality, bring it up to video standard, and they're on a guaranteed winner. "Do yourself a favour, take a look," Laurence says. Gold bracelet dangling, he starts moving his glass rapidly around the tabletop, leapfrogging the sticky circles that blotch its surface. "Two thousand pounds would do," he says. "Or less."

Leaving the pub, we take a stroll through the streets behind King's Cross Station. Silent, barely lit, they seem deserted. Then a car cruises past, its headlights sweep the shadows and the walls are lined solid with waiting women. For a moment they hang fire, motionless, like so many birds on a wire. The car slows, starts to crawl, and the women rush forward into the pool of light, jabbering and pleading. Their voices skitter off the warehouse walls, across the railway tracks, getting shriller and more urgent every second, until one of them is chosen, the car pulls away again, and those left behind drift back to the dark.

Some of the girls hail Laurence as we pass. One asks him for the lend of a tenner, much to his disgust. "I haven't got time for this," he grumps, and we climb the Pentonville Road, towards the Copenhagen Street estates, where he lives. He says he could use a spliff, a little night music, but he doesn't invite me inside his flat. "The maid hasn't been," he explains, straight-faced. So I stand outside in the walkway, among the graffiti. SICKOFANS UNITE, one reads. There is a small scrub of lawn at my feet, more mud than grass. A discarded hypo has been wedged between two clods of earth, primed to stab the unwary.

When Laurence emerges, I point out the trap. "That isn't cricket," he says. Then we're off on our travels again. Back down the hill to the station, past the group of loafers outside Joe Coral's, the drinkers in the shop doorways, the woman with the wild-flame hair singing "Wannabe" and the fallen football fan, naked to the waist, stretched out on the pavement beside the Chinese Methodist Church, until we arrive at McGlynn's.

The pub itself is closed by now, but we sit down at one of the wooden benches, resting our bones and waiting for a man, a friend of Laurence's, to pick us up and take us to a party in the flats across the street. The man never comes, but it doesn't matter. The night is warm and full of echoes, and Laurence hasn't done talking.

He tells me about Jamaica, about Streatham, about Copenhagen Street; discourses at length on the republic, and Pamela Anderson's tits; sparks up spliff after spliff. The smell of hash in the heavy night air makes me drowsy and I make a mess of my notes. "I can't abide sloppiness," Laurence berates me, and walks me across Argyll Square to the Hotel Montana, where I'm staying. Two North Africans are lounging by the park railing, arguing in wailing, singsong voices. Laurence listens in for a few moments, then taps me on the shoulder, goodbye.

"Fierce dreams," he says.

ONE MORNING I read an article in *Time Out* about Odinism. This is a growing religion, apparently, and among its new adherents are a number of extreme right-wingers, formerly of the British National Party. Intrigued, I call the magazine and ask for contacts. Among the names I'm given is Mary Carson, Researcher.

When I ring her number, a deep-voiced Derry woman answers. She says she comes from Pennyburn, not a mile from my own childhood home, and she has an accent you could butter bread with. Lulled by its succulence, I form an image of red hands and muscular forearms, the type of Derry woman I recall from childhood, piling out of the linen factories at dusk or hanging up clothes in the huddled backyards, a gaggle of brawling infants at their feet.

When we meet outside a pub, though, I'm confronted by a street urchin. Mary Carson in person is tiny and crop-haired, and her clothes—boy's trousers, striped undershirt, purple boots—come straight out of *Oliver!* She hardly looks fit to be let out alone.

We sit upstairs on a flat metal roof. The hot and rancid air of the night city, the chains of fairy lights in the beer garden below and the pounding bass of the pub jukebox combine to conjure up a funfair mood. Despite this, we start awkwardly. Mary Carson seems shy. She glugs fizzy water and blushes furiously. Then she fixes me in the eye. "That lager is poison. It even smells like death," she begins, then blushes again. A moment's silence, and she has another stab. "I'm thirty-three," she says, but I don't believe her; she can't be a day past eighteen. Downstairs the jukebox is playing "Smells Like Teen Spirit." "C'mere till I tell ye," Mary says. And the words start pouring out of her.

I've never heard speed-rapping like it. Derry people are known for fast, flapping mouths, but this is in a class by itself. A pure force of nature, unstoppable. Her pallid, heart-shaped face thrusts forward, as if pushing against a strong wind; her skinny child's arms start to pump. She balls her fists, punching at air, and the heels of her purple Doc Martens drum the roof, and the night turns blue with her language.

One of her back teeth has gone missing, but the tooth next to it is gold. And this seems characteristic. The world she describes is all black holes and blinding flashes, with nothing in between. Her motto? "Leap before you look."

She's new in London and its greatness still amazes her. "The first time I walked into the West End, I almost tripped over my chin." In Derry, she feels as if she knows every soul she passes—them, and their families, too. Her father is Willie Carson, the great photojournalist, whose pictures define the town, both in and out of the Troubles. The full Carson tribe, counting cousins and nieces and nephews, numbers over eighty. "I can't spit without hitting a blood relative," Mary says. But in London she's nobody; the universal stranger: "Wild free."

She's here on a mission, she says.

After she left school, love and pride in her father steered her into journalism. She became the first Catholic to work for the *Londonderry Sentinel,* then moved to Belfast, where she had a stint as a TV presenter. "I lacked focus, but. My head didn't know which way my arse was pointing." Then one night she went out with her friends Roisin and Neil, a black Englishman. A group of skinheads spotted them—two white girls, out with a black—and went apeshit. Mary told Neil to run for it and he did, but the skinheads were not to be cheated. They cornered the girls and started to beat them up. At first, Mary took it passively, trying to cover up, but the beating didn't stop. "They kept punching us and kicking us, the kicking was worst, and I knew they were going to kill us there. The boy who was over me was so gone with frenzy, his saliva dripped on my face. I saw Roisin being held with her arms behind her back while one of the skins delivered karate kicks to her stomach. And that's when I lost it. I let out this mortal scream and started lashing out. Screaming and cursing and jumping on their backs, I was possessed. Them boys must have thought they'd tackled a she-devil. Two she-devils, because Roisin was whaling them, too." Then Neil came back with help, and the skins dispersed.

Her adrenaline was pumping so hard, she couldn't feel pain. While Roisin was carted off to hospital with a suspected collapsed lung and shattered abdomen, Mary refused all help. "I just wanted to go home, get some sleep. A bit of peace." But later that night she collapsed. The skins had kicked her so hard, they'd caved in her womb.

The damage still hasn't healed. Some days the pain becomes so ferocious that she can't move for it, she just sits in a chair and shakes. Her incapacity enrages her, but she doesn't hate those who caused it. "I can't," Mary says. "I owe them too much."

In a sense, those skinheads had redirected her life. While she was laid up in hospital, she found the focus she had been wanting. "When you're stuck in bed, immobilised, you can either think or vegetate, and I'm not a fucking courgette, so I gave my mind some hard exercise. I thought a lot about the Troubles. I'd seen my town torn apart, people I loved destroyed, and the bloodshed seemed never-ending. At one time, that filled me with total blind hate. I could have joined the IRA or anything else that was going, I was that desperate to lash out. But now I felt something new. I thought about them skinhead boys and what they'd done to us, and it seemed fascinating to me. For someone, anyone, to be so filled with anger that they'd set on a total stranger and kick them inside out—what would make you act that way? What would you be thinking while you were at it? And how would you feel after? I had to know those things."

Since arriving in England a few months ago, she's been trying to track down answers. As a researcher, she's met and made friends with fetishists and pagans, hardcore neo-Nazis, techno anarchists, even skinhead Loyalist bikers—anyone she believes has things to teach her. "I tell them what I am, a Derry Taig. If they can't handle that, fine. You'd be surprised how often they can, but."

And what has she found out? For a moment, the flood dries up and she pauses to think this one over, her face scrunched tight in concentration, a schoolgirl stuck at sums. "I've found out there's a lot to find out," she says.

Immediately, the floodgates open again and a hundred more stories pour through. She tells me about her husband, who comes from a Larne family as staunchly Protestant as her own is Catholic; about her brother, who plays bass in a punk band and works for the Catholic Truth Society; about her sisters, and her cousins, and her friends, and all their love affairs; about Derry, the centre of the universe; about passion; about faith. "I'd die for those I love," she says, and makes it sound a promise.

I keep pouring her more water; she knocks the stuff back by the quart. "You're very quiet," she says at one point, as though I might have an option. But I'm quite content to be gagged. Though I've known her less than two hours, she already seems part of my life. She tells me about a friend of hers who keeps a slave, and another friend who swallowed too many airsickness tablets and saw a little man come crawling through his letter box, and yet another friend who just may save the world. Everyone she knows seems to be either a master or monster; every act is a life-and-death drama. In her refracted heat, I feel my own life intensified.

Someone in the beer garden tosses a glass. It smashes

against the wall beneath us, scattering splinters at our feet. "The natives are restless," Mary says. And so is she. The city is packed with wonders; she needs to go out rampaging. "You wouldn't believe the brilliance," she tells me, heels drumming, and then she is on her feet, whirling round the roof. I've got to see Carl Cox, she says. Until I do, I haven't lived. To witness one of his all-nighters, with ten thousand dance maniacs going out of their brains, and big Carl, the way he handles them, controlling them with his beats, bringing them up and up till the whole multitude is ready to explode, then easing them back down, then whacking them again, taking them right over the top: "Delirium!" she cries. Her purple boots scrunch wildly on the broken glass, and she acts out the madness, puffing out her cheeks and swelling her gut to mimic the massive Carl Cox, pogoing wildly from spot to spot to flesh out the crowd. "The smell of the armpits! Oh, the oxters!" she says, and she raises both her arms on high. "Heaven wouldn't smell that sweet."

The jukebox is turned off, the fairy lights are snuffed. For a split second, there's silence, and I grab at it. I try to explain the journey I'm making but the details don't seem necessary. Mary keeps nodding her head, as if she knows all this anyhow and, in any case, it doesn't matter. Something I wouldn't attempt to name has passed between us. We have become connected. When I stop blethering and the night's quiet is restored, Mary asks me no questions. She doesn't bother to enquire when the journey starts, or where it might be headed. Just turns up the soles of her boots and gives them a sharp rap. "Lead on, big lad," she says.

MOST DAYS WE arrive at McGlynn's around noon. We settle down outside, at our favoured corner bench, and loaf away the afternoon, poring over the republican tabloids. That means the *Mirror* and the *Star,* but never the *Sun,* which Mary abhors for its evil doings in Ulster, in Liverpool, and elsewhere: "I wouldn't wipe my arse with it," she says. "I've got too much respect for my shite."

These are days filled with stirring tidings. A black gunman has painted himself white to avoid detection as he robs a NatWest bank in Croydon. A sudden outbreak of trolley rage in a Wakefield supermarket has left a customer spread-eagled and bleeding over the Mr. Kipling cakes display. In Bristol a male model turned Ecstasy dealer is spared imprisonment when he bursts into tears in the dock, claiming to be too pretty for jail. And in Selly Oak, an old folks' club, hoping for a lottery handout, has changed its name to the Gay Gnomes.

McGlynn's stands at a crossroads—St. Pancras Station to the north, the Cromer Street housing estate to the south, fertile back alleys to east and west. As for Whidborne Street, where the pub itself stands, it's a local version of the Via Dolorosa.

In the course of an afternoon, half the drifters in King's Cross pass by, many of them repeatedly. They're like bit players in an amateur play, who have to keep circling to flesh out the cast: Bangladeshis and Bengalis shopping at the Asian corner shop, dope dealers ambling over from Argyll Square, shirtless five-bellies searching for a spot to vomit, small boys flogging digital watches, body-builders preening, lipstick lesbians signifying, commuters, prostitutes, gang kids, drunks.

Most of the players, defused by heat and the foul air, are after nothing more turbulent than a shady spot to get smashed in. The Cross is set in the pit of a deep valley, where the River Fleet once flowed, and the miasma survives. All the rot of the city summer is gathered to a fullness here. "This is a vale of putrefaction," a nun says to me in a checkout line one day.

Nuns are in short supply. After all, this is *notorious* King's Cross, the tabloid adjective as automatic by now as *wartorn* Bosnia or *glittering* Las Vegas, even if the police have been conducting one of their periodic purges—Zero Tolerance, in the fashionable cant phrase—and many of the prostitutes have temporarily moved on, down the road to Paddington, or up the hill to Barnsbury.

The purge is mostly cosmetic. In a few weeks or months, the Paddington police will take their own turn at playing street-sweepers, and the girls come streaming back. For the moment, though, the Cross is oddly serene.

Argyll Square, lined on both sides with cheap hotels, is normally the heart of the action. I remember missing a train one night and trying to find a room. The first place I tried, the door was opened by a mumbling woman in a floral muumuu, who showed me a room in the basement. The room had no windows and no furniture, just a trestle bed with a soiled pillow. On inspection, the soiling appeared to be blood. "Blood, yes," the woman in the muumuu agreed, then brightened. "But not fresh."

This time around, I'm staying at the Hotel Montana, which is palatial by comparison. My room has a Monet print on the wall, *The Artist's Garden at Giverny*, and its very own sink to piss in. As for Argyll Square, which I recall as dark and murderous, it is now brightly lit, and there is a children's playground. Some of the hotels have been condemned, their interiors ripped out; others, refurbished, have started to take American Express.

"Street girls are dying," the man at the front desk tells me. Not because of Zero Tolerance, though; it's a matter of changing tastes. Most punters these days prefer to have sex by appointment. "Call up and make a booking, go to the girl's nice flat—they feel safer that way, much, much."

Purge or no, the rituals of bought sex are still everywhere. Every morning the clean-up crews remove last night's crop of ads from the phone boxes—"Greek goddess, oral and anal," "Exotic Asian temptress," "Paula, blonde transvestite," "Young English Rose"—and every noon a fresh batch appears. I watch the eternal struggle from inside the Caledonian Café, where I like to eat a late breakfast. Sometimes I'm joined by a woman called Celia, who works as a call girl's maid. A hard-boned woman, all bumps and angles, she looks forbidding in repose, with an almost lipless mouth, but she dearly loves to talk. Though born in Naples, she tells me, she has lived in London for thirty years. "More English than the English, that's me; I know what drives the Englishmen happy," she says, and looks at me expectantly, waiting for me to ask what. When I fail to speak up, she gives the answer, anyway. "Naughty boys, spanky bottoms—they all want the big comeuppance."

Celia likes it that way. She has been working as a maid for almost fifteen years, but her present young lady, Diana, is the first dominatrix she's been employed by, and she's never known life so restful. Diana's clients are always on time, always well-mannered, and they never try to bargain. "None of the silly macho business, trying to be the prize ram. Just slap me, please hurt me. Put me in pieces, sweet as pie."

This is the wave of the future, she thinks. Girls like Diana will dispense with their pimps, and even with direct sex. "The fucking ends always in tears." Whips are more hygienic and vibrators more fun. "You ask any girl, they tell you the same thing. They hate the men, they hate men's sex, they only like men's moneys. If they want to have nice love for themselves, they must wait to see their girlfriends."

As part of this cult of progress, Celia doesn't indulge in a full breakfast, merely nibbles. There are five cans of air-freshener inside her shopping bag, she informs me—three of them peach-scented, one strawberry and one fragrance-free. "This is New Britain," she reminds me. "The age of enlightenment."

Laurence, to my surprise, agrees with her. "These pimps, nine times out of ten, they're worthy to have their balls cut off," he tells me, the next time we talk. And what about the girls? Do they really despise all men? "'Course they do, and quite right, too."

I run across him often, going about his appointed rounds. The Cross is like that: once you've learned to block out the commuters, it becomes its own self-contained world and the same faces keep repeating—drinkers, dealers, even the cops—like a set of Happy Families.

The subject of Pamela Anderson and her film recurs, and this time it won't go away. Finally, nagged into submission, I agree to give it a look.

The footage is kept stored at a friend's house in Highbury. This friend is a squat, ginger-haired Glaswegian called TP, short for Thomas Paine—"My mother was strong for Liberty," he explains—and he lives in a room crammed wall to wall, floor to ceiling, with dirty magazines. Some of these are collector's items. "Every copy of *Juggs* ever printed," TP says, gesturing at one treasured pile. There is even a near-priceless issue of *Rear View,* printed upside down by a printer's error.

In the midst of all these riches, carved out like a First World War trench, is a narrow runway with an overstuffed armchair at one end and a VCR at the other. A single plastic tulip, passion-pink, blooms in a jam jar. "Take a seat. Relax," Laurence tells me, but only when he's already claimed the armchair. So I park myself on a stack of *Lesbo Lickers,* and the screening gets underway.

It proves an anti-climax. The film quality is so blurred, the loop itself so jumpy, that most of the action is indecipherable. There does seem to be a busty blonde involved, and she appears to act well on the going, but whether that blonde is Pamela Anderson, or the director's cousin, or Margaret Thatcher, come to that, there is no way of telling.

"Let me think about it," I mumble, the reel having run its course; and Laurence doesn't argue. "It's still a bit rough in spots," he muses. "Needs a drop of fairy dust, don't you think?" It's as though, having dragged me here, he considers his work done, honour served. By the time we start back towards the Cross, he has already switched tacks and is touting the mega-million potential of take-away jerk chicken.

When I return to my post at McGlynn's, Mary is already waiting with the tabloids. Seven spectators and eleven competitors have been injured at the annual cheese-rolling contest at Cooper's Hill, Brockworth, near Gloucester. The most seriously damaged is a man who suffered a head trauma in a hundred-foot fall down the hillside, as he tried to avoid a bouncing eight-pound Double Gloucester that had rolled off course.

I am happy here. We have the whole afternoon for holiday, and Mary's hair has been dyed coal-black, with strips of pillar-box red. Behind our backs is a vacant house for rent. A lone terraced house with nothing on either side, it sticks up like a last tooth. Mary covets it fiercely. "It would make a wild headquarters," she thinks. For what? "Public works." Such as? "Kicking arse."

A Portuguese woman called Elsa wanders over to our bench. She is stylishly dressed in a houndstooth tweed suit and white frilled blouse, and she has been drinking. "My father was a lawyer, a very big man, he was secretary to the great Salazar, but don't become a lawyer, darling, a lawyer is a liar. I was the perfect young lady, I was raised by the nuns. I was a stewardess with Aer Lingus, all the stars flew on my plane. Elizabeth Taylor and Richard Burton, the great Robert Mitchum, he spoke to me in person. But now what am I?" she demands. "A peace artist, that's all."

A young Somalian woman, stick-thin and haunted, hunkers down on the pavement, with her back against a brick schoolyard wall and her skeletal knees raised to her chest like a praying mantis. Some of the drinkers at the benches jeer at her but she seems to be impervious; just stares at them, chain-smoking. "She gets raped almost every night," Elsa says. "She's used to it."

In the early evening, when the heat of the day has lost its evil and mothers come out to stroll their babies in prams, a heavy-legged transvestite in a green glitter dress, scarcely more than a curtain fringe, stops beside a bench full of construction workers and slowly raises his arms, so that the skirt rises up and exposes his balls.

"One thing I'll never understand," Mary says, watching him. "Why did God put creases behind people's knees?" Then she rises and goes home to her husband, and I move off towards Russell Square, where Aidan Dun, a poet, is reading in an art gallery.

He's written an epic poem called "Vale Royal," on the mystical and magical significance of King's Cross and St. Pancras. Plucking at a guitar as he reads, he simpers each time he reaches a choice line. But "Vale Royal" itself has force: "And so I came to the place called Pan Cross, / And the plain of Good Luck, / Where the workers with golden hands / Are building the Cathedral of the Sunchild / Beside the river, on the cone of high land / Above the flashing downward race of the Fleet."

At the interval, poet and punters mingle in a shady courtyard, networking like mad things, while I take refuge at a corner table. The man next to me is a gaunt West Indian with grizzled beard and a bowler hat. I ask him his name. "Edgecombe," he replies. "Johnny Edge."

For a moment I can't quite place him. Then it clicks.

Johnny Edgecombe is the man who fired six shots into the front door of Stephen Ward's mews house in 1962, demanding that Christine Keeler come out and talk. The man who detonated the whole Profumo affair, blew Harold Macmillan out of office, and so gave the Anglo Club a whack from which it never quite recovered.

If the republic has founding fathers, Johnny Edge would be one of them. But he hardly looks a gunslinger now; certainly not a wreaker of cataclysms. Instead, he seems the complete jazz hipster, all grace and irony. Smiling serenely on Aidan Dun's flaunting, he might be watching a rowdy child at play, and every time he finishes a sentence, he laughs far back in his throat, *heh heh*.

What does he do these days? Mostly sits in his room, he says, and listens to music. He has written a novel, also his memoirs. I must visit him some time.

Before I can question him further, a joint comes round and he gets distracted. But I take him up on his offer, which brings me, a few days later, to a boardinghouse in Blackheath, where he occupies a top-floor bedsit.

Jazz posters on the wall, pictures of his three daughters on the mantelpiece. "Have a cup of rose-hip tea," says Edge. His face by day looks older and harder used than it did at the gallery, but his manner is still courtly, both he and his room immaculate. Late-afternoon sunlight slants in through a high window and Stan Getz plays "Desafinado" on the radio.

Edge shows scant interest in general conversation, or in who I am, or why I'm here. All he wants is to tell his tale. "England was an accident," he starts off, speaking carefully, in measured cadences, the way people do when they've had too much time to stew. "My father was a famous man. Captain Johnny was his name." That was in Antigua, where Edge was born, one of eight or nine children "that I know of," and Captain Johnny sailed the *Perseverance*, a two-masted schooner, hauling rice from Suriname, cotton from Barbados, gasoline from Trinidad.

As a child, Edge itched to join him. "My mother and

my four brothers, they all tried to get me to fly straight, to wear shoes and go to school, walk that respectable line, heh heh, but my whole desire was for the sea."

At sixteen, he was a pantry boy on a cabin boat. He wanted to get to New York, to join up with Captain Johnny and hear some jazz, but his plans kept going awry. He jumped one ship and stowed away on another, did jail time in Galveston, then in Durham, and wound up in Tiger Bay, the tumultuous Cardiff waterfront, running with the hustlers and the hookers, the crapshooters. From there, he moved on to London. Worked a few scams in Bond Street jewellers, posing as an African prince while his confederates helped themselves to any loose rings; lived with and on prostitutes, and got busted for it. Then he came upon Peter Rachman, the slum landlord, and Rachman set him up in a Notting Hill shebeen.

That was his shining hour. The shebeen not only offered after-hours' drinking, but gambling, music, dope. "I used to get all the real top London villains coming down, not just petty criminals or smash-and-grab guys, but people with major money in their pockets."

Slumming white trendies like Stephen Ward and Paula Hamilton-Marshall adored the place. This was the early sixties, of course, when black still meant forbidden fruit: "I was terrified that my mother would find out that I had coloured friends," Christine Keeler would say later on. Never mind a black lover. "I felt that I could not face my friends and relations ever again if that came out in public."

The fatal moment, according to Edge, came on a beautiful summer Sunday. "I was strolling along by Hyde Park, sucking on a joint and eyeing all these beautiful continental women, heh heh, not a care in creation, when a cab pulled up." Inside was Paula Hamilton-Marshall and her friend Christine, cringing in a corner. "I thought, What's wrong with this chick? Right away I knew this was a bad trip. But I got in the cab anyway."

Keeler was on the run from Lucky Gordon, another

Jamaican, with a razor he was itching to use on her. She hid out with Edge for the next six months. It was a stormy period, though not without compensations. "The only times we would fight were when she thought I wasn't giving her enough attention or that I was taking her for granted, then she'd get really emotional and try and humiliate me until I'd have to respond by giving her a slap. After that, she would be really lovely, you couldn't ask to meet a nicer girl."

On Edge's birthday, they went to the All-Nighter in Wardour Street to celebrate. Lucky Gordon was there and a free-for-all broke out. "Screaming and knife-waving, tables overturned, plates and mirrors shattering." And Lucky, a notorious cutter, ended up getting cut himself.

Edge and Christine Keeler took refuge in a friend's house in Brentwood, but Christine soon got sick of it. The world that she really cherished was Stephen Ward's—the West End, furs, fancy cars. John Profumo and Ivanov, the KGB man, were lovers who could give her all that; dark meat and ganja were merely diversions, and now they'd lost their savour. First chance she got, she snuck away to Ward's mews house.

When Edge tracked her down there, pounding at her door, she flung a pound note at him in quittance. "That made me quite annoyed. She was trying to treat me like some slave." Edge was carrying her gun, a little Walther .32. "I just wanted to talk to her. Get into the house and give her a good spanking." Still she refused to open up, so he started shooting. "I thought it would be like the movies, one shot and I'd be in." But the lock never budged.

The trial that followed was a farce. Keeler had gone on the lam to Spain and the taxi driver who'd driven Edge to the mews had since died of a heart attack, so there were no eyewitnesses. "No case to answer, still they gave me seven years. Hoping to hush the whole thing up, y'understand, but it blow in their faces anyhow. The war minister and the hooker and the Russian spy, Lord Astor down at

Cliveden, Mandy Rice-Davies in the witness-stand, saying, 'Well, he would, wouldn't he?' Profumo lies to Parliament, but he's found out, he has to come clean in the end, Macmillan's government goes down the drain. And nothing is ever the same again."

Edge served five years. "Bitter times, man, the injustice of the thing, all the lies." When he was released, he had a stab at the straight life. He took up with a Danish au pair, eighteen to his thirty-five, and they moved to Ireland. Opened a tearoom in Tralee and sold craftwork; had two daughters together. "But it didn't last. Nothing does." They moved to Copenhagen, the marriage broke up, and finally Edge, for all that he'd suffered at England's hands, came back to London again.

Why did he return? "It's what I knew," he says. He ran a mobile jazz discotheque for a time, dabbled in various businesses, but nothing really worked, and now, past sixty, he finds himself at loose ends. "Not too much shaking, man." His two daughters in Denmark, and a third who lives here in London, help him keep the faith. Even so, he gets frustrated. If he had the funds, he'd be home in Antigua, mucking about on boats and smoking good herb, but cash and himself have long been strangers. "You could say I'm currently resting. By necessity, heh heh."

So he sits in this room and plays his jazz, and sometimes the phone rings. He hopes that someone will publish his memoirs or at least his novel. Still, he carries a feeling of remove, as if, for all his affability, his real focus is somewhere else.

Time and again, as we talk, he keeps returning to that night in the mews. "Sometimes it feels like my true life end right there, in the space of those six bullets." The sun is off his face; John Coltrane is playing "Giant Steps"; it's time for another rose-hip tea. "You never get free," says Edge.

THIS IS THE great day. The day of the night when England takes on the might of the world and the world is beaten, no, destroyed. Football is coming home.

The republic is in carnival, boots stomping, flags waving, all the streets in King's Cross swarmed by fans and my lunchtime bench outside McGlynn's commandeered by five lads with one letter each stencilled on their foreheads—large white letters with red and blue trim. Between them, the letters spell EGLAD. "What happened to the two Ns?" I enquire.

"Lifted, weren't they?" says L.

I try to buy a sandwich at the bar but everything edible has already been devoured. All that's left is a pickled egg, and I sit gnawing at its rubber carapace, while "Three Lions on a Shirt" plays endlessly on the jukebox.

There is a man at the next table with the most prodigious belly. More than just a belly, really—a fabulous beast, the stuff of legend and song. Naked above a pair of Union Jack shorts, it grows out of his lap, dead-white and hairless, like a separate being. On a woman, it might shelter octuplets.

The man himself, whose name is Les, is unimposing, bleary-eyed in flip-flops and black socks, not worthy of the magnificence of his middle. And he seems aware of this; is happy to defer. When he speaks, he keeps up a constant rubbing and stroking, a series of little love taps, as if the belly is the true oracle, his mouth just the messenger.

Three other men are at the same table, and they bask in the reflected glory. "Hearken to King Gut!" one of them keeps crowing, each time the belly scores a point.

When the others go back to work, Les swings King Gut like an overstuffed coalsack in my direction. "Mine's a Tennent's," he says, and starts to talk about 1966, the last year that England ruled the world. "The day we won the cup, that was the best day of my life," he confides. The worst, too, as things turned out.

He was seventeen at the time, studious and law-abiding. His family lived in Tottenham, his father worked at a garden-ornament factory, his mother was a dab hand at floral arrangements. There was a good job waiting for Les with his dad's firm but he had wider ambitions, he couldn't see spending his working life with a bunch of gnomes and plaster Bambis. "I was handy with words, I could always turn a phrase. Advertising, I fancied that strong. Dreaming up some flash slogan, then seeing the ad on TV."

He used to sit up late, working on imaginary campaigns. *I O It All to Ovaltine* is one he still remembers: "I didn't have a clue, just a knack." But World Cup Final night changed the playing field. No chance of J. Walter Thompson after that.

Simply put, he got drunk.

He went down to the King's Head. Till then, the most booze he'd ever swallowed was a glug from his dad's beer or a few swigs from a bottle of ginger wine Jacko Manville stole from his aunt, over behind the Methodist chapel. But this was a night that had no limits. Everyone was piled in the pub together, old and young. "Didn't matter your age or the state you were in—if you could get it down you, they'd keep pouring it." Les started on pints, but he didn't fancy the taste, so he switched to cherry brandy, then tawny port, then anything he could lay hands on. "It seemed only right. My patriotic duty."

At some point in the proceedings, a car got nicked. Les and three friends of his, none of them could drive, but that didn't seem to matter, not tonight, so they pinched this car from outside the pub and took off. And they hit a woman. Killed her. A middle-aged woman, mother of three, crossing the street at a red light.

Les wasn't driving himself, he was in the back being sick at the time, but of course that was no excuse, he got blamed like all the others. Then certain other matters came to light—"nothing serious. More like unfortunate"— and his goose was cooked. Instead of joining an ad agency, he did a stint in Borstal, which taught him another trade: Basic Crime.

Not that he's complaining. "I was a big boy, wasn't I?" All in all, he'd done quite nicely for himself. He may not have ended up as a star copywriter, but he doesn't starve. He is a plumber, married with two sons in the motor trade and a daughter training to be a nurse. And Dawn, his wife, is a gem. "All woman, all heart, and lovely with it." If she hadn't had polio as a child, she could have been a fashion model, a film star, anything she fancied. Instead, she's had to settle for Les: "But never a word of moaning, not a squeak."

Still, he can't help wondering how his life would have panned out, where he would be now, if England had lost that final. "I'd probably be some toffee-nosed git, a pain in the arse to one and all, myself included." But maybe not. "I might have been a bit sharper, more on the ball. Slimmer, anyway."

He's done all right for himself. "I'm sufficed." But sufficed doesn't mean complete. "I know there's something missing, there has to be more somewhere." Every so often, he gets this odd restless itching inside and he can't seem to sleep. Sometimes he'll put on his best suit, stand himself a night out in Soho. "I pass myself off as a businessman on the town, a big-shot exec. Sounds stupid, I know, but it happens, right? I flash this wallet full of nice crisp banknotes, morning-dew-fresh-picked as they say, and help myself to a bit of A-1 crumpet. Champers all round, and I puff myself sick on a Romeo y Julieta. Regular Champagne Charlie, that's me." He gives King Gut a sharp pinch, then a reassuring pat. "Old fat fool," he says fondly.

His table is a mess. All the time that he's been talking, in between petting his belly, he has kept crumbling butt-ends in the ashtray, and now the ashtray has overflowed. Tiny curls and sprigs of tobacco lie scattered everywhere, mulched in with lager slops. "Just look at the state of this," Les says tetchily, as if the muck were someone else's making.

But what can you do? The whole country is a pig wallow.

Take Tottenham. When Les was growing up in the fifties and early sixties, that whole area was a pleasure. Tidy streets, well-kept houses, hard-working people with jobs and regular payments. You got the odd trouble-maker, admittedly. Teddy boys were strong round there and you could find some serious brawls of a Saturday night at the Royal. Nothing out of order, though; just fists and the occasional flick-knife. Not like now, when you take your life in your hands every time you stroll round the corner for a quick beer.

Something needs to happen. Something big and dramatic to help stop the rot, to turn back the clock. A miracle of sorts. Like beating, no, destroying the world.

"That's the magnitude of the moment," Les says. Reading the papers this week, he's been reminded of a film he saw once. It was nothing famous, not even a full-length feature; just something on late-night TV. Years ago now, he can't even be sure of the title: "*The Two Doors,* or something. Load of bollocks, really." For some reason, though, the story has stuck in his mind.

"There's this feller called Don, an American bloke. Pretty much your Average Joe, married with kids, a house in the suburbs. Anyhow, he gets a new job. A big promotion, his dream come true. But his first day at work, when he shows up at the office, no one shows him where he's meant to sit. Instead, he finds these two blank doors facing him, with no way of knowing which one he's meant to use. So what can he do? He makes a blind guess. Picks the one on the left. And he walks straight into Hell."

Don finds himself trapped in a giant fishtank, forced to watch while everything and everyone he loves goes to ruin. "He sees his old neighbourhood turn into a snake-pit. All the neighbours start feuding, there's fires and murders every night. Then his wife, she can't cope without him and she turns into a boozer, a rat-faced old biddy who picks up men. His son is framed for embezzlement and goes off to jail, his daughter gets killed in a plane crash. And Don himself, all this time, he's powerless to help."

The years drag by, he grows old and weak. Then one day, when he's just about given up hope, he finds himself back at the two doors. "And this time, of course, he chooses right. Charges out into the sunshine. And the world is just as he left it. Wife, kids, car, house, all present and accounted for ... choir of angels on the sound-track ... The End."

Well, that's America for you. "You don't know whether to laugh or cry." When you think it over, though, the parallels are uncanny. "In nineteen sixty-six, we walked through the wrong door. England did, and I did, and we've been paying ever since." But tonight the circle will be completed. "History repeats itself, but this time we get it right." Back into the sunlight, and the world just as it once was. "England for ever. Number one."

And if England loses? "Can't happen," says Les, and gives King Gut a quick whack for support. "It's in the bag." He would bet his house on that. "Sometimes you just know, deep in your heart," he says. "Call it fate."

AT THE FINAL whistle, when England has lost, Mary stands up in the pub and says with calm finality: "Well, that's the death. Now bring on the wake." So we go down to Trafalgar Square.

There is going to be a riot. Everybody in the pub says so. There's bound to be major trouble, and we'd have to be mad to get involved. But that's not the mood in the streets. Even in defeat, the England supporters keep on jubilating.

If anything, the mood is more exultant than ever. The singing and chanting, the flags and rattles flying, the wordless roaring—all of it has gathered to a final careening madness.

Once in Trafalgar Square, the fans set up headquarters at the foot of Nelson's Column. Shoulder to shoulder, three ranks deep, they form a phalanx; a rabble army, uniformed in T-shirts and DMs and St. George's warpaint. All round the square's perimeter, meanwhile, tourists with cameras line the stone balustrades, avid for a show.

For a long time, the spectators have to make do with singing. The fans are drunk, all right; and their songs, when you can catch the words, are obscene. But still no sign of a riot.

The police presence is more threatening. Mob squads and attack dogs, walkie-talkies, bullet-proof vests—they look primed and ripe for battle.

On the steps of St. Martin-in-the-Fields, I ask an

armoured lawman, complete with shield and Plexiglas mask, how things are going. "Not good. This lot is out of control," he says, indicating the singing fans, the middle-aged fathers walking their infant sons around the rims of the fountains, the teenage bimbettes with their halter-tops and pierced belly buttons singing Spice Girls' hits. Below us, a boy falls to his knees and is violently sick. "We've got a situation," the lawman says.

This is surprising to me. Football riots don't self-ignite; they need expert orchestration. And the police have gone to great lengths to ensure that none of the top conductors are available. Most of the known ringleaders have been lifted in well-publicised dawn swoops, and those who evaded the raids and made it to the match tonight have been headed off, coralled before they can reach Trafalgar Square. The revellers at Nelson's Column are leaderless, and seem impotent.

When "Three Lions" begins to pall, we stroll the streets behind Whitehall and Pall Mall, where the heart of the Empire once beat. In the gardens by the Athenaeum, there's a party of young things in evening-dress, sipping champagne. The girls have bare shoulders and plunging necklines, and their escorts wear white tie. Peering over the iron railings, I meet the glance of a stately brunette in black velvet. Her white breasts are monuments, her smile more dismissive than any curse.

The night is hushed here. Trafalgar Square is a minute's walk away but these buildings are like citadels, they kill all noise from outside. Sitting at the top of Duke of York Steps, all we can hear is a distant high-pitched wailing, tinny and distorted like a cheap cassette.

A lanky youth plods by, hand in hand with a small child. The child, who looks about seven, is carrying a miniature Union Jack and has an outsize St. George's flag draped across his back. His stumpy little legs, oddly bowed, seem almost too weak to support him. "I'm pissed, Chris," I hear the child say, but something is not right here, the voice is much too deep for his age, the tone too battle-scarred. "I'm pissed and I want to go home," he says, then turns his face to the light.

He's a dwarf, and he is crying.

As he goes home, so do we. Mary heads for Kentish Town and I go back to the Cross. Just as I arrive at Argyll Square, however, a pack of youths comes barrelling past. "It's going off!" they yell, and I turn around, go lumbering in their wake.

By the time I'm back at Trafalgar Square, the mood has soured fatally. Most of the fans are still singing or splashing about in the fountains but some have clambered onto the barriers, shouting taunts at the attack dogs and their handlers. And the police seem hot to hit back. The dogs, positioned some twenty yards from the edge of the crowd, strain at their long flexile leashes, which can be played like fishing-lines. Now their handlers begin to unreel these lines and the dogs rush forward in frenzy, almost into the fans' faces. Only at the last lunge do the leashes snap tight, so that the animals are frozen in mid-pounce, front paws thrashing.

A few charges like that and the fans catch the drift. Their leaders may be missing, but you don't need to be a pro to know how to play this game. The first bottles start to fly, the Nazi salutes begin and a new chant goes up: "Come and have a go if you think you're hard enough."

The law needs no second bidding. Extra riot squads are called up, armoured cars loom from under the massive arches of the Mall. Safe behind their helmets and shields, the police make a baton charge into the square, trying to sweep the crowds out. But the crowds have nowhere to go. Charing Cross Road and St. Martin's Lane have been blocked off. They are trapped.

For the spectators at the balustrades, this is everything they could have hoped for. Youths are led past with blood streaming down their faces. Drunks fall and are trampled underfoot, women scream and children are handed up through the crush. Then there's a second baton charge, a blind-panic rush to nowhere, and a bottle shatters at my feet. One lad, on his knees, is searching for lost teeth. And still, bizarrely, the singing keeps on.

Suddenly, the trap seems sprung. Northumberland Avenue, where the riot squad has massed thickest, is mysteriously vacated, and the fans, flushed from their cage, go racing along it, smashing windows, overturning cars and setting them alight. The riot has been achieved.

And I go home to bed.

What with the woman sobbing in the next room, and the Turkish youths disputing about Allah outside my window, and my cot that has no real mattress, just a shallow strip of foam that feels stuffed with ball-bearings and rusty nails, I don't sleep soundly.

Even when I doze off at last, I am soon awakened again, this time by a lamentation in Argyll Square. A man's voice, hoarse and broken, is keening.

The sound rises and falls raggedly, as if the man is rocking himself to its rhythm. YEEENALAAAN! YEEENALAAAN! he seems to be crying. A Muslim incantation? A call to prayer, or dirge for the dead? But no. When I look out of my window, it's only Mac, one of the drinkers from across the square.

Squatting by the park railings, he suckles a can of Special Brew. Glugs deep, then keens again.

YEEENALAAAN?

No. That isn't it.

EEENA LEE ANN?

Not quite.

EEENGALAAAN!

But of course.

ENG-A-LAND!

What else?

JOY RIDING

THE WOOLLEN HAT does it. An evil-looking object, orange and mangy, it makes me think of a ginger cat that had been fed through a meat grinder, but Mary treasures it. She wears it jammed hard and low across her eyebrows, so that her face is cut in half and all you see are fierce eyes, greedy mouth. She looks like a road warrior.

She's found us transport, a pygmy Rover Metro, in a rental yard off the Finchley Road. It's such a runt that it should only have to pay half-price at parking meters. Still, it has a rakish air, a definite jut to its strut. Its paint-work is a lurid teal and it sings to itself as it travels. We name it Teal Wheels, our journey the Teal Wheels Tour.

I don't drive. Not that it matters, because Mary isn't about to surrender the wheel. Being on the same scale as the Metro, she feels that she alone understands it. Orange hat rammed into place like a battle helmet, books and spare clothing wedged under her bony arse, she pushes her seat forward as far as it will go, the steering wheel almost nuzzling her breasts. Then she puts her foot down, and we hit the motorways.

She drives like a speedmaster working a video game. Cruises at ninety, flips lanes, ducks and dodges, curses and whoops, all with perfect command. Smokes her own cigarettes, smokes mine, guzzles junk snacks, gulps water and plays techno tapes so loud the bass sounds like a rock crusher. When I shut my eyes, which is often, I feel as if

I'm trapped inside some monstrous compactor. It seems a righteous way to go.

When the pounding stops, we are in Bristol. "A tidy wee spin," Mary says, and takes off her orange hat. Without it, she looks almost feminine. "Food," she says. "Give me food."

THE KEY WORD in Bristol is *blagging*. It is one of those terms, like *camp* and *funky*, that isn't easy to define, though everyone knows what it means: hustling for people too lazy to really hustle. True hustlers live off risk, fuelled by outrageous conceits, but blaggers merely look for soft options. They don't knock down doors, just ease through the cracks.

We've settled in Montpelier, an area where the blagger's art attains its highest perfection. No one here seems to work and not many break sweat. We hang around the paved space at the foot of Picton Street, outside the corner shop. Joints and white cider go the rounds and dealers make calls from the phone box. From time to time, a stray dog takes a dump. That passes for a commotion.

A loafer's paradise, and lovely to look at—Bristol is, quite literally, a golden city. Much of it is built of Bath stone, which gives everything a burnished glow. Though Montpelier isn't its most glamorous quarter, a certain distinction endures. Narrow village-like streets, Victorian terraces, backwaters, all a little run to seed but now beginning to gentrify, the squats and boarded windows counterbalanced by window boxes and hanging plants. There is a quietude about the place, a shabby ease, that works itself under the skin, sucks out all rawness and rage.

In the evening, we wander up the hill to a pub called the Cadbury House. "All human life is there," we've been informed. So we climb. And we climb. Bristol is full of heights that look like pleasant hikes from below but feel like cliffs once you come to tackle them head-on. Perhaps that's why the pace stays so slow. Or perhaps it's the sleepiness of the light, which is soft and blurry, oddly opaque, and makes everything look subtly distorted, as if viewed through a sliver of glass.

To walk inside the Cadbury House is to step straight back into the sixties. Long hair and beards, tie-dyed T-shirts, girls in leotards and ethnic jewellery. One man sitting at the bar is still reading *Steppenwolf.*

Only the music is new. Strange for such a sleepy town, but Bristol has always been a musical powerhouse, from Rock & Roll down to acid jazz and trip-hop. The Wild Bunch and Massive Attack, Tricky, Portishead and Roni Size all gestated hereabouts, and some hung out at the Cadbury House. "They'll stick up a plaque one day," the man reading *Steppenwolf* muses. "'Tricky blagged here.'"

The music, in large part, is an off-shoot of the city's mixed history. As a great port, Bristol has always been cosmopolitan. Blacks were first brought here by the slave trade, then stayed on when the trade collapsed. After the Second World War, numbers of West Indians settled in St. Paul's, the quarter abutting Montpelier. It wasn't much of a place, just a few run-down streets round Grosvenor Road, but it became a magnet, not just for blacks in other neighbourhoods but for young whites on the razzle, seeking blues dances and dope. A loose alliance grew up—hip blacks, white wannabes. The riot sealed the pact.

It blew up on 2 April 1980, when twenty lawmen raided a joint called the Black and White Café, looking for drugs. In the resulting ruckus, a black social worker, Dr. Prince Brown, suffered a torn and mutilated trouser leg. Incensed bystanders, both black and white, started throwing bottles and bricks. The law fought back with truncheons and dustbin lids. Petrol bombs were set off, shops looted, banks and local businesses destroyed. By the time the smoke cleared, over a hundred arrests had been made.

Penny-ante stuff by global standards, but in England,

where riot was still a rarity, it proved to be a signpost. Within a year, there had been other, bigger explosions, most violently in Brixton and Toxteth, and the pattern of spasmodic civil skirmishing that ran through the Thatcher years was established.

St. Paul's still carries the scuff-marks. The action end of Grosvenor Road has shrunk to perhaps a hundred yards of shops and community offices, facing out on a triangular green, but the atmosphere is not genial. A few brothers give us a stare-down as we stroll past, and one, perched on a low stone wall, spits in the rough direction of my shoes. He looks as though he wouldn't mind a spot of trouble, but not right now, in the heat of the day, while he's still digesting his lunch.

Other parts of Bristol are lazy by choice but the lethargy here has a sour, mean taste. Nothing to do and nowhere to go. The studs lounging on the corners all look exhausted; sick and spent with idleness.

We find ourselves outside the headquarters of the Justice for Marlon Thomas Campaign. It's a disused shop, its windows plastered with flyers and want-ads. Inside is Marlon's brother, Leroy.

He is a cool item, Leroy. A sharp dresser, a mover, quick with words. When we ask about his brother, he hands over a fistful of pamphlets.

One night in 1994, apparently, a group of young blacks visited Bob Wilson's Fair on Durdham Downs and suffered savage beatings, allegedly by workers with the fair. Marlon Thomas, then eighteen and a student at Brunel College, took the worst of it. He spent months on the critical list and still hasn't fully recovered. As for the fair workers, five were arrested, three charged with attempted murder.

That's where the pamphlet leaves it, but we want to hear more. Were the fair workers found guilty and, if so, what sentences did they receive? Did Marlon Thomas receive compensation? And exactly how has justice failed to be done? Leroy says he'd be happy to tell us all. Only not right now. He is too busy making plans for the upcoming carnival. It would be better if we talked in the morning. "Just give me a shout on the mobile," he says, and ushers us back into the street, with its reek of waste and dulled rage.

So we call him in the morning. And the next day, and the day after that. But Leroy is forever too occupied. "Tomorrow. In the morning. Tomorrow," he keeps saying, until at last the message gets through, and we let him be. We are in a land of *mañana*.

Once we've got that clear, everything else seems to fall into place: the city's languor, its passivity, even the filtered softness of its light. The whole atmosphere is not really English but subtropical. Some weird trick of osmosis, perhaps left over from its slave-trade days, has slowed and thickened its pulse, so that it seems less akin to Gloucester or Cardiff, say, than to Galveston or Savannah, even Port-au-Prince.

That may be how the music evolved. Out of racial diversity, and time to spare, and the whole climate of blagging, not hustling. In this climate, the slurred, saturated delivery of a Tricky makes perfect sense. He might have things to say, urgent statements to make. Only not right now.

As we wander through the town, one name keeps cropping up. Sapphire. A black transvestite.

He has been around for ever. Or since the eighties, anyhow. Back then, there used to be a club called the Dug Out, where worlds collided: black kids from St. Paul's and Eastville, white kids from the tower blocks, bohos, students, punks, Clifton trendies. It was a basement warren, dark and grungy, with carpeting that stuck to your feet, making you feel you were sinking in quicksand. A place where people could just fall by and loiter. The Wild Bunch started as DJs there. And Sapphire was its court jester.

Jester, and stirrer, and resident outrage, all rolled into one. While everyone else sat and nodded, he'd dance in sequins and a glitter skirt, sky-high on amyl nitrite. Pull straight white kids off the floor and give them blow jobs in the toilets. "He got away with murder, but he had style," we hear. "Buttocks wouldn't melt in his mouth."

Since the Dug Out's death, he has moved on to its successors—the Blue Mountain, Lakota, Club Loco. He seems to embody the city's climate: its fecklessness, and also its lack of restrictions, its casual mix of straight and gay, black and white, and everything in-between. But lately he has become elusive. Nobody is sure where he lives now, or how to contact him.

Days of search get us nowhere. Every club and bar knows him, but none can pin him down. Like Miss Susan Brown in the Professor Longhair song, he walks right in, he walks right out, and no one knows what the girl is about.

Then late one afternoon, when we have almost abandoned the quest, Sapphire comes to us. We're grazing at the corner shop on Picton Street, discreetly stalking an aubergine, when Mary glances up and beholds a man in sandals and an ankle-length floral skirt, vividly made-up, watching her with eyes full of yearning.

The make-up can't camouflage the mileage. One old admirer, reminiscing about Sapphire in the Dug Out days, called him a bombshell. If so, he's now a bombshell of a certain age. Still striking, but frayed around the edges and deeply depressed.

He isn't interested in talking to me. In typical Bristol style, he doesn't turn me down flat, just sloughs me off. Besides, he is far too busy with Mary. Leaning over her, clutching at her hand, he starts to pour out his soul. He's a lonely man, he says. His life is empty, he has no comfort. "When I was younger, it was party, party, that was all I needed," he says. But now. Oh, but now. And he clutches her hand tighter, a man clinging on. His eyes are cavernous with longing and Mary can't wriggle loose. So the two of them stand locked, Sapphire in his sandals and floral skirt, Mary in her schoolboy's trousers and purple boots and ratty orange hat, while the cider drinkers stumble around them, and the dealers work their phones, and all of Bristol drowses. "The love of a good woman," says Sapphire. "Is that too much to ask?"

A WOMAN IS screaming blue murder.

Moving towards the sound, I turn into Stoke's Croft, the main road that flanks Montpelier and St. Paul's, and see that she's fighting the law. A big-boned girl, dressed for damage in ripped fishnet tights and a lime-green minidress, she straddles a traffic island, clinging to the bollard, while trying to kick a cop in the balls. The cop has her pinned by one arm, seems to be trying to calm her down, but the woman isn't having any. *Cocksucker,* she calls him. He doesn't like that.

Catching me watching, the woman struggles harder. "There's my husband," she yells, and she tears herself free. The cop takes a few steps in pursuit, then changes his mind, lets her go. "You took your fucking time," the woman says to me, and she links my arm, starts marching me down the street.

For a moment I think we've met before, but she says not. "You don't know me from Adam Ant," she confides. Still she doesn't let go of my arm. She keeps dragging me along Stoke's Croft, her fingers grappled in my sleeve. There is a patch of dried blood on her dress, her face is swollen and blotchy, and she's missing some teeth, yet there is a wild beauty in her. "I want a drink," she says. So we go in the Old Pint and Pie.

The pub is brand-new, loud and garish; it reeks of bleach and disinfectant. The woman orders a vodka and bitter lemon, and bums one of my Sweet Aftons. "Sweet life, my love," she says. Her voice is a soft Devon burr, warm and buttery. She takes a drink, a deep shuddering drag. "He called me a dirty slapper. Told me to bugger off home," she tells me. "He called me fucking mad." And it all comes piling out, everything that's banged up within her, as if she can't hold it a moment more.

Her name is Martha. She comes from Exeter. She's married with three children but her husband isn't the man she loves. The man she loves is called Nelson and he's here in Bristol somewhere, or at least he's supposed to be, only he's gone lost, he has been missing for months, and that's why Martha is out on the streets, she's trying to find him again.

"I'm in this town seeking," she says, and the phrase typifies the way she talks—she has a sweet tooth for language. When she asks the barman for a second drink, she calls it an equaliser. And when she speaks of passion, she says, "I dropped dead in love."

Two years ago, she was back in Exeter, living on Heavytree Road, and her life felt well in order. Keith, her husband, was working in a bookie's and her three daughters—Moira, Vanessa and Kylie—were all in school. Money was tight, because Keith left most of his wages at the bookie's, but that was nothing new. The day they'd met, he was in the Turk's Head, poring over the form. Martha had just turned eighteen and she felt hot, game for anything. She was wearing fuck-me shoes and a dress cut down to there, up to here. When Keith scored a winner, he bought champagne. Six weeks later, they were wed.

The marriage wasn't good, wasn't bad. The main problem was that Martha liked sex and Keith, like most men, really didn't. But at least she had safety. That meant the world to her.

Her family had been travelling people and her whole childhood had been lived on the edge, barely staying afloat from day to day, constantly moving on. "There was nothing for us in England, just aggro and abuse, a load of shite. So we tried Ireland instead, but that was worse." She remembered dirty-arsed little towns in Offaly and Cavan which drove them out with stones, and once, in Roscommon, someone set light to their caravan in the night. "No mercy, they tried to burn us alive. I woke up in a cloud of black smoke and my mother slapping me, trying to get me to shift. Me and my brother Paul crawled out through a broken window. We were all over cuts, black from ashes. But it's my mother I remember most. Seeing her slumped down in the grass, like, on her knees, sort of stunned. She had a terrible gash on her forehead, it was really pumping. And the way she looked at us. Shaking and sort of dazed, with all the blood—it was like a trapped animal."

After their caravan burned, they'd given up on Ireland and come back to Devon. But the family was destroyed. "My dad went to jail and my mum went down the pub." Her mother had always liked a drink but now it got the best of her. She started having trouble with the law. Fighting and disturbing the peace, chucking bricks through plate-glass windows. Finally, she passed out with a lit smoke and set fire to the hole they'd been squatting in.

At the time this made no sense. Later on, though, Martha came to learn a bit about the occult and the true nature of curses. "My mum, when she was still herself, she was basically an earth person. Very firmly rooted, and fire doesn't like that. So it has to try and destroy those roots. That's why the fires kept pursuing her, see? They were trying to claim her for their own."

Soon after the second burn-out, Martha was put into care. She was eleven, and full of trouble. "I was strong into cutting; my knife was my best friend. Sometimes I cut myself, my arms and legs, and sometimes I lashed out. One time I sliced up a boy who told the teacher I had crabs. Big lad, he was, but I soon whittled him down to size. Oh, and cats; I was death on moggies."

There was more. Stuff she doesn't want to dig up now. "It's too confused in my mind. I was mad, my love. And madness makes a mess." But she can pinpoint the moment when she started to heal. "I was in this café in Exeter centre. A coffee bar, like, and I was eating this sticky bun. Well, the bun was stale; I couldn't get it down me. So I started playing silly buggers. Sticking my tongue through the middle, sucking at the cream filling, and the cream got spread all over my face. When I looked in the mirror, you never saw such a sight. So I thought, Fuck it. Might as well go the whole hog. And I did. I started grabbing up cakes off the trolley. Chocolate éclairs, rum babas, meringues; anything I could lay hands on. Smashing them in my face like paint bombs or throwing them at the other punters, just going berserk and screaming out laughter, I couldn't stop. Then the manager started running towards me, and of course I didn't have the price on me, I didn't have fucking 10p, so I took off. I went charging through Guildhall shopping precinct, dripping chocolate and jam and clotted cream, and into Cathedral Yard. They have these craft fairs, I call them Bitsashit Boutiques, and I started racing up and down between the stalls. I was yelling stuff, I don't even know what. I was totally gonzo, off the wall. And then this hand came down on my arm. A dirty great meat hook, really strong; the sort of grip you'd expect on a body-builder. But when I looked up, it was only a priest. So he asked me what's up and I told him straight. 'I'm mad,' I said. But the priest didn't blink. He just said, 'God bless you.' Then he let me go."

It mightn't seem like much now. Priests are supposed to bless you, that's their job. But to her, right then, it was a life-saver. "I took it as a sign. I went off down Fore Street, down to the river, and when I got there, I tried to wash myself clean. I stuck my whole head in the water, hair and all, only some of the chocolate wouldn't come off. Never mind. I sat down on the bank and waited to dry off. It was a fair day, nice and mild. There was one of those old barges, with the bright paintwork and polished brass, and the boy that owned it was up on deck, messing about. Drop-dead gorgeous, he was; the build of him. I wouldn't mind some of that, I thought. And then I thought, God bless me. And, stupid cow, I broke down crying. I was that happy, you see."

Soon afterwards, she got involved with an occult group in Beacon Lane. Nothing heavy; no black sabbaths or animal sacrifices. They were sweethearts, mostly. But they helped her to grow. Made her understand her own powers—that her life was in her own hands, to shape and control any way she dared. "To start with, that just meant taking my clothes off a lot. But gradually I went deeper. I learned to block out negatives. I discovered myself as a goddess."

It was this goddess who got married. And the same goddess who birthed her three daughters. After a few years, though, she started to lose her way again. Because of Keith and his horses, they were constantly in debt, so they had to live in shite digs. "Two rooms above an Indian takeaway, and the stink of curry got on everything. My clothes and hair, the sheets, even the kids' toys. I should have named my girls Papadum, Vindaloo and sodding Biryani. But it was a roof, wasn't it?"

She started drinking hard, just like her mother, and soon it took up all her time. "I'd heard that drinking before breakfast is the end. So I stopped eating breakfast. That way I didn't have to worry, you see."

At least she didn't have the girls to bother about; they'd gone to stay with Keith's mum. "Well, I thought it best." With the stink of curry downstairs, they couldn't get their proper sleep, and they were falling behind at school.

One wet Tuesday lunchtime, she was walking down Heavytree Road, feeling sick. She had a lot on her mind and a fair bit of vodka on her stomach. All she wanted was to wash herself away. So she went in the Royal Oak. And that's when she dropped dead in love.

The pub was almost empty. A man was playing darts by himself. Nelson, his name was; she'd seen him around.

He worked on building sites, a scaffolder, and hung around with a gang of Jamaicans. Not that he was black himself, just mixed: "What you'd call coffee olé."

In the past, she'd never fancied him much. "He always acted like he was God's gift. 'I'm a hard man, look at me.' You know the routine. 'Get down on your knees and beg for it, you bitches.' All that macho posing, it got up my nose."

Today, though, he looked different. Maybe it was the light or maybe just her mood, but he seemed softer somehow. When he stood by the window, aiming his dart, his colour was warm and gold, almost glowing. Martha was sitting at the bar, nursing her vodka tonic. He smiled at her. Just a quick sideways crinkle, nothing blatant. Then he threw his dart.

They didn't have to discuss a thing. The man just finished his game, then sat down beside her, waited while she polished off her vodka tonic, and then they fucked.

Nelson was moonlighting as a security guard and he had the use of a trailer, but it was like tackling an obstacle course to get there. Past a barbed-wire fence and a pair of guard dogs, across a sea of slushy mud, and when they reached the trailer, it was a total pigsty, piled high with rubbish. "I've seen cleaner cesspits." But none of that made any odds. There was a mangy old mattress, like a nest in the middle of all the debris. It was a mass of cigarette burns and water stains. "Fire and water, I saw that in a flash." Which was a bad omen. Opposing elements meant clashes, discord, betrayal. "I knew I was bollocking fate." And she didn't care. "It was a bed." So she fell down across it.

From the moment Nelson fed her that first smile, she'd lost all will. He could have had her on the pub floor if he'd wanted to, between two packets of crisps. She wasn't easy by nature. He made her easy, that's all.

Water snuffed out fire. "I went down and under, and never came up." For the first days and weeks, they met secretly. Nelson had other women, she knew that, but they didn't worry her. "I was invincible, my love. No woman alive could stand against me." Nelson was planning to leave Exeter soon, move on to better things, and she'd be going with him. "We were never meant to get stuck and die in a nothing town. Some people, that's their destiny, but our destiny was more."

Keith didn't want to let her go. "He said we should start again. He said we belonged together. Man and wife, he said. Well, I panicked. I saw my whole future; it was a black hole. I just sat there, breathing in the fumes of rogan gosht and chicken tikka masala, and I felt that sick, I couldn't shift."

She spent the whole afternoon drinking, choking back dread. Then, like always when she drank, she brought out the matches. And the flames brought her out of her trance. When she felt the heat, it broke the spell. She doused the curtains, stamped on the rug. Then she packed a bag and caught the bus to Nelson's trailer.

"He was a bit offish at first. Said he was his own boss, thank you very much, and he didn't fancy being pressured. But I soon made him sweet. *Ve haff our methods, you know.*"

Nelson had a half-sister, Joy, who lived on the outskirts of Bristol. A white girl with a white militant husband, a hardcore Aryan Power man, an all-white housing estate. Brother and sister had never been close. Close enough, though: "She had a spare room, an empty bed."

What about her children? "I thought of that. Of course I did. I thought about it for days, and I cried a river, and all. But I couldn't help myself. If you'd ever loved a man, you'd understand. I had to have him."

The atmosphere at Joy's was tense. Tony, her husband, wouldn't say one word to them. Wouldn't let Nelson eat off the same plates or drink from the same glasses, wouldn't even let their sheets in with the family wash. His hostility had no teeth, though. He was unemployed, hadn't had a job in years, while Joy was a nursery-school teacher. That made her the breadwinner. And she said they could stay. "She called it family honour. It means you can hate each other's guts, but nobody must know."

Withywood, the housing estate, was a pit. Only three miles south of the city centre, but it seemed another world. When it was first built, in the fifties, it was meant to be a model community, stuck out in the countryside, healthy and unspoiled, with hills and farms nearby and fields full of live cows. "A Club fucking Med, from what I heard." But the shine had worn off long ago.

Uneasy in Joy's house, she spent her days roaming. Nelson had work as a scaffolder in Hotwells and she was on her own. She hung around the housing office, which was built up and protected like a fortress, or she made excursions to Dundry Hill. Mostly, she just walked at random. "It was all run by gangs, the whole estate; ramrodders, joyriders, crackheads. Anyone that wasn't mad like me was scared to come outdoors." But nothing scared Martha, not then. "That's the thing about love, it's a bulletproof vest."

Some weekends Nelson took her on excursions. "Clifton Downs, the Avon Gorge, the Suspension Bridge, I thought I'd dropped into a magic city." More often, though, they stayed in bed. "That man just touched me and I climbed walls. Flew out the window, my love. I went around the world and never left my sheets."

They didn't talk much; there was no call. Unlike Keith, Nelson was a man of acts, not words. "I didn't know him, really. No one did. Joy told me once, in all their childhood, she never seen him cry. Or laugh, come to that. Not a belly-laugh, full out, like a human being."

Then, one Thursday night, he failed to come home. No sign, no message, not a word—he just didn't show up. "He's done a flit," Joy said, right off. But that couldn't be true; it couldn't. Martha sat up all night by their bedroom window, and at first light she started walking. It was March, a raw day, and she wasn't dressed for it. A short skirt and leather knee-boots, high heels at eight of a morning, she must have looked a right tart. But she wanted to look hot for him. Knock his eyes out when they met, so he'd realise what he stood to lose, come back to his right senses.

She walked all the way to Hotwells. Cars kept stopping, horny bastards offering lifts. She could have caught a bus, of course, but she preferred to slog on by foot. "I was like a pilgrim, sort of." Toiling up the hills and spilling back down; crossing rivers, islands, canals; feet blistering, toes crushed. "Well, it felt for the best to suffer. I thought it might help my chances."

When she reached the site Nelson worked on, though, they told her he'd left yesterday. Asked for his cards at the day's end and simply walked away. Martha stood in the gateway, looking up at the scaffolding, and when the fore-man told her what was what, everything in her fell apart, she burst. "I pissed myself, didn't I?" Then she fell in the pub on the corner. All this time since she'd been in Bris-tol, stuck away in Withywood, she'd hardly touched a drop. "Tony Aryan used to sniff my breath. He thought I was a degenerate, he made that more than clear. Because I loved a mongrel, you see." So she'd stayed on the dry, just to spite him.

No point in further sacrifice. By the time she got back to Joy's that night, she was stinking. Tony Aryan took one look at her and slammed the door. Then he opened it again; handed her an envelope. It came from Nelson, dated yesterday. Inside was fifty pounds in mixed notes, but no letter, not a word.

The raw mean day had turned to an even dirtier night. There was an evil wind, and Martha, still dressed in miniskirt and high heels, had no defences. "I wanted to crawl in a hole." But none of the holes around Withy-wood were safe. She was alone out there with the gangs. "In that kit, I might as well have hung a Rape Me sign round my neck." So she started walking again, back into the city, whipped and wet and drunk as she was. The buses had stopped running; there were no taxis about. "I ended up kipping in a bus shelter near St. Mary Redcliffe, wrapped up in a cardboard box. Just for the night, I thought. Just this once."

The worst thing of all was not understanding. She had to track Nelson down, wherever he was, to get their problems sorted, make things right.

The first place she looked was back in Exeter. Maybe he'd felt homesick or maybe one of his used bitches had got her screws into him again. No dice, though; nobody had seen him, hide nor hair. And she'd run out of money. She called on Keith, in hopes of a quick sub, but he wouldn't front her the skin off his arse. When she asked to see her girls, he went completely ballistic. Raging and ranting, you couldn't talk sense to him. "He never considered my feelings. Never once." All he could see was his own hurt. Men and their fucking egos, it was always the same.

After Exeter, she tried again in Hotwells. Asked the foreman if Nelson had ever talked about other towns, and he reeled off a whole list. Worcester, Newport, Bridgewater, Avonmouth, Bath. So off she went again. Hitchhiking mostly, pounding the roads. But not a sniff anywhere. More than likely, the foreman had just been playing with her. Still, she kept slogging on.

It was mad, of course; she knew that. If she had been in her right mind, she would have cut her losses long ago. But that was love, wasn't it? The way she felt, there was no life without him. No life worth saving, anyway. When she'd failed to find him on the road, she came back to Bristol and set up vigil there. Sooner or later, he was bound to pass through. When he did, she would be waiting.

"I'm chained to the railings, I am," Martha says to me now, and crosses her wrists as if cuffed. We're back on the streets, and hours have passed. From the Old Pint and Pie, we moved on to Jazmin's Café for a slice of Jamaican rum cake, and then to Our Lady of Ostrobrama for a quick prayer, and in all that time she's barely paused for breath. The words keep thrashing and flailing, the stories multiplying. Still she shows no sign of exhaustion.

She has been hunting Nelson for almost four months. Each week she does a fresh circuit of the city's building sites by day, and its warehouses and office blocks by night, in case he's taken work as a security guard. Sometimes she checks Withywood, sometimes she tries the law courts. Mostly, though, she just hangs round the city centre, in hopes of a chance sighting. So far there's been nothing, but she won't admit to doubts. "He'll turn up all right," she tells me. "I'm being tested, that's all."

Money is a problem. So is finding a bed. Some nights, if the weather is evil, she dosses down in a shelter, but more often she sleeps rough. There's a place called the Pit, near the bus station, where people congregrate. An outsize concrete dug-out, hidden from the traffic above. In daytime it has shops and stalls but after dark it belongs to the homeless.

The Pit is the closest she comes to safety these days. "I have good friends there, they watch my back. They know my ways, how I can get wild, but they don't judge. Well, how can they? They've been there themselves."

One man, in particular, has been good to her. He's known as Sergeant Colin, because he wears fatigues and army boots and he spends his days standing guard outside the empty building where the recruiting office used to be. "A man of principles, he is. A rock." Still, she can't stay in the Pit for ever. There are too many fights and she doesn't get enough rest. "I need to look after my head. If I don't, I get all wound up, and then at times I go Bang." There have been incidents; the law has been on her case. "Matches, and the drink, and my big mouth." She's under too much stress.

Some of it might be Bristol's fault. When you get to know the place as well as she has, you start to see through its cracks. The things that you liked at first—the slowness, the tolerance—turn out to be only apathy. "This isn't Shangri-la, I'll tell you that for nothing." But then, what is? "All I know is, it's out there. It exists." Once Nelson shows up, and they get back together, they're going to see the world. "Sometimes I think San Francisco. Or maybe Mexico." Or maybe they'll take to the skies. "He promised to teach me to hang-glide one time." Or again, they might end up living on a beach. "How does the Bahamas sound, my love? What's big and blue and wet?" Drifting out on the tide, sun-drenched, with a bucket of rum punch. "I'd drown in that any day."

Once Nelson shows up. The funny thing is, though he's been gone all these months, she feels he's coming closer every day. He could be down the next street or sitting inside the next pub. "I just have to keep on seeking," she says, downing her drink, and leads me back into the city.

As we turn on to Stoke's Croft again, she steps straight off the pavement, not looking, into the flow of traffic. I grab her arm, drag her back, but she isn't the least bit bothered. Twisting free, she just laughs. Broken teeth, wild eyes, bottled hair; the ripped tights and the lime-green minidress. No bus or car has her number. "This one's for burning," she says.

O N OUR WAY out of Bristol we visit a sailor named Cedric Reeve, who lives on a Chinese junk. Grizzled and shaggy, he looks like a pirate and his attitude is blunt. "When I checked this morning, I wasn't dead yet," he tells us. "So I'd say this is a fair day."

The junk, *The Fortunate Cloud*, is moored in a marina on Spike Island, surrounded by sleek modern yachts. Modelled after the style of the early Ming dynasty, its sides are embellished with ornate carved dragons and there's a slavering demon at its prow. On this bleak and rain-lashed morning, framed against a backcloth of cranes and industrial blight, it seems impossibly exotic: a boat out of an opium dream.

Reeve himself is sixty, a man of volcanic energies. Born in London, he used to manage a lifeboat museum, now defunct, and he built his junk, which he calls "the carcass," by hand. This took some doing, because he'd damaged his spine in a fall and was half-crippled at the time. Then, when *The Fortunate Cloud* was finished and finally in the water, he found he had multiple sclerosis.

"A bit of a problem," he calls this, dismissively. It failed to prevent him from sailing to Shanghai and back, or surviving a gunboat attack in the Taiwan Strait. He won't be confined to a wheelchair, has thrown away his elbow crutches. And now he's about to set sail once again. "I'm moving on. Penzance, this time," he says. His head is massively imposing, with wild bushy eyebrows and a great bone for a nose. Squinting up at us from under the hood of his oilskin, he looks indestructible. But he is too busy to talk. "I'm under the gun," he informs us, gruff but not discourteous. "The world doesn't stop. Why should I?"

On that note, he dives back into the guts of the Chinese junk, and we retreat. Soon we're zipping down the motorway towards Devon and Cornwall, buffeted by a fierce gale. I keep picturing Reeve, all beard and eyebrows and wild wilful heart, chugging through the same storm to Penzance, while *The Fortunate Cloud* groans and spits dragon's teeth, yet endures.

"Dauntless," Mary says. This is her word of the week. And it comes to my mind again when we reach Cornwall, and find ourselves in Fraggle Rock.

The Rock is a New Age travellers' site, a few miles outside Liskeard. It's stuck away down a side road, only a few yards off the A38, but invisible to passing traffic. In the wake of the storm, the caravans and trailers are awash in mud and the road is a sea of puddles. A man named George appears through ranks of children and dripping curs to see what we're about. He has a tight, wiry body and a challenging gaze. "What do you want to know?" he asks me. "Everything," I reply.

We've found the site through a friend who doubles as a social worker. A liaison between Fraggle Rock and the outer world, she has warned us to expect a chilly welcome. "They don't trust strangers," she says. So here I stand, up to my hocks in spit and slurry, while George weighs me up, then opens his mouth and does not shut it again.

So much for English reserve. Leading me through the puddles to his van, George keeps talking a blue streak. His living space, steamy with wet heat, is crammed with mattresses and fat cushions. George squats cross-legged on the bed, I hunker on the floor, other travellers drift in and out. Some look battered, others merely drenched, but the atmosphere is comradely; they seem joined in a common cause. "An endangered species, that's us. They keep trying to stamp us out but we won't oblige," George remarks. "We're professional survivors."

"Who's they?"

"Government, the police, the Southern Intelligence Unit in Devizes, they all want us gone, and why? Because we don't live by rules, and rules are all they have, without rules they'd have no control."

This speech sounds ominously pat. Reaching under his mattress, he starts to pull out documents; newspaper cuttings, legal papers, correspondence. He waves them at me to demonstrate his point, and that point is always the same: travellers are victims.

Why do they get so much grief? "We're seen as a threat, right? We don't fit, so we must be wiped out. And many of us have been, too. Busted, banged up in jails, dispersed. Ten years ago, we felt like an army, but how many's still left today? Five thousand? But you'd think we were a horde. A human plague, right? Drug fiends, rapists, scum. And what's our crime, once you get past the scapegoating? We don't know our place, that's all."

In George's case, this is largely because he's never had a place to know. Born in Lincoln, he grew up without family or structure. "I was in care homes, detention, Borstal—the full comply-or-die programme." He was always taught that he was a freak, a total no-hoper. Then he went to a free festival and found out he wasn't alone. "Suddenly I saw that we were a tribe. Freaks like me, right? We could have a life, after all."

It was the start of the eighties, glory days for dissent. The movement that had kicked off with Flower Power back in the late sixties had spread and deepened its roots. For most, it was still a summer sport, a chance to grab some cheap drugs and cheaper sex, work up a tan and blow off a few rebel clichés. But there was also a core group, in for the long haul. "People like me, we had nothing to go back to. The road was all there was. So we made it our home."

Travellers came from all kinds of backgrounds then. They might be old hippies or punks or New Age mystics or anarchists or junkies, but their differences weren't important. "We all shared the same spirit, we all believed. The world was going to change." George marched and chanted with the Anti-Nazi League, played in a punk band, toured the country with Circus Normal. In winter, he scraped by. And in summer, when the festival season rolled round, he felt a free man.

The key gathering, of course, was Stonehenge, the annual free festival to celebrate the solstice, and celebrate the celebrants. "You'd meet the same people each year, it was like one huge family. A mass of music and light, as far as you could see. People, just people, that's what it was. Humanity, feeling good." But all that had changed on 1 June 1985; the night of the Beanfield.

Exactly what happened depends on who you're talking to. The consensus, though, is that a loose coalition of powers—local landowners, the police, the county council—got together and decided that they didn't want any more of these dirty, hairy, drug-addled people messing up Stonehenge and its surrounds. The National Trust and English Heritage took out injunctions against the coming festival. Then the law went into action.

Each year a ramshackle regiment of brightly painted vans and buses, trucks, London taxis, fire engines and old bangers, grandly titled the Peace Convoy, made a ceremonial approach to the festival site. In 1985, the procession numbered some 150 vehicles. Close to a village called Shipton Billinger, they were met by the police. There were 1,363 officers on hand. The road was blocked off with mounds of gravel and the convoy trapped, but the travellers broke through a fence and took refuge in a beanfield. There followed some hours of stalemate, with the police ordering the fugitives to come out and be arrested, and the fugitives refusing to budge. Finally, the police attacked. Using riot gear, shields and truncheons, they stormed the vehicles, smashed in windows, broke teeth and noses and heads. TV camera crews followed them, recording the bloodshed, but the police were undeterred. "I'm not here to bargain," said Assistant Chief Constable Grundy, the operational commander. Four hundred twenty arrests were made.

"That did our heads in. We never got over it," says George. Squatting in his nest of documents, he waves one arm jaggedly, disjointedly, like a maimed bird. "One day we felt unstoppable, the next we were dog turds, right?"

The terrible thing about the Beanfield was that it couldn't happen, and yet it did. Growing up English and white, you took certain limits for granted. If you rattled their chains, the police might snap at you, even rough you up a little. That's how the game was played. A bit of aggro to ginger things up; a pleasant fizz of paranoia. But not this. Not these science-fiction terminators with their batons and flying boots. That wasn't a bit of bother, it was terror. "People thought they were going to die."

The road was never easy again. Confidence drained away, and travellers went on the defensive. If they tried to stop, the authorities moved them on; if they protested, the riot gear and attack dogs came out.

The Criminal Justice Act and the Public Order Bill had tightened the screws still further. Anyone with a choice had given up, got off the road. "We're down to the hard-core now." A few battered dissenters like George himself, assorted alcoholics and junkies, a scattering of petty criminals. "They've whittled us to the bone."

Cornwall is one of the last counties where travellers can set up camp in relative peace. Even here, though, times are hard. A few months ago, there was an incident when one of the kids at Fraggle Rock was accused of disappearing a bottle of wine from a nearby liquor store. Two policemen, one male, one female, came on site and insisted on searching every van. When the travellers resisted, things turned nasty. That afternoon about seventy police in full riot gear descended. "Helicopters, dogs, flashing lights, the lot. But who could blame them?" asks George, all innocence. "We were nine adults and eleven kids. A lethal force."

Since then, there's been a constant feeling of unease. Police harassment is only part of the problem; travellers themselves are changing. Many sites have been ravaged by violence and heroin use, though Fraggle Rock is better than most. "There's not as much idealism now, it's been beaten out of a lot of us," George admits.

Joints do the rounds. So do mugs of tea. One man, stoned out of his tree, seeks advice: should he come down or double the dose? Another reminisces about his last stint in jail. "I'm better off here," he concludes.

One figure dominates—a tall, muscular man with cropped hair, high cheekbones and a wry, self-mocking smile. His name is Gilles, born in Paris and raised in Leicester, of theatrical stock and, so he claims, five generations of unwed mothers.

By early evening the rain has moved on. The site is bathed in warm sunlight and everyone has emerged from their vehicles. Gilles holds court beside a guttering fire, while his partner, Sue, keeps watch. She's a striking, weather-burned woman, radiating strength. Like Gilles, she gives off a sense of self-containment but in a darker, fiercer style. While her man speaks freely, all smiles, she keeps her guard up. "I talk. She thinks," Gilles explains.

The site at this hour has a backstreet feel. Travellers sit lazing outside their vans, drinking lager and smoking roll-ups. It's Saturday night, and some are planning an evening in the pubs. George is meeting a one-time Fraggler called Skank, a transvestite welder. Others just want to soak up the warmth. One of them asks what I'm writing. When I tell him, he looks disgusted. "D'you want to know the secret of life?" he demands.

"I wouldn't mind."

"Don't get banged up in Winson Green."

Cars roll out in a posse, taking music and laughter with them. When they're gone, Gilles stretches his long limbs and starts to roll a cigarette. Kids playing in the slushy mud, mutts snuffling at our feet, the dying sun on our backs and junkyard shambles all around—it's a peaceable scene, and Gilles wallows in its ease. "I've spent my life looking for my gang, a group I could fit in with, and this is it," he says. "My place, my politics and my strength are here. Fraggle Rock is my street."

He talks with the assurance of a born phrase-maker. Anecdotes and philosophies roll off him seamlessly, but they don't come off sounding slick. Instead, they feel shaped by hard experience. "When you arrive at a site like this, I don't care who you are, you come naked. Some people may show up with a lot of fancy ideas, full of utopian dreams, but they never last long. Hardcore travellers, the ones who endure, have no choice. They've lost everything, their jobs and homes, many times their families as well. They've done time, or they're on drugs, or they have mental problems. The nine-to-five world has no further use for them; they're seen as garbage. No one will accept them, just us. We're always here, and we take in anyone who asks. No exceptions and no conditions. None."

In his view, there are worse fates than bottoming out. "The man who loses everything, or the woman, I guarantee their main feeling, when the last of it has gone, will be relief. At last they can stop struggling; there isn't any point. They're down to bedrock, and guess what? They're still breathing."

What was it that Cedric Reeve told us, peering out through his beard and the squalling rain? *When I checked this morning, I wasn't dead yet. So I'd say this is a fair day.* "My sentiments exactly," says Gilles.

He used to be a businessman, a conman, a wheeler and dealer. He made fortunes and lost them, went bankrupt, ran afoul of the law. "I was always one for thinking big. When I was about nineteen, I designed a new-fangled toothbrush and applied for a patent. I thought I was going to be a millionaire. I went to all these trade fairs and picked up loads of free samples that I'd sell off to chemists. Pure profit. Then Customs and Excise raided us. We hadn't been paying our VAT. That was the end of Gilles, boy millionaire."

Other, murkier adventures followed. "Let's just say I was in a lot of shit and I didn't know how to get out." In the end, out of options, he simply abandoned ship and started over. Along with Sue and the kids, he took to the road. They lived in the back of a taxi, in a railway hut, in a ten-foot trailer, in a tent. Once they were stranded in a storm, miles from anywhere, when they stumbled on an abandoned bus. "A magic bus! Out of fucking nowhere!" They swiped it, fixed it up, then passed it on. "That bus saved lives, I'm telling you."

When local authorities began to cut off other havens, they took refuge in Fraggle Rock. That was four years ago, and they haven't stirred since. "This is our home, it's as simple as that." Still, if the site gets shut down one day and they're forced to move on again, the loss will not destroy them. "It's a flexible life, travelling; you can't afford to put down roots," Gilles says. A wolfish grin splits his face. "We're not so much *Down and Out in Paris and London,* more fucked up in Liskeard and Saltash."

An eavesdropper starts humming "Me and Bobby McGee." "Right you are," says Gilles. "We're all old hippies under the skin; just a bunch of washed-up anarchists. I've always liked extremists. The power of radical thinking, no matter what form it takes. My mother's a full-blown Maggie Thatcher Tory, dyed-in-the-wool, but I have a lot of time for her. At least she's got beliefs; a passion. Rather an ardent fascist than a half-arsed liberal."

"Fuck that," the eavesdropper says. "They had the right idea when they strung them up from the fucking lamp-post."

"The fascists or the half-arsed liberals?"

"The whole fucking shower. And writers, too."

Another roll-up and another beer defuse the moment. A few yards off, Sue is rounding up children, doling out food, yet still keeping watch. "I lack her stamina," Gilles muses. "She'll stand at a supermarket cheese counter but she refuses to take a ticket. She doesn't believe in being called by a number, she finds it demeaning." She also refuses to live off state hand-outs, though Gilles himself is not so picky.

The dole aside, he supports his family by trading in scrap and by raiding the skips outside Safeway's, rescuing food that's past its sell-by date. "We had whole chickens last Christmas, fifteen-pounders, and curry for Boxing Day." Other supermarket chains, like Tesco's and Sainsbury's, pour bleach on their discards, ostensibly to ward off rats: "But we're the real vermin in their minds."

Always, when he starts waxing high-flown, his sly wolf's grin deflates him. What fuels him most deeply, I feel, is not militance but an insatiable curiosity. "At one time in my life I used to drive past hitchhikers. Can't imagine it now," he says. "You see someone standing by the verge in a suit and his engine has blown up. Well, you have a joint in your hand and the kids are screaming, you don't really want to stop. But, what the fuck, you do anyway. The guy scrambles in the back, then he gets a load of you, the convict hair, the tattoos, and of course he's terrified. You can see him thinking: *travellers . . . anarchists . . . weirdos . . . LET ME OUT OF HERE!* But he's stuck. So what can he do? Hope for the best. Just like us all. Try to hold his piss. And what happens then? More often than not, he starts to talk. Maybe it's nerves, maybe something else. But flap goes his mouth, anyhow. And out comes . . . what? Anything, everything. The whole mad world . . ."

The connection may be fleeting. That doesn't make it trivial. "I have a sixteen-year-old son. He's selfish, loud, aggressive; all the things a sixteen-year-old should be. But he would never, no matter what, leave someone standing by the road." A dog trots up for a scratch, and Gilles obliges. "That's progress for you," he says.

It's growing late; the light is fading. "Everyone alive

wants answers. My own way of looking for them is to sit about in caravans and read books and mind my own business, which might be strange but doesn't strike me as vicious." He ponders. "You know what I'd really love to do? Write a book about people's thoughts at one given moment; seven twenty-nine on a Tuesday morning, say. Knock on their doors and ask them what they're expecting. Little green men from Mars like I am, or Christ, or a lottery win." The dog lifts its leg; Gilles smiles his crooked smile. "Or simply a big bang, The End."

CORNWALL IS a strange land. Or three strange lands in one. There is the ancient country of Celtic mysteries, and ye olde country for tourists, and the hard-scrabble, broken-down country that most of its people inhabit, as poor as any in Europe.

Driving it, we're never sure which of these countries we're in, from one mile to another. Up on the wilds of Bodmin Moor, we get lost in a wilderness, all boglands and tarns and distant tors. A herd of shaggy wild cattle blocks our path at a crossroads, heads lowered to charge. But where do the signposts point? Kids Kingdom and the Legendary Last Labyrinth, Shire's Adventure Park and the American Spirit of the West.

The old industries—tin, china-clay, fishing—are all dead or dying. Nothing's left but the ruined engine houses and chimneys of the mines and the bizarre lunar landscapes of the worked-out quarries with their monstrous white pyramids of waste. As for the coast, it's mostly chalets and caravan parks.

At night, when we stop at old market towns—Liskeard, Bodmin, Launceston—the main squares are plastered with posters for craft fairs and arts festivals. By nightfall, though, the restaurants are closing, the pubs half-empty and the streets virtually deserted.

Mary shuts herself up in a phone box and calls home. She's too short for the receiver to nestle naturally against her chin and has to strain upwards, neck tense, chin thrusting, willing herself to lift-off.

Locked out, I sit waiting and watching. Sometimes a gaggle of teens slouches past, bored stiff and raging. On a wall in Bodmin, one of them has scrawled the motto, I WANK, THEREFORE I AM.

Away from the towns, the roads turn cart-track narrow, rising and falling like roller coasters, and the hedgerows are riotous with wild flowers. As a schoolboy, I knew all their names off by heart—toadflax, skullcap, hound's-tongue, stork's-bill—but now I'm not sure which is which. Once we drive through a cloud of white butter-flies. Two miles on, a Stealth bomber zooms out of a field. "They're just trying to confuse us," Mary says, and it's true enough. The whole time we're in Cornwall, I feel myself adrift, as though I've lost some crucial clue.

The feeling is most acute in St. Neot. Superficially, this is a standard-issue Cornish village, picturesque and twee, with roses clustered round the cottage doors and a sixteenth-century Creation window, all crimson and gold, in the parish church. Yet something about the place nags my memory; some allusion I can't nail. I wander through the churchyard and study the gravestones. Nothing there. So I drop to my haunches and try sniffing the warm, wet earth. Still nothing.

Two nights later, midway through my sausage and eggs and beans and chips, I suddenly make the jump. Of course. St. Neot is Grace's birthplace. "The old womb and thumb-suck," he calls it.

With remembrance comes a sharp goose of guilt. I haven't seen the old boy in ages, it must be almost eigh-teen months. That's far too long, so I call him up. Too late. Val, his wife, tells me Grace dropped dead the week before Easter.

Val herself sounds philosophic. He was only sixty-eight, but an old and exhausted sixty-eight, she says, and his heart caved in. "His meter ran out, that's all," she sums up. She's a nurse by trade, Val, and not much given to drama. But I'm not so sensible. I have known Grace since I was sixteen, and I always assumed he'd be around for ever.

Our connection goes back to my first summer alone in London. I was working, more or less, as a packer in the basement of the Army & Navy Stores. It was a menial job at menial wages, stuck underground in dead air, fiddling about with bits of string. No red-blooded Saxon male, in those days of easy employment, would sully himself with such piddle. It was work fit only for women and foreigners—Trinidadians, Nigerians, Poles—and for sixteen-year-olds without a clue.

In this early form of the republic, the women talked fucking all day, in castrating detail. "Love is a game of inches," one told me. She was a redhead, born in Wakefield; Teresa, named after the saint. I was terrified of her. She was always taunting me, daring me to show her what I'd got. "I bet you've got Irish disease, all you Micks are the same," she said, and waggled her little finger at me, shrieking with laughter. Once she followed me into the Gents and started to hoist her skirt. Her thighs were mottled and bruised, raw-looking. I ran.

Teresa thought I'd fled because I was queer. That was what she told the other women, anyhow. They took up the refrain and left a used tampon on my workbench. Teresa called me her Wild Irish Rose. Hilarious, she thought it was.

At the time I was dying for the love of a girl in sky-blue shorts, but she wouldn't look at me. At night I lay, hard and sleepless, aching for her touch, only to straggle into the basement come morning and get jeered at for a fairy.

It was a Nigerian who saved me. His given name was Aki or Okee, I'm not sure which, but everyone called him Hockey—a squat, low-slung figure with too many teeth for his mouth and muscular footballer's thighs, which he liked to show off in tight jeans. A gentle spirit, he was always quick to cover my mistakes. One night he invited me back to his bedsit after work.

He lived in Balham; we rode down on the bus. When we reached Hockey's stop, he was met by three other Nigerians, who thumped his back and hugged him, not like a man back after a day's desultory toil in a basement, but like a hero home from the wars. "What news of the Army and Navy?" one asked.

"I blow them up, boom!" Hockey answered. When he laughed, his teeth were crooked and crammed but dazzling white; they made me think of tumbling skittles. "Boom!" he shouted.

The bedsit was just round the corner, top floor in a red-brick semi-detached. Hearing us come in, the landlady popped out from behind her kitchen door. She didn't look at all like the harridan landladies in films. She was youngish and elegant, with bright red fingernails and a filmy white blouse that showed off her bust. She didn't care much for the Nigerians, though. "You know my rules. *No Guests*," she said. "They are no guests, they are all my brothers," Hockey told her. "And this," he added, pushing me forward into the light, "this boy is my fine son."

Struck dumb, the landlady let us pass. Upstairs, a miniature flag of many garish, clashing colours was tacked to Hockey's door. When I asked whose flag it was, he told me it belonged to his local football club back home in Lagos. "I miss my kickers," he said, and a look came into his face then, a haunt of such unredeemable loss that my own woes seemed nothing.

The rest of the evening is blurred to me now. What I remember is sitting on the floor of Hockey's room, drinking sweet home-made liquor. Not being practised, I got stinking drunk right away, but it didn't seem to matter, because the Nigerians did, too. They sang a native song and tried to teach me the chorus. Then we sang "God Save the Queen."

It was a pivotal night for me. For the first time since arriving in this strange land, I felt touched by something shared, and the feeling set me free. I started combing the London streets, hot for adventures and strangeness. I didn't know what drove me but I knew what hit the spot. One night, when I was coming home from work, a dark girl called out from her window, promising pleasure beyond all enduring. "I'll suck your spine out through your eyeballs," she cooed, smoky-voiced, "and back through your arsehole again."

Another night, searching for a pub, any pub, that would sell alcohol to minors, I stumbled into a bar on the Bayswater Road. It was full of men in very tight trousers, who seemed strangely happy to see me. Before I could find out why, someone large and billowy in a low-cut floral frock had swooped to my rescue.

This was Grace.

I'd never seen anyone like him: six foot two, pumped and buffed; a lantern jaw, blue with stubble; silky, corn-blond hair worn in bangs, Prince Valiant style; mountains of Man-Tanned muscle; and then his dress, a filmy number in peach and chartreuse, with a fetching primrose pattern.

I didn't feel much threatened. Grace's act was too theatrical, too camp for that. Besides, there was a gentleness about him, a backhanded straightness. He was a born protector.

From the moment he saw me, he took me over. For the rest of the summer, he served as my private tutor in London, its pleasures and perils. His friends, not all of them gay, were musicians and gamblers, pot smokers and sometime whores. A few of them blanked me but most were tolerant. Either way, it didn't matter much. Tucked under Grace's massive wing, I was guaranteed safe passage.

For most of the week, he lived in semi-concealment. He drove long-distance lorries, lived with a married sister in Maida Vale. His gay life was mostly confined to a body-builder's gym near Carnaby Street. He'd been a professional wrestler once, working under the name of Doctor Doom, but all that sweat and resin gave him allergies. Now his ambition was to be a creature of leisure.

His Cornish roots showed only when he wore civvies. In drag, he used standard camp argot. Out of costume, however, he could be almost butch. His accent changed to a slow Western drone and he proved a fierce man with a hammer. He was always fixing windows and broken hinges, or running up a quick shelf or two.

The only strange thing about him, to me, was that he didn't feel strange. It was his born gift to make all human doings seem natural: "Just follow the bouncing ball," he liked to say.

The summer ended and I left London, though not to return to Derry. I spent the next years in Newcastle-upon-Tyne; didn't so much drop out of school as plummet; tried playing tenor sax, with dire results; drifted back to London; dabbled briefly with working, then opted for writing instead; and ended up in a Paddington bedsit, a minute's walk from Grace's new flat.

By now, he was a housewife, and looked it. Having reached his mid-thirties, he'd given up body-building and his muscles were starting to run to flab. Even so, when he went out on the razzle and decked himself in full finery—ball gown and heels, say, or a veiled Ascot hat—he could still be an astonishment.

His life wasn't simple. In the sixties, transvestites weren't yet the fashionable gender-bender icons they have become. Even a mobile brick shithouse like Grace had to duck and dive, learn to lie. His lover, Pompey, a merchant seaman from Portsmouth, had to pose as a long-lost cousin when he came home between ships.

When Pompey was at sea, Grace paid the rent by working as a part-time bouncer, part-time freelance milliner. But his great passion was for the horses. We'd sit in his kitchenette, which he preferred to call the conservatory, and scope out the form, as Grace slaved over a bonnet, a veil, a feathered cloche. "Work, work, work, but what the fuck?" he'd say, resplendent in a lacy peignoir or his favourite Chinese housecoat. "So far, so grandiose."

That was one of his pet phrases. In Grace's world, life's ups and downs were basically irrelevant. What counted in the end was mileage—how much you packed in, how greedily you enjoyed it and how little you felt cheated at the death. "Only a cheapskate looks at the bill," he believed.

Sometimes he talked to me about St. Neot. It was a sorry little place, he said, full of dirty minds and evil tongues, but he missed it, even so. One day he must go home.

Much about his Cornish days remained shadowy to me. His father had been a farm worker, he told me once, and Grace himself grew up in a yard full of pigs. I picked up a vague impression of wild winter storms, of hard graft and short rations. But the main emphasis was on swaddling clothes. "I just wanted to have babies," Grace said. "Always did, from kindergarten up."

He used to haunt an abandoned rectory in the wilds of Bodmin Moor. "I wanted to be married and live there. That was my great fantasy. To do the place up, bring it back to life. Then I would be the little wife and helpmate, bringing up the kids, fetching speckled eggs from the henhouse for their breakfast and helping them with their schoolwork, while my husband, the vicar, sat shut up in his study, puffing on his pipe and writing Sunday's sermon."

Looking back, what amazed him was how cut and dried the whole thing had been. As far as he could recall, he had never felt guilt or gone through any form of inner struggle. "I was born, not made," he insisted. "Just call me Original Sin." By the time he arrived at puberty, he was already pushing six feet and weighed over thirteen stone. "Fat as butter, darling. If you'd spread me on Mother's Pride, you could have fed a regiment."

Joining the Army Cadet Corps had knocked off the lard. It had also launched him on an endless round of sexual adventures, which he kept buried like a cache of old dog bones, to be dug up whenever he felt the urge to reminisce. Not that he went in much for graphic description—his style was arch suggestion. One of his lovers had been nicknamed Harry the Horse, I remember, but Grace just batted his eyelashes when I was gauche enough to ask why.

The Army Cadet phase had finished him for St. Neot, and for many miles around. "My reputation lay in tatters." He was sixteen and massive, built like a Sherman tank, but the village street erupted in wolf-whistles every time he took a stroll. "I wouldn't have minded, not really, but half of the bastards had had me. The married ones were the worst. They always are."

So he packed up and headed for the cities. He did stints in Plymouth and Southampton, then moved inland to Oxford. He worked on building sites, carried the hod. Took up body-building and won a shelfful of trophies. Played two-fingered piano in pubs, and sort of sang. "Where Have All the Flowers Gone?" was his big number. "I was the Marlene Dietrich of Cowley." But he still wanted to have children.

By this time, his pet fantasy had moved on from the rectory and the pipe-smoking vicar. What he wanted now was Aristotle Onassis. A yacht, a sundeck, and his very own billionaire, lightly grizzled round the edges, who would bathe him in champagne, then bless him with three children, two boys, one girl.

Instead, he'd got Pompey.

As for the children, he made do with surrogates. I suppose I was one of them. But I was too old for him, really. His mother's heart beat strongest for the under-tens. The neighbours' kids were always running in and out of his flat, juicing him for sweets or change. He swore at them, but always succumbed. The children, in return, called him Auntie Grace. They trusted him absolutely.

Was he happy? "Mustn't grumble," he'd say, and nothing more, whenever I asked how he was doing. The only hint that he might be unfulfilled came one night when we dropped in at Ronnie Scott's jazz club. Blossom Dearie was appearing. At one point, she sang "Someday My Prince Will Come." I looked across at Grace, and his mascara was a mess.

In the meantime, he kept on racketing. Burning the candle at both ends wasn't simply a pleasure to him, but a sacred duty. By the seventies, as middle age took hold, the strain was beginning to tell. Rather than be seen to clean up his act, though, he decided to switch playing fields. He wasn't ready for St. Neot yet, so he and Pompey retired to Dorset, where they ran a village pub. For a few years, we drifted out of contact.

The next time I saw him, he was taking lunch at Jimmy's in Frith Street, an old favourite of ours. He was tucking into the souvlaki with the same zest as ever, but he didn't look fit. "Good, healthy living, it's killing me," he confided. Too many cream cakes and chocolate éclairs, too many Cutty Sarks too early in the day—he'd bloated up to close on eighteen stone. Pompey had decamped with some trollop from the Inland Revenue, the pub had gone belly-up and everything was shot to hell. But was Grace defeated? "I'm just getting warmed up," he said, and ordered the baklava with extra whipped cream.

From then on, we kept in casual touch. Grace tried a series of jobs—barman, carpenter, bookie's teller—without quite hitting the spot. He even claimed to have done a stint as an undertaker's greeter, but the culture of grief was not his speed. "I'm searching for my niche," he told me. He was nudging sixty then.

These were awkward times between us. Grace lived in Highbury, I lived in New York, and when we had reunions, he liked to pick a neutral spot. "Let's meet halfway," he always said, meaning Soho. We would share a few pints, a Scotch egg or two, some desultory racing chatter, and then we'd part, neither of us having said one word that mattered. Yet I loved him.

Our meetings grew more and more sporadic. Then one night, out of nowhere, he phoned. Could he see me the following day?

We chose a pub near Holland Park. When I showed up, Grace was already waiting, impeccable in a double-breasted blazer, a fresh white shirt and a tie adorned with crossed cricket bats. He had lost a haystack of weight, looked thriving. What surprised me most, though, was his companion—a small, toffee-coloured boy called Tommy, three years old and devastatingly good-looking, who kept referring to Grace as Dad.

Grace himself took this in stride. "It's what I am, after all. His progenitor," he said, dead smug. He flashed a bland and fatuous smirk, basking in my bewilderment. "I'm a family man, aren't I?"

Tommy's mother, he told me, was a Trinidadian nurse and they'd been together six years, married almost five. "The happiest days of my life," Grace claimed.

The only reason he hadn't mentioned this earlier was that Val, Tommy's mother, was a serious person, a tax-payer and churchgoer, who had no time for fecklessness. Grace's racier sides, and the friends who went with them, were strictly off-limits. "I showed her one of your books," he said. "It didn't pass muster."

That was why I hadn't heard from him much. So why get in touch now? He looked uneasy. Playing for time, he bought the boy a fresh Coke. "It's a bit embarrassing, really," he said at last. When I studied him closely, I noticed a creeping greyness beneath his surface well-being, a slackening and falling-in of muscle tone, especially around his mouth. "What's embarrassing?" I prompted.

"Life. Just life." He kept his eyes on Tommy, who was vainly trying to blow up a burst bag of crisps. Our table was stuck in a dark corner but winter sunlight was stream-ing through a window above our heads, slanting across the pub's wooden floor. "I'd like you to write up my story," Grace blurted. "We could work on it together. What's the phrase the agents use? *Get into bed.*"

In that moment, with the pale sun lighting up the bar, and the second pint lying warm and flaccid in my gut, it didn't seem such a bad idea. *The Book of Grace*, why not? We talked on for a while, made a few rough plans, dug up some dead tales. Then we parted. "To be continued in our next," Grace said as we embraced, two old dogs. But something came up, and I left town.

Now I stand in this phone box, in this little Cornish town, staring at a message scratched into the coin box. Noel ❤ Bob, it says. Outside, the rebel teens go by, shouting about wankers, and I think of that lost summer, when Hockey was my father and Grace my Man-Tan mother. Then I see Grace in that last pub. The greyness beneath his skin, the pinched look around his mouth. At one moment, between stories, he paused to sip at his beer, take a nibble on his Scotch egg. "It would be a shame to just vanish," he said, offhand. Then we talked about something else.

TRAVELS WITH MARY are all helter-skelter. As we whirl around the republic, I feel as if I'm riding on her coat-tails, barely clinging on. Whenever we make a pit-stop, she flies out of Teal Wheels as if slingshot. By the time I lumber out behind her, she's already hit full stride.

She is a human magnet. The moment she stops racing, decides to give her boots a break, people start to gather around her. Drunks, derelicts, Romeos and wide-boys on the make, storytellers, argufiers and every manner of craicsmith come flocking to feed off her batteries. Her energy and hunger act on them like instant speed.

Her passion has been bred in her, at least in part, by Derry. It is a town fierce with life, both terrible and heroic; a town of non-stop and outrageous theatre; a tragic town, always on the verge of cataclysm, yet fuelled by humour and cock-eyed hope; a town, above all, of prodigious self-belief.

The one word that keeps returning is "hope." For Mary, it is the prime mover. When she launches herself into one of her patented hymns of praise, adulating a new writer or techno DJ or political visionary, her diatribes always end on the same note: "It's given people new hope. Now they know they're not alone."

In my own cosmology, hope is beside the point and being alone a state of grace. But Mary will have none of that; she thinks it ungodly. "We have work to do," she keeps repeating, as she charges ahead of me. Wrongs to right, lives to mend—for her, the republic isn't a conceit, but an article of faith. So she rampages through its badlands, St. Joan in purple boots, while the faithful flock to gape and wonder.

Authority is less impressed. The trouble starts when she gets off the street and into offices. She's too intemperate, altogether too raucous for corporate taste. Her work history is dotted with blow-ups, fatal confrontations, for reasons she can't quite fathom. "I only told him to get his head out of his arsehole," she'll say, looking back, and shake her head in bafflement.

She's easily stung. Every slight, intentional or otherwise, knocks her sprawling. But she gets right up, primed and firing. Sometimes the results are murderous. Friendships are laid waste, lives turned to shambles. "Why can't she mind her own business?" a former friend complains. But that's exactly the point. To Mary, the whole breathing, brawling world is her own business, for better and for worse.

July rolls around and, with it, Orange Day. Swinging north, we head for Southport, to watch the Loyalists in action. It's the only town in England where they'll be marching for the Glorious Twelfth. According to a misprint in the local paper, "a much lager attendance" is expected this year.

Not just lager, but bitter and spirits as well. Mid-morning, when we roll on to the seafront, the drinking is already picking up nicely. The streets are lined with day-trippers, out on a family outing; carloads and chartered buses full of them, luxuriating in the summer's warmth. They've come equipped with sandwiches and sunblock, Union Jacks and a limitless stock of brews.

Southport itself is stylish: a Victorian resort, complete with pleasure gardens, arcades and the world's oldest and longest iron pier, all essentially intact.

Beneath that pier, I visit the Gents—scalloped tiling and

marble sinks, a slow drip of icy water and a soldierly line of Edwardian urinals, full-length and dazzling, that glory in the trade name of Adamant. An elderly man in a battered tweed jacket wanders in and takes up position beside me. The jacket smells of mothballs and stale ale. Together we stand, stiff and straining, eyes front. The old man achieves a weak trickle, just enough for dignity. Then he takes one step back. A waggle, a shake, a quick buttoning. "Fuck the Pope," the old man says.

Outdoors, the marchers are ready to start. I take up position by a statue of Queen Victoria, next to a 1900 calliope, advertised as "suitable for all classes." Far down the street and around the corner, I can hear the first strains of "The Sash My Father Wore."

Marching bands and baton-twirlers have gathered from all over Lancashire and beyond, some ferried across from Ulster, and the titles on their banners are a Loyalist roll of honour: Liverpool Young Volunteers, Crown and Bible Defenders, the Derry Walls Concertina and Accordion Band, the Garscule Rising Sons of William, Johnston's True Blues, the Lily of Toxteth, the Star of Southport, the Shankhill Protestant Boys. But how circumspectly they tread, how muted their song and dance. The Orange Day marches I've watched in the past, clinging to my mother's hand as a child in the Derry Diamond or cowering behind a sandbag near Drumcree, were stark and terrible affairs. The black bowler hats, the Sash, the curlew shriek of the fifes and the booming of the lambeg drums—these were symbols full of dread. But this! A day's romp at the seaside; whelks and rock and Kiss-Me-Quick hats. As the bands straggle up the street, wheeling past the dead queen, they seem no more fanatical than a school outing, and far less threatening. Some of the bandsmen are laughing and winking; a few, unthinkably, are black. They even stop for red lights.

Mary can hardly believe it. "Yer a load of poofs," she shouts out. A few skinheads give her a hard stare, but not one makes a move. Too busy sucking their ice lollies.

The cavalcade comes to rest in the pleasure gardens, with beds of roses all around, gaudy pinks and yellows, and posters for Abba: The Tribute. Flopping down on the lawns, the Orangemen lay aside their fifes and drums, strip off their tunics and relax. A ragged chorus rises up, roughly to the tune of "Danny Boy": "Oh, Mammy dear / The Pope's a queer / He takes it up the arse." Then the drinking starts in earnest.

Back in the town centre, the party's already going full blast. All along Lord Street, with its glass-covered arcades and stolid Victorian emporiums, the drinkers roam in loose packs. The alley behind the Scarisbrick Hotel is wedged solid with skinheads and others, standing, sitting, sprawling full length. Women singing "No Surrender," children dolled up as William and Mary, and one Asian youth, in maximum boots and a plastic bowler, chanting pie-eyed in praise of Ian Paisley. I ask him why. "He walks on water," the Asian says.

Baffled, we take refuge inside the Captain's Table. Instantly, I'm plunged back into my childhood—ladies with gloves and blue rinses, Eddie Calvert and Alma Cogan on the tape deck, Knickerbocker Glory for afters. But even here decorum is under threat. A fifty-year-old Lolita in hot pants and a *Remember the Boyne* T-shirt is weeping quietly in a corner, dabbing at her eyes with her Union Jack. Then a Scouser comes in, selling clockwork monkeys. "Gerry Adams, going cheap!" he cries. Outside in the alley, an infant in nappies, held aloft by his proud father, is bashing away at a lambeg. Over their heads hangs a banner—FOR THE THRONE IS ESTABLISHED BY RIGHTEOUSNESS—and Max Bygraves sings "We'll Meet Again," complete with heavenly choir.

I go ten rounds with a banana split. I'd rather be drowned in a butt of malmsey, but I'm not drinking, and Mary never touches a drop. Strange to walk cold sober through these flowing rivers of booze. Broken glass and slopped alcohol are everywhere, and the sweetish sick reek of lager in the heat. Lovers lie in doorways, half-stripped. Some men are down on all fours, felled oxen; others just keep chanting "No Surrender."

And it's still early. Mid-afternoon, with the sun high and no end in sight. "Can you picture the night?" Mary asks, and I think of *Barnaby Rudge*. The Gordon Riots, London burning, and Protestant mobs with their cry of No Popery. And those nightmare scenes when the looters break into the distillery and gorge themselves to death on raw alcohol, while fires rage below in the cellars, and men and women sizzle, too drunk to save themselves.

On a side street, taking a breather, I pass a man of sorrows. He owns one of the holiday hotels, Brae Mar or San Remo or Sunny Bank, and he's standing in a postage-stamp scrub of front garden, forlornly wielding a water bucket. "They've pissed on my roses," he tells me. Long strands of hair, dyed bright ginger, lie plastered across his bald pate. "There was no call for that," he says.

Back at the statue of Queen Victoria, we squat on the curb, surrounded by boot boys. "Next stop Blackpool!" I hear someone shout, and there's a rush to action. The boot boys jump into cars, take off. And Mary, watching them go, doesn't hesitate. "Time to burn some rubber, buster," she says. So we race them to the Tower.

IF SOUTHPORT is liquid, Blackpool's a flood.

We never know what's hit us. One minute we're cruising through suburbs in the gathering dusk, street after drab street of terraced housing, not greatly different from any other Lancashire town. The next, spat out on the Promenade, we're plunged into a mass madness, where B&B stands for Bedlam & Babylon.

What are the chief ingredients? Flashing lights, bared flesh, ear-splitting din. Hip-hop and jungle, rock and house and reggae, pounding from pub doorways, up from cellars, out of coaches and car windows. Teenage girls parading in microskirts and halter-tops, two by two, their thighs stark-white as plucked chickens. Drunken grannies on the rampage in T-shirts proclaiming *Over Thirty and Feeling Dirty*. Hard lads in squads, chanting football slogans. The mingled odours of spilled beer, frying grease, sewage, bleach. Double-decker trams festooned with fairy lights. Street-hawkers peddling willie-warmers, electric yo-yos, gin-flavoured rock. Three piers, and seven miles of murky brown water. And, overlooking the whole inferno like a gargantuan neon lighthouse, the Tower.

I gulp. I breathe deep. I dive in.

Where to start? With a stick of the gin-flavoured rock, and a *Wine Me, Dine Me, 69 Me* T-shirt. "That's meant for the lasses," the souvenir salesman warns me, rolling his eyes like an old-time blue comic of the Max Miller school, but I buy it anyway.

I fall into the maelstrom and am swept along. Within an hour, I'm washed into a karaoke pub, where a poor man's Engelbert Humperdinck sings "Release Me" with such delirious passion that the veins on his forehead stand out like purple wires; a gay bar called The Flying Handbag; one club full of half-naked ladies done up as mermaids, another full of half-naked men done up as Santa's elves; shooting galleries, haunted houses, rocket ships; a virtual-reality pinball machine, with myself as the ball; and back again, more or less intact, to the Tower.

Along the way I lose touch with Mary. The last I see of her, she's beating up some hapless sailor who's spoken out of turn. Then the human current tugs me under again and, by the time I resurface, no more Mary.

Without her, I run out of gas. So I make my way to the Tower Ballroom, where they play a more elderly game.

This, not the Armageddon outdoors, is the Blackpool I've always imagined. A genial, tacky place, peopled by gypsy fortune-tellers and comic landladies, fat men snoozing in the sun with spotted hankies over their faces, fat women gorging on sticky buns, donkeys on the sands, and courting couples riding the Big Wheel. Gracie Fields and George Formby, and Reginald Dixon at the Mighty Wurlitzer.

Reginald himself is dead and gone now, with only a plaque for remembrance, but his world survives in the ballroom, a full-blown Edwardian fantasia, all gilt and stucco and chandeliers.

"Bid Me Discourse, I Will Enchant Thine Ear," reads the carved motto above the stage. A dance band in tuxedos plays quicksteps and foxtrots, but the gleaming hardwood floor is half-empty. Middle-aged women shuffle awkwardly in each other's arms, taking it in turns to lead; a little girl, aged five at most, dances with her father. Then the dance band takes a break, and it's time for the organist. Antiquated but still game, the Wurlitzer lumbers back into life, complete with its arsenal of sound effects—castanets, sleigh bells, train whistle—and one old man heaves a sigh. "I caught my first dose of clap here," he confides. "Well, not right here, of course, but after, up in Talbot Road. Big girl, blonde, her name were Rose. Ten bob." He stares bleakly across the floor at the couples twirling, the three gilded graces above the proscenium arch. "Nineteen thirty-nine, August, last month before the war. I were just eighteen," he says, and turns his back. "Ten bloody bob."

Far above the dance floor, I take my ease in the empty second balcony. From this height, the couples look like wind-up toys. Up among the chandeliers, under the gilded ceiling, it's still the fifties. England has won the war, and the young queen is every man's sweetheart, and half the world's map is pink. While you're young and fit, you work, you make babies, you save. And when you're old, you come dancing.

The illusion doesn't last. As I start to make my descent, I pass two women on the marble stairway. They're huddled against a wall, swigging from a smuggled bottle of rum. Glasgow women, loud and brassy. As I go by, one asks me for a kiss. She has a Betty Grable figure, high-bosomed, wide-hipped, and a helmet of black lacquered hair. Her breath, when she slithers up close, is strong but warm. "I lost my husband here," she says. "My husband, her brother, the dirtiest bastard in Parkhead."

When she says *here*, she means it literally. The bastard in question dropped dead where we stand. "Heart attack, over and out. The medics came running, double quick. But not so quick," his wife recalls fondly, "that I didn't have time to give him a kicking first."

Her name is Moira; her sister-in-law is Jean. The husband died twenty-two years ago, but they come back every summer, to mark the anniversary. "Spit on the sick fuck's grave," Moira says. "I would do worse, only I'm a lady."

What keeps their hatred so fierce? Moira isn't telling. "Never mind me, I'm drunk," she says. She coils an arm round my neck, then changes her mind, takes a whack at the rum instead. Jean starts to laugh and Moira joins in. "His face as he fell," she says.

Their laughter pursues me down the stairs. By the time I reach the dance floor again, the band is back, and so is Mary.

She's dancing with a man in his early eighties, spruce and trim, who moves as if he's floating on air. He sweeps her through foxtrots and quicksteps, rumbas and paso dobles, then steers her over to me.

For half a century, he says, he used to come here with his wife each summer. Now that she's dead, the ritual endures. "I try to keep myself up to the mark, on the ball. Not let myself run to seed like some," he explains. "She wouldn't like that, my wife. If I went all soft and flabby, she'd think it wasn't apt."

It is a lovely word, *apt.* "I'm partial to it myself," the man concurs. His name is Stanley, he comes from Wirral; when he worked, he was a plumber by trade. "I never studied language before, didn't have the time, but I'm getting quite colloquial. It keeps me young, I find. A new word each day, a couple of nights out dancing each week, a spell of Blackpool each July, that's my recipe," he says, and he spins on his way again, clasping a fresh partner. "*Panacea*, now there's a word for you."

The weight of all these memories—Rose and the clap

on Talbot Road, Moira's dead bastard husband, Stanley's fifty years in the ballroom of romance—is starting to bog me down. The band is playing a slow waltz, treacle-thick. "Delectable," Stanley calls out, spinning by, and I grab Mary's arm, rush her back into the streets.

If anything, the pace has intensified. It's the heart of the night now, and crowds descend on the pubs like packs of Visigoths, knocking back two or three drinks for every round, then rushing on again. We are accosted by a dwarf on stilts selling peppermint-flavoured condoms. Then we're in a transvestite cabaret called Funny Girls. A heart-stopping boygirl in black leather thighboots and a black leather tunic cut just below the crotch is singing "Send in the Clowns." A little later, I stand slavering on the front, drowning in the smells of frying onions, while Mary consults the Gypsy Petulengro. A papier-mâché dragon with two heads asks me for a light. Five minutes pass and Mary emerges, flush with good news. "All my dreams will come true," she reports. And we rush on. Try to breathe the sea breezes, but the stench of sewage drives us back. A girl dressed as a seventies' disco princess—flared pants and polyester and chains—wants to lure us into Jellies for a *Saturday Night Fever* bash but we can't stop. We keep beating against the tide, past the arcades and strip joints, the barkers and tattooed love boys, the musclemen flexing, the jailbait pouting, the hash and E and bad cocaine, till we reach Pleasure Beach, the amusement park, where all things are biggest and best.

We enter a land of pink lunar mountains, limpid blue waters and subterranean grottoes. Drifting on a slow boat through the River Caves, we are transported to ancient Egypt, the jungles of darkest Africa, mysterious China and the ruins of Machu Picchu. Afterwards, I sit dreaming by a Hawaiian waterfall, looking out across the Atlas Mountains at the moon, while Mary rides the Pepsi Max Big One, the world's highest, fastest roller coaster. Every-one is screaming. "I died happy up there," Mary says, shuddering but ecstatic, when she returns to earth.

Then it's long past midnight, and we're back at our lodgings, trying to slip in on the sly, not to disturb the sleepers. But our caution proves meaningless. The bar is called Karaoke Island and a woman with big frosted hair, black-spider eyelashes, a full paint job, is belting out "It's Now or Never" for an audience of one young couple, a purple-faced Scotsman and the cat, in tones that could wake up Elvis himself.

I feel as if I've reached the final leg of an odyssey. Hard to believe, when I think of Queen Victoria's statue and the morning sunlight in the pleasure gardens, that it's just been one day. I sit stupefied on the red Naugahyde banquette, retracing my steps, while the karaoke singer moves from "Feelings" to "Anyone Who Had a Heart," and on to "Unchained Melody." I've got a blister on my left heel, and my eyes are raw and stinging. The singer asks me for a tune but my mind is blank. There must be some song I know; every mother's son knows a song. But what? The Scotsman suggests "Danny Boy." No, not that. "Let me think," I say, and I try, I really do. Instead of a golden oldie, though, what comes to me is the image of the old man pissing in the Gents beneath Southport Pier. Mary tells me to sing "The Sash," and I wouldn't mind. If I could just remember the words.

THE FIRST TIME I saw Liverpool, in 1965, it was an imperial city. A mighty port, a great roaring northern metropolis, with its own language and laws, its own universe. As I walked out of Lime Street Station, I was confronted by a wind-blown banner, slung between two massive Victorian piles, proclaiming SECOND TO NONE.

What impressed me most about the place was its absolute self-containment. Unlike other provincial cities I'd been in—Newcastle, Manchester, Birmingham—it displayed no obsession with London. No sense of awe and, equally, no envy; merely an amused condescension. Londoners, in Mersey mythology, were a flabby and flatulent race. They preened and postured, and gave themselves all manner of airs. But they had no bottom, no real life. Once you stripped away their pretensions, they were void.

How different from Liverpool! Scousers were sharp, Scousers had wit, and Scousers would always inherit the world. Just look at the Beatles. The whole living planet had gone ape-shit about those lads, the Fab Four. Only their home town was unimpressed. "Not a bad band," seemed to be the general verdict. The best in the world, perhaps, but not the best in Liverpool.

The same attitude was common to all the great arts—football, drinking, pub-talking, sex. I fell among the Liverpool Poets, then in their first flower. Adrian Henri and Brian Patten, Roger McGough and Paul McCartney's half-brother, Mike. They were giving a reading in a cellar, not far from the Cavern. The room was jam-packed, no air to breathe, and the crowd burning up. When each poem was done, they didn't just clap politely, as Londoners would have done, but yelled and whistled, stomped their feet, in some cases hissed.

At the end, there was a free-verse jam session, open to all, at which the audience, on the whole, proved more adept than the billed poets. Dockers, students, nurses, layabouts—they all took their turn, till their voices seemed the whole city. Dry, sardonic, earthy and rhapsodic, bombastic and just plain filthy. But cocky, above all. Infinitely sure.

After the gig, the poets and most of their public retired to a flat in Mount Vernon, where they proceeded to drink, talk and fuck the night away. By the time I left, it was morning. I started walking back towards the city centre. And what I saw then was magnificence. The Georgian squares, the monolithic heft of the Anglican Cathedral, the Cotton Exchange, the Royal Liver Building, St. George's Hall—the whole place was vivid with life and bravura, the urban equivalent to a cock's crow.

I WAS a working journalist by then, cushy on expenses. So I stayed at the Adelphi, the palatial Victorian flophouse near the station. It was a monstrosity, yes, but quite superb—a fantasia of gilt and chintz and sweeping stairways, where my bed seemed the size of a small ocean liner and even the faintest nod of my head brought people rushing to fawn on me, bring me treats. This was the first grand hotel I'd ever stayed at, and it has always remained, in my mind, the La in La Dee Dah.

Now I'm going back, though I know that's rash. Not to stay overnight; a room would be risking too much. But simply to take a cup of tea? With maybe a cucumber sandwich? What possible damage could that do?

I am meeting a man called Harold May. A retired

schoolmaster, he wrote to me a few months ago, criticising a book of mine. His letter was testy but pithy. "Your grasp of the subject and your command of syntax are both sadly wanting," he wrote. In a flash, I was fourteen, ink-stained and scrofulous, in the back row of Mr. Connolly's class. I'd failed Eng. Lang. Again.

As punishment, he suggested that I write about Liverpool, with himself as my tutor. It was a rich subject, he said, and had been his lifelong study. "I pride myself that my expertise in this field is neither superficial nor specious," he wrote, clearly a dig at myself. But recent events had wounded him deeply. Though Liverpool was a great city, its decline was also great, and it now stood on the edge of ruin. "This has become a horror story," he claimed.

Certainly, the years have not been kind to the Adelphi. The chandeliers have survived intact, and so has the vast vaulting lobby, as solemn as any cathedral. Still, the atmosphere is musty, the glitter faded and glum. Not to kick a dowager while she's down, but my cucumber sandwich is tragic.

Harold May is a tall man, lean and austere, who wears his black suit, starched white shirt and solid black shoes like a uniform, and sniffs at my own disarray. "There are no standards any more," he says. He sips at his Earl Grey, one lump; gazes blankly around him. "The world has lost its mind."

He is seventy-seven, a widower, a gentleman of leisure. His wife died six years ago, after forty-seven years of marriage, and life hasn't been any good since.

He still lives in their terraced house in Anfield; the same house he grew up in. There was a famous murder done in Wolverton Street, just around the corner. William Wallace, an insurance salesman, was accused of braining his wife, Julia, with the proverbial blunt instrument. Tried, convicted, then released on appeal. "He wasn't the murdering type," says Mr. May. "But the notoriety did him in. Killed him sure as hanging."

Still, he must not digress. The essential point for me to remember is that he remains in his childhood home. It's too big for him, really: "Too full of memories." Yet it's memory that sustains him. When he isn't remembering his wife—or their daughter who drowned in Lake Windermere, the wet summer of 1958, when she was nine—he returns to even earlier times. His own school days, most of all. Those days when he lived for cricket.

"Would you credit it, young man, if I was to tell you that the greatest moment of my life, the act that gave me deepest pleasure, was securing the autographs of the complete Lancashire XI, the day they defeated Yorkshire at Sheffield." His Uncle Jack had taken him. Driven him all the way from Liverpool as a belated birthday gift. "August Bank Holiday, 1937. Paynter and Washbrook, Duckworth and Sibbles—where would you find the like of those names today? Or Iddon, whose bowling put the Tykes to the sword? Eighteen and a half overs, three maidens, nine wickets, forty-two runs. But there, I must not bore you."

Across the lobby another old man, who might or might not be a member of Status Quo, is preening in black leather and bragging loudly about blow jobs. "Profoundly distressing," says Mr. May, averting his eyes. "Where was I?"

With his Uncle Jack in Sheffield, in the summer of '37. On the way back across the Pennines, they stopped in Castleton and Uncle Jack had his autographed scorecard framed. "I kept it on my bedside table, but I was frightened it might get broken, so in the end I locked it away. I kept it in the bottom drawer of my desk." And there it remained for sixty years. Until his wife was three years dead, in fact. There seemed no more cause for precautions then. So Mr. May let it out.

"I treasured that card. It was my prize." He offers this in a clipped and hurried undertone, as if it were slightly shameful. He doesn't wish to sound foolish, he says. All his life, he has striven for exactitude and reason. His wife used to call him a dry stick. "But old men turn maudlin. That is the nature of things."

They also crave company. Until recent years, he rarely touched alcohol. The odd glass of sherry, or a bottle of sparkling wine for that special occasion, but nothing stronger. He's seen too many other teachers lured down the primrose path; there is no future in it. To this day, no one would call him excessive. But he does enjoy something warming of a night. Ginger wine, or perhaps a whisky mac.

A few months ago, he took to frequenting a nearby pub. Not his local; he wouldn't care for his neighbours to see him. Instead, he favoured an anonymous drinking house a mile from his home on the edge of a housing estate. Rather a rough crowd, he says. Loud and brawling, some no strangers to crime. They called him Grandad and asked him about his sex life. "Are you getting it?" they said. "Getting your end away?"

Appalling vulgarity; there is no excuse for bad manners. But somehow Mr. May has learned to live with it. "At my age, one contrives to adjust, or there is no contact whatever."

Besides, one boy in the pub crowd seemed cut from finer cloth. A soft-spoken youth, with clean fingernails; Derric Johnson, his name was. Sometimes, when it wasn't a darts night, he would sit down and engage in civilised discourse. He gave the impression that he was genuinely interested in Mr. May's past, and the times he'd lived through. The wars, the political ferments; above all, the great sporting moments. Had he ever seen Billy Liddell? Dixie Dean? What about Golden Miller?

Normally, these wouldn't have been among his topics of choice. "Cricket is my game. I was brought up to believe that football and racing are common." Still, you couldn't spend a life in Liverpool without acquiring a smattering of sporting lore. The questions stirred memories he didn't know he possessed, and he found he enjoyed sharing them. Until this Derric Johnson appeared, he hadn't realised how badly he missed conversation—"the rites of social intercourse." Now he found himself waiting for the boy to come in each night and

feeling let down when he didn't appear. "It's not digni-
fied, I know. No fool like an old fool, and so forth. But I
couldn't seem to help myself."

Sometimes he suspected it might all be a tease. He
would catch Derric sniggering with his pals and wonder if
he himself was the target. But, face to face, the boy
seemed so sincere. A good-looking lad, too, strongly
made; if not for his broken nose, he would be downright
handsome. And he couldn't have been more respectful.
Called Mr. May "Sir," and always enquired about his
health. Asked about his house, his Persian cat, his library.
"Imagine that," he kept saying. Until Mr. May's suspi-
cions were all smoothed away, and he opened his heart.

He talked freely about Sheffield, and Iddon's 9–42, and
the autographed scorecard; and Derric seemed genuinely
impressed. "I'd love to see the scorecard sometime. A
thing like that, it must be priceless," he said. Obsequious
almost. So Mr. May invited him into his home.

Of course he knew it was rash. He read *The Times,* just
like anyone else, and was familiar with the vicious things
young men do. Burglary, assault, grievous bodily harm: "I
was not unaware of the dangers." They didn't deter him,
however. He had been rational and careful his whole life.
Now he determined to take a blind leap. "I thought of my
poor wife. After our daughter died, she was always taking
in strays. Cats and dogs, birds with broken wings. I never
let her keep them, I thought it was unhygienic." Not that
Derric Johnson was a stray. But he was young, and he
needed moulding. "I thought of him as a protégé."

When they reached the house, they drank a glass of
ginger wine in the parlour. Nobody but social workers
and Mr. May's niece Cyndra had been here within the
last year, and Mr. May became aware, for the first time,
that the house reeked of damp. Derric was wearing a blue
sweater, which looked nice on him, but he was bothered
by the cold. His face got flushed and he started to cough.
Mr. May offered him another drink, or a warming mug of
cocoa. No. The boy wanted nothing.

"It was quite an awkward situation. To tell the truth, I

felt at fault," says Mr. May. He wanted to offer comfort but he didn't know where to begin. In the end, at a loss, he slunk upstairs to his bedroom and fetched the framed scorecard.

When he returned, Derric was waiting in the hallway and the whole atmosphere had changed. The air was charged with tension, the threat of unpleasantness. Derric took a look down the list of signatures—Eddie Paynter, George Duckworth, Frank Sibbles—and then he looked at Mr. May. There was something wrong about his eyes.

For a moment, Mr. May thought the boy was going to kill him. Beat him senseless, or crush his skull. But there was no physical assault; no drama of any sort. Derric simply slid the scorecard from its frame and held it against the light. Then he tore it in little pieces. And dropped the debris at Mr. May's feet.

"Is that sanity?" Mr. May asks me now, draining his Earl Grey and looking round for a waiter to bring him a whisky mac. The man in black leathers, sprawling under the chandeliers, has progressed to whips and anal sex, and Mr. May looks weary unto death. "What world are we living in?" he asks.

REUNITED WITH MARY, I try to repeat my route of that first morning in 1965, after I'd left the Liverpool Poets. I travel Mount Vernon and Chinatown, along The Boulevard, and by backstreets down to the Mersey. Much of the basic structure is extant; at first glance, it seems the same great city. Then I look again, and I see it's just a shell. The docks and warehouses that teemed with work, the streets that never stopped roaring—they're half deserted now. Around Park Lane and St. James Street, names once glorious, we pass block after block of bricked-up windows, barbed-wire defences, To Let and For Sale signs. The great Victorian merchant houses still loom, soot-blackened, tremendous. All around them, though, are empty pubs and abandoned shops; a wasteland.

How can it be? Merseyside was once home to three

million souls; the second greatest port in the Empire. Ten miles of shipyards and docks, 100,000 men employed, half the total exports from Britain, and shipping lines whose names were a litany—Blue Funnel, Pacific Steam, White Star, Cunard, McAndrews, Elder Dempster. Even in the sixties, when trade had already started to fall away, only London outranked it. Now the Mersey can't even compete with Hartlepool and Immingham.

The three million has shrunk to around 600,000. The wharves and piers stand deserted. Only one dock remains in business, and that's in Bootle. Now it, too, is standing idle, because of the dockers' strike. When we drive around it, we see a few protest placards, but no picket lines block our road and nothing moves, not even a gull.

As for the great warehouses, those brick Calibans, heroic in their monstrosity, some have been turned into yuppie flats and others into tourist traps.

To catch a whiff of the latter, we take a wander round the Albert Dock, which politicians claim is the pride of a new, reborn Liverpool. In its pomp, it used to handle tobacco and copper, palm oil and cotton, coffee and jute. Now it's a place of museums, and acres of chain boutiques; a shopping mall with pretensions.

One man in the whole antiseptic sprawl makes eye contact as we pass. A gangling, off-balance figure, he's selling books from a stall. The books all have the same title: *I'm Not Drunk, Honest!* The man's name is Hal Lever, and this book is his history.

His voice is oddly slurred. At first, it isn't easy to make out the words, but it's just a matter of finding their rhythm, adjusting to a different pulse. He used to be a seafarer, he says. "I was a beggar for adventure." Then he had his accident. "I was going to work in a minicab and we hit a tanker. I was unconscious for three weeks. When I came round, I couldn't walk, couldn't speak. I had lost my memory, I had two broken wrists, a fractured skull, I was paralysed. The doctors thought I wouldn't recover, they sent me to a psych hospital. I was there five weeks, then my memory came back. When I realised where I was, I checked myself out. Went down the town to tell everyone what had happened. But nobody would talk to me. The minute I opened my mouth, they thought I was mad or drunk."

Every pub Hal went into, people told him not to make trouble. When they threw him out, he'd argue back, which only made things worse. Then he developed a thyroid problem. "My speech got really bad then. I was in the hospital a long time. No way to pass the time, and people couldn't, no, they *wouldn't* understand the words I said. So I wrote a novel, instead. *Exiled in Paradise*, similar to *Lord of the Flies*, only better. Then I wrote this book; my story. Sent it to a publisher, but they sent it back. Said it was a good book, only wouldn't it be better, more dramatic, if I ended up a drug addict?"

Nothing broke him. "I've been defeated many times but never defeatist." When all else failed, he went out looking for sponsors. The actress Emma Thompson helped him; so did others. "I had five thousand books printed and published. Twenty-ninth September, 1994. Now I sell about sixty books each week, also T-shirts and pens. To this date, I have sold eighty-three hundred pens." Yet people still look at him funny. "They might be more aware, but tolerant? No." For most, he's still a man who stumbles and sounds drunk: "Not quite the full shilling." And that would never change. "I'm human. I was not invented. Despite common belief, I was born of two parents." But how many feel connected to him? "Few," he says. "A precious few."

THERE ARE WHOLE neighbourhoods that look like bomb sites. We'll be walking up a terraced street, perfectly normal. Then we turn a corner, and find ourselves in no man's land. Nothing but mud and shattered brickwork, holes in the ground where the houses used to be. Sometimes there is a printed notice from this or that agency, announcing plans for future development. More often, there's just emptiness.

We set up base in Toxteth, the heart of the Liverpool 8 district. Its reputation is all riots and gangsters and drug killings. What we find, instead, is a mangled magnificence.

The area's proportions are full of grandeur. The broad expanse of The Boulevard, the Victorian pavilions in Sefton Park and the great mansions that ring it—this must all have been stupendous once, when shipping magnates lived and ruled here. Now the ornate gates are rusted and the statuary defaced, all the thousands of glass panes in the Palm House shattered. A Sponsor-a-Pane scheme has been launched to replace them. In an area where unemployment runs around eighty per cent, it isn't an easy sell.

Mary has a friend, Tom Calderbank—Scouse Tom—who is a young local activist. He helps run *The Dingle,* a community paper, and lives just off Sefton Park.

He occupies a ground-floor flat in a big rambling house that resembles a fortress under siege. When we ring his bell, there is extended foreplay with locks and bolts, then Scouse Tom appears at a crack in the door. Eager eyes, long hair worn back in a ponytail. Wide mouth already talking.

His living room is spacious, the kind of room that calls out for a grand piano, but it has to make do with the standard post-hippie trappings: drawn curtains and candles, tapestry, a string of beanbag birds adorned with little bells. Though he was an academic star at school, there's no paying work for him in Toxteth. So he concentrates on *The Dingle,* and on scouting grant money to support it. "We're in a grantocracy here," he says. "That means we spend half our lives sitting on our arses and waiting."

For twenty years, rescue funds have flooded in from local government, from Westminster, from Europe. Countless schemes have been set up and then dismantled, two-year plans and five-year plans, regeneration projects like Objective One. Government ministers have flown in and proclaimed that the Pool is on its way back. Snazzy offices have been opened, glossy brochures printed up, and many solemn-faced men in suits have waxed fat in the process.

The whole area could be renamed Quango City. When Tom thinks of the money that's been pumped into Liverpool 8 over the years, he gags. "There's been about six billion so far, spread over the last four decades, and here we are today, still living in shit."

We take a walkabout through the late-afternoon stillness, down empty streets, past silenced pubs and abandoned shops. Afterwards, we sit in Toxteth Park Cemetery and watch the blackbirds peck at the graves. "You need to meet my mam," Tom says.

His mother is Maggie Calderbank; she's a woman of flame. Dark and strong and handsome, she sits in the front room of her semi-detached, in a cul-de-sac called Green Gables Close, and makes it feel like the epicentre of the world. "Strange. Very strange," she says. "For twenty-two years I lived in Greeta Street, and now I live in Green Gables Close, and yet I've never moved! Like if you're no longer called a street, you might stop acting like a street. You're called a close, so you might behave, y'know, in a middle-class way, the way that people in closes behave. But we're not fooled. They fool no one but themselves."

Maggie's style of rhetoric is earthy, deep-rooted. "I'm one of those people who've always said what I feel," she tells me. "If the truth hurts, well, that's just tough. I'm not going to shut my mouth just because I might get people agitated or cause dissension in the ranks. I know what I know, and I say what I believe. I believe that the city of Liverpool has been deliberately destroyed by the British government. We were too much; there was too great a passion and a spirit here, and it had to be crushed, and the easiest way to do it was to break the unions, take away all the industry and businesses, create vast unemployment, provoke a riot, then give the city the blame."

This is the kind of theory that causes Southerners to

sigh and roll their eyes skyward. Maggie knows that, but doesn't care. "They stitched us up," she says. "Liverpool's a mess, no one wants to invest in us, there's no more jobs. All that's left is the fiddle, right? When people used to fiddle, it was part of Liverpool's humour, y'know; if you could work a fiddle, that was considered great craic. But now you have no alternative. Because there's no real work here, and if you do find something, it's so low-paid that you can't take care of your community charges and your rent and your fuel bills, and then buy food and put clothes on your back, much less go out and have a good time. Your only way out is crime. And, of course, that makes it easier all round. They're building all these new prisons and they have to fill them, haven't they? Well, why else would the prison service be getting privatised? All the industry is going to be fed into the jails. It'll be inmates that make the furniture, finish the clothes, and for what? Two and a half pounds a week? So what business is going to come into a city like Liverpool and open a factory making jeans, paying people two hundred pounds a week, let's say, when they can funnel it into the prisons and get their lovely jeans made for next to nothing?"

She started life in Granby, now the heart of Toxteth's black ghetto and widely considered a no-go area, though not by Maggie herself. When she talks of growing up there, she makes Liverpool 8 sound like Shangri-la. "It was fabulous, that's all," she says. "The liveliest place in the world. So many people from different countries were arriving when I was a kid. By the time I was five, I had tasted the foods of the world. A Chinese family, I used to eat in their house. West African families, I'd eat with them. Pakistan and India and even Tibet, it was fab, and it made life, y'know, more alive. To think that all these people, from everywhere around the globe, they'd heard of Liverpool, they'd heard of Granby, and this was the place they'd chosen to come, out of the whole world, I thought that was a magical thing."

The feeling of safety she had then; the stability. "There

was everything here you could possibly want. Shops, swimming baths, a library; there was a picture house right on Granby Street, the Prince's Picture House. We called it the Bughouse and that's what it was, flea-ridden; a lot of those places were. But it was beautiful. It wasn't exactly the cleanest, and your feet stuck to the floor, but when you looked at the plasterwork that was in there, y'know, these huge great plaster scrolls on the ceiling and down the sides of the screen, gods and goddesses all over the shop. Every Saturday afternoon I'd be there, cheering on Roy Rogers and cursing all the Indians to get shot. I was a child of my era, very much so, and Saturday was my mad day. From one o'clock to four in the Bughouse, and then we'd run over to Warwick Street. There was an ice-cream place called Cadwallader's, a tiny shop, much smaller than this room, but they made the best ice cream in the world. They'd put this great lump on top of the cornet, it was just huge, and then the man serving, he'd get this little bottle of raspberry syrup. He'd stick it down deep into the ice and then he'd lift it up, and it would be like a red fountain. It used to spill over at the sides, running down your hands and everything, and that was Toxteth then, in the fifties, the early sixties, that was the life we had."

Not that there were no dark places. But the darkness was in herself. From the age of six or seven, she was aware that she had psychic powers. Everywhere she went, she felt images pressing in on her: other people's thoughts, their feelings, sometimes even their futures. And this terrified her. She found it so oppressive that she feared to ride on a bus. "People used to think I was travel-sick but it was just the noise in my head, like a million insects bashing up against a window. I'd be on the bus with forty people, say, and all the thoughts that were in their minds would come crowding over me, the whole busload of them at once. In two minutes I'd be swamped, and I couldn't shield myself, it knocked me dizzy. I was aware of things unbearable to know."

She also had an obsession with death. "I was very, very

afraid of the end. When we were kids, every time that someone in the neighbourhood died, my mother used to drag us round to visit the corpse. Very often she'd be called on to wash the body, and she would, y'know, it was the old way. Someone would knock on our door and say, 'Old such-a-body's died.' And my mam would say, 'Hang on, I'll fetch the Dettol.' She'd round up the Dettol and TCP and cotton wool, then off she'd go, and she would drag us with her. She dragged us around every corpse. So I didn't like death; didn't like the smell. To this day I can't abide the smell of TCP. I associate it with this one occasion, when the smell was absolutely awful and my mam was using the TCP to try and mask it. The woman had died of cancer and my sister was there, she was putting up sheets across the windows. She was up on a ladder, and she fell; landed on the corpse, smack on. The force of the impact must have caused the cancer to start evacuating the body, and the room was filled with this god-awful stench. And that, to me, was the smell of death. The odour of corruption."

Maggie came from a tribe of merchant seamen. "My grandfather was at sea, so was my dad, and me myself, when I was fifteen, I wanted to go as well. My dad said no, it was no life for a woman, he wouldn't let me sign on. But it's in my blood, even so."

When she came to be married, she chose yet another seafarer, as if to make her voyages through him. They're not together now, but they made this home and had two sons, Tom and Matty. Maggie raised them while her husband was off at sea, and then she became a social worker, part-time at first, but later, after 1981, the year of the riot, with a crusader's passion.

The riot was the watershed. Before that, there were problems—unemployment rising, businesses failing, streets torn down, shops gutted, families moved out—but the community was still strong. Afterwards, that strength was gone, and it has never returned.

The London press called it a race riot. For Maggie,

though, it was simply people versus police. "It was never black against white; it was a political statement. Toxteth just said, 'We're not having this. We're tired of being treated like crap.' All of us were one on that. But blacks, of course, they were treated worst of us all, so their protest was the most extreme."

Those few nights of letting off steam, the stone-throwing and looting and overturned cars, were paid for at dreadful cost. A white boy died. And Toxteth became a dirty word. "The riot was the stick they used to beat us with. From then on, it was like they could do anything they wanted and when we tried to fight them, they just shrugged and said, 'Well, it's Toxteth, y'know, what can you expect?'"

To counter the hopelessness, she plunged herself into work. "Nineteen eighty-two, I went to work for the Toxteth probation service and became the co-ordinator of the Toxteth Victim Support scheme, which I did for a year. And during that year, I also helped to reopen a community centre, established two luncheon clubs and a hairdresser's for the elderly, established a youth club. So it was quite a busy year. And then I was attending courses. Drug-awareness courses, AIDS courses, welfare rights courses, and I set up a group for parents of disabled children." Children like Matty, her youngest, who's autistic.

He is twenty-two now, Matty. All morning, while his mother has held court, he's been in the back garden, watching the birds. Now he comes indoors and sits on the floor by the coffee table, poring over a giant box of sweets. He's a system of raw energies, all joy and terror and nothing between; a bright-eyed boy with fine bones and a wild tangle of hair, which he continually fusses. He takes an instant shine to Mary, keeps her plied with jelly beans, but I only rate the odd gumball. "I'm in charge here," he tells me. Yet he is defenceless against surprises. The flicking of Maggie's cigarette lighter, the barking of a neighbour's dog—these make him shy like a startled horse. "I don't like bad bangs," he says.

"Hard lines," says his mother, her eyes loving him. "It's all bad bangs round here."

She gave up social work at the end of the eighties, partly to care for Matty and partly to care for herself. "I was running on empty, completely used up. So I thought, Right, now it's time for me." These days she writes stories and songs, and makes a little pin-money telling fortunes. "I do tarot cards, palms, crystal balls, runes, I do Chinese horoscopes, I do dream interpretations. But I'm not a fortune-teller really; that's the wrong title. More than fortunes, I'm a *feelings*-teller. I'll identify what's going on inside you, and also why. Say you have a problem, I can pin down where in the past it's come from, and what you need to do to correct it. I help people lift the dead weight from their souls, so they're freed to move forward again."

As she sits smoking, talking, she attracts a constant stream of visitors. People seeking advice, people in need and people who merely require a cup of tea. Maggie attends to them with an even hand, then settles back into her thoughts, which always return to her city. "We're going to rise up," she says. "Any day now, I can feel it, we're going to throw off the shackles and take back what's rightfully ours. We used to be a mighty oak, now we're just an acorn, but we can't be kept down for ever. If we ever get our guts back, Liverpool will declare independence. They'll end up building a great big wall around us, and they'll think they have us walled in, but that's where we're going to fool them. The wall won't keep us in, not us. It'll keep them out."

Traipsing round the city centre at the weekend, I'm reminded of something that Grace used to say: "When human life is extinct, there's always students and tourists." They are the only paying customers on view, milling around the Albert Dock and the Cavern, the students decked out in hip-hop glad rags, the tourists in shell suits and trainers.

Lacking a viable present, the city is avid to package its past. Whatever hasn't been destroyed has been turned into theme parks. On the Mersey ferry, they play the old Gerry and the Pacemakers record virtually non-stop; and when you venture into the narrow, dank streets around the Cavern, you're carpet-bombed with Beatles' schlock. The original Cavern was razed years ago to make way for a parking lot, but that doesn't deter the pilgrims. They take pictures of the blank space, and of themselves standing in it, then retire to a new, fake Cavern across the street.

"Welcome to History," a taped message blares. But, theme parks aside, precious little has escaped the wrecker's ball. I'm reading *English Journey*, a travelogue by Beryl Bainbridge. She was born and raised in Liverpool, and there's a traumatic passage when, coming home on a visit, she stands at a window in the Adelphi and surveys the wreckage of Church Street. "All the landmarks I remembered, gone without trace," she writes. "No Boosey and Hawkes with the ukeleles in the window and a life-sized photograph of George Formby, smiling just to show you how easy it was. No gunsmith's with its velvet drapes and pheasants stuffed with sawdust, and Johnny Walker in his breeches, who once had leapt in coloured lights across the hoarding of the public house, toppled forever from the sky. No ice warehouse, no Bears Paw restaurant, no pet market. Gone the parrot humped in its gilded cage in Blackler's store. Obliterated the gloomy depths of the Kardomah Café; burnt as old-fashioned the red plush sofas of the Lyceum tearooms; slung into the refuse tips the potted palms and the nickel-plated water jugs." And she concludes, despairing, "Someone's murdered Liverpool and got away with it."

And yet, it's not that simple. Each time we think the body's stopped twitching, and we're ready to nail down the lid, it ups and gives us the finger. We visit the offices of the dockers' union, the sites of the Toxteth riot, the graveyards of demos and gang wars, and the stench of defeat is so sulphurous, it chokes us. So we take shelter in the Bleak House, aptly named, in the Dingle. Nobody's talking, and few can afford to drink. Then a little squit of a man comes in and announces that McManaman is God. And another man says, "Macca? He couldn't score with a two-quid hooer." And then a woman chips in, saying, "Steve Heighway now, he was gear." And the first man raps back, "Heighway? More like a cul-de-sac." And suddenly the whole pub is up and raging, and the city's last rites are on hold. So long as there's still football, and water in the Mersey, the game's not up. "They may have cut off my bollocks," as one man says. "But my dick doesn't know that yet."

On a Saturday lunchtime, we stroll the terraced streets around Goodison Park. Everton is playing Newcastle United and the whole neighbourhood, basking in rare sunlight, is in carnival. All the houses, two-up, two-down, have their doors wide open. Big-bodied women are sitting on the stoops with their stockings rolled down and dresses hiked, soaking up the heat. Kids in their Everton shirts, fresh out of the wash, are playing space wars. At every corner, men peddle rosettes and scarves, glossy photos of Duncan Ferguson. Meanwhile, on a patch of waste ground, a gospeller holds up a placard: "Heed God's word." But just a mile away, in Anfield, a scrawl on a wall strikes a more pragmatic note: GOD GRANT US, it reads.

OUR JOURNEYING ends up at a community office on Smithdown Road, bang in the heart of Toxteth, where we meet Yinka. Olayinka Yesufu, Nigerian by family, Wavertree by neighbourhood, spitting mad by disposition. "D'you want an angry man? I am your angry man," he says, subjecting me to a staredown. But when I don't blink, he relents, and leads me upstairs into an empty office, where he proceeds to lay himself bare.

Stocky, muscular, very dark, he has the body of a bare-knuckle middleweight, but his face is all movement and light. It changes with his mood, and his moods change constantly. One moment he's brooding, his heavy mouth twisted with loathing; the next, eyes gleaming, he starts talking about living alone in a lighthouse, somewhere off the west coast of Ireland. "I'm not a macho, macho guy," he says then. "My name means Child Surrounded by Honour. I can be a hard bastard when I have to, but only in the cause of Right. Some days I feel age-old, other days I'm a child in a man's body, and sometimes I'm both at once. To be honest, I'm unique."

He sees himself not as a single entity, but as a series of fragments. "I'm ripped apart in so many ways—African, British; streetwise, academic; media-ambitious, hate the media; passionate believer, don't give a fuck. The challenge is to blend them."

He's always been scholastically gifted, yet fiercely aware of his isolation. His primary school was overwhelmingly white. Then he moved to Arundel Comprehensive, where there were 20 blacks, 800 whites. When he achieved Grade 1s in his CSEs, his headmaster's only response was to ask him if he'd cheated. "That was the goad I needed," he says. He went on to take a BA Honours in History, writing his dissertation on slavery. But academia doesn't really suit him. "I'm too revisionist. I always go against the grain and they don't like that, they just want a peaceful time. If you rock their boat, they won't give you jack."

For the moment, he's wavering among a career in politics, or the media, or possibly business. "Whatever I do, I want to matter, but that's so hard to achieve here." The work system is set up for mediocrity. "Just get your grant and shut up." His eyes roll up, so that only the whites are left showing. "They keep papering over the cracks. Meanwhile, the building collapses."

Later on, he takes us on a guided tour. We follow the trail of the riot. The original flashpoints have been torn down; turned into closes or simply reduced to rubble. Regeneration schemes have produced a stylish new hospital, some decent housing and some spectacular white elephants: gated ranch-style homes, with landscaped gardens, Saabs and Volvos in the driveways, privatised policing.

For contrast, Yinka steers us to Mount Vernon and the Anglican Cathedral. Rosy pink by day, its vast sandstone mass has turned a livid bluish-brown in the dusk, as if God's got a dodgy liver. But it's not the cathedral itself that we're meant to inspect. A narrow gate leads to a long and precipitous stone stairway, taking us down into a sunken graveyard. Walls like sheer cliffs, lined with tombs, surround us on three sides. A monstrous blackbird flaps its wings above our heads. The city seems miles away.

"This was its own city once," Yinka says. A necropolis, hectic with Calvary crosses, marble angels, ornate family vaults. Now all that has been vandalised or cleared away. The graves that survive are plain flat slabs, sunk in the earth. Most commemorate merchants, among them slave traders. "They're the ones that made Liverpool. Made it great," Yinka says, his face unreadable in the gathering murk. "This is where it all begins."

And where does it end? We take a walk along Granby Street. Its area encompasses every style of urban blight that Liverpool 8 can boast—festering terraces, abandoned and bricked-up shops, police cameras, graffiti, wasteland. Somalis live here, and Asians, and West Indians. "It's a dumping ground, really," Yinka says. "But the media loves it." Every time there's a new gang murder, the TV crews roll in, instant outrage at the ready. "To them, there are no human beings in Granby, just sound bites."

It's dark now; a warm, soft night. Some men are sitting at a table on the street, outside a little café, and we join them. The mood is amiable, no hint of threat. Joints are smoked, and their benefits discussed. "A little draw never hurt no soul," one man says. An armoured police car with bullet-proof glass cruises past. The men outside the café watch it idly, without comment. When I look at

Yinka, however, he looks stricken, his face taut with fury. "If I was walking by myself, they'd lift me," he says. *"Look, a nigger with attitude—let's have a piece of that."* He rises up, starts back towards Teal Wheels. Sits huddled in on himself, not talking, until we're back in the city centre. Rage has drawn his skin so tight across his cheekbones and around his mouth, he might be wearing a mask.

"I won't be had," he says at last. He takes a deep breath and blows it out. "They all want me in the ghetto. Whites and blacks, it's all the same; even some of my best mates. They want me to pick sides. Any side, it doesn't matter. Just so long as I label myself. Stick myself in a pigeon-hole."

That isn't a game he's willing to play. "I have to make my own road. Me; myself. I have to deal with Liverpool and it has to deal with me, the two of us together, down to the very end."

Somewhere in Everton, high on a hill, we stop at a park. The whole of Liverpool lies sprawled below us, from Aigburth to Bootle; Yinka looks down on it in silence. Gradually, the tension leaves him. All rhetoric drains away and his voice, when he speaks again, is private. "I love this city," he says. A pause. "I hate this city," he says. Another pause. "I love this hateful city," he says.

I HAVE A DAUGHTER, Lucy, who lives in Greater Manchester, in Salford 7. It is a tough area, often featured in TV documentaries about inner-city blight, and her street, though by no means the worst, exists in a state of semi-siege. Half the homes are up for sale and many others have been taken over by dope dealers. She doesn't do a whole lot of late-night strolling.

One morning I set off across the Bury New Road into a neighbourhood where I've been warned not to venture. Thirty years ago, any one of its terraced streets might have been the model for early Coronation Street, the working-class TV soap. Now the houses are mostly abandoned, their windows bricked up, their front doors shielded by steel-plated armour. Where residents hang on, the roofs are festooned with barbed wire and prison bars protect the living-rooms.

Deep inside one house, I can hear the shrill of a burglar alarm. This strikes me as strange; the house appears impregnable. Sheet-iron, cement, broken glass—who or what could work its way through that lot? "Search me," says a man passing by. "Rats, maybe. All I know is, alarm's been ringing two days, and the cops haven't turned up yet."

"But a man could be trapped in there," I fluster. "Shouldn't someone take a look?"

"Better not," says the man crisply. "He might still be alive."

Any more dithering on my part dies with the arrival of two skullheads, one sporting a *British Bulldogs Bite Back* T-shirt. The way he looks at me, he seems to be sniffing breakfast, so I take my leave. Round the corner, up the back lane, out on to a wide expanse of waste ground.

There's nobody and nothing here, just a burned-out car, one dead dog. Then a lone runner comes into view. A boxer in a hooded tracksuit, out doing roadwork, throwing punches at air.

Bantamweight, I guess, or maybe fly; no more than five foot two. The slight figure is struggling in the rough going—I can hear breath rasping, feet scuffling in heavy workboots, but the runner keeps slogging on regardless. As our paths cross, I get a hard, flat stare from under the hood. The fighter is a girl.

She looks about fifteen; cropped hair, chalk-white face. *Don't say a word. Don't even think of smiling,* her silent stare says, *or you're a dead man, fatty.*

A few days later, I see her again. This time she's hanging out with the brew crew who sit around the earthworks in Piccadilly Gardens. She isn't drinking herself, but seems to take ease from the company. The get-stuffed stare is gone, and she doesn't object when I strike up conversation.

Her name is Megan; she claims to be eighteen. Her life's goal is to become a world champion kick-boxer: "Well, anything in the martial arts. Karate, capoeira, t'ai chi, escrima, I've tried the lot. But kick-boxing is the best. I don't have that much power but I know how to use my fulcrum."

Without her tracksuit, she's stick-thin, androgynous, all mouth and bruised-looking eyes. Her jeans and T-shirt are several sizes too big for her—she looks like a small child in dress-up. Still, she claims to be a killing machine. "I know all the pressure points." She holds up a pair of minuscule hands and slices the air with karate chops. "Any bastard that threatens me, I could turn him to dog-meat, easy as piss." But damage is not what she's really about. "The point is to defend, not destroy." She sees herself as a protector, not just of herself, but of the weak and endangered in general. "See this lot?" she says, gesturing towards the brew crew. "They're as soft as shit, most of them. Anyone can push them around; the filth, social workers, gangs. To me, that isn't right. They're all my family, in a way, and I won't see them abused."

Her role as avenging angel extends to all victims. She'd like the job of castrating child molesters, and she knows some fancy methods of torture that she's saving for slum landlords: "The ones who target the old and sick. Just give me a few minutes, and they'd be old and sick themselves."

One of her role models is Nelly, a homeless woman who spends her life roaming the city centre, feeding the pigeons. For Nelly, it is a crusade, and anyone who tries to stop her risks a mortal kicking. "Dead on," Megan says. "She's protecting her own, that's all; she's sussed. Some people think she's gone in the head, they want her off the streets, because she keeps feeding bread to the birds. They say it spreads disease but that's shite. This whole city's diseased, anyway—how can bread or birds make it worse?"

I ask how she started kick-boxing. "I wanted to be able to hurt someone," she says. "Not to actually hurt them, that's not it. Just to be able to."

She comes from Cheetham Hill, the youngest of five. Her stepfather used to work in a factory making plastic footballs. In those days, he wasn't too bad, but after he got the sack he turned ugly. He started using heavy drugs, which didn't suit him. The heroin was OK, it only made him a zombie, but the crack drove him out of his box and he tried to have sex with her. She was ten then, eleven, and he wouldn't leave her alone, so she had to leave home.

"Slept rough for a week, then the busies picked me up. I was all over nits, my arms and legs, everywhere, you could hardly see me for bites." She was taken into care and lived with a family but that turned out even worse: "Don't ever mention weedkiller," she tells me cryptically. "Wire-cutters, neither."

Since then, she's survived by her wits. For a time, she went back to Cheetham Hill, lived in squats, stayed alive by petty thieving. There was a girl gang that she ran with sometimes but gangs aren't really her style. She's basically a loner.

For months she slept in basements, a disused church hall, a condemned warehouse. She didn't think a lot of herself, she thought she was just rubbish, and she kept getting into fights. Drinking and brawling, getting barred from half the pubs in Cheetham Hill: "The Empress, the Cleveland, the Robin Hood, you name it, I got my arse kicked there."

One night, legless, she started acting up in the Magic Box. When the bouncer threw her out, she kept trying to kick him but he held her off with one hand, the way a dad does with a little kid. She'd have given anything to whack him but there was no way. At last she gave up trying, just went limp. Then he gave her a clip round the ear, not too hard, but none too gentle either. "Know what that's called?" the bouncer said. "Self-defence."

That stuck with her. The power of self-reliance; she liked the idea of control. So she decided to take up boxing. She went to a couple of gyms but they ran her off. No girls allowed. Then she tried karate classes but that was too boring, all the ritual and bowing, she didn't have the patience. But there was this fella she knew. Big fella, built like a tank, used to play rugby league for Warrington. He'd learned martial arts in Strangeways and he traded her lessons for oral sex.

Well, giving head, it was nothing to her. "A lot of bother about fuck all." Some people might say she was selling herself but she was only cashing a ticket, using what she had. "It's not like a blow job is love."

So far she's been training for almost a year, and she can really tell the difference. Her arms are still like pipecleaners, no amount of weightlifting seems to make any difference, but her wind, her stamina, her body control are all competition class. Even better, she feels strong inside. "It's like *the bastards can't beat me. No way can I be owned.*" On one triceps, she sports a tattoo of a howling she-wolf; on her calf, another says MAKE MY DAY.

If only kick-boxing had a bigger following. In America, it's a big-time deal—world tournaments, TV coverage, serious money—but it's still a sideshow here. When Megan tells people what she does, they either blank her or laugh: "There's so much prejudice. Blind ignorance," she tells me. "You'd think I bit the heads off toads."

A light rain has started; time for another run. Circling the earthworks, she starts to do warm-ups; stretching, twisting, her pinched white face stark with effort. One day, who knows, she might make it to the States, become a big name. "Then you could say you knew me when." When what? "When I was nothing." Or, no. She isn't supposed to think like that. Negatives are degrading; they take away her power. "When I was something," Megan says, as she starts running. "I just didn't know what."

MANCHESTER HAS fascinated me since childhood. When I was nine, my parents were given use of a gatehouse in County Donegal. It stood at the edge of a large Anglo-Irish estate; a land of forests and lochs and purple hillsides. Two or three times a year, we went up to the big house to pay our respects. While my parents took tea with the landowners, I was left free to wander.

Usually, I went exploring in the kitchen gardens or rowed a leaky boat around the lily pond. There was one day, however, when it was raining too hard to go outdoors and the only way for the adults to get shot of me was to park me in the library. It was a warm, dark room like a cave. The wooden floor smelled of soap and plum-scented wax, and that's also how it tasted when I sampled a bit on my fingers, and then a bit more, till the whole inside of my mouth was coated with soapy plum wax and I felt pleasurably sick.

I thought I was probably poisoned, a warming thought on a wet afternoon. Having only minutes to live, there seemed little point in starting a whole book, so I passed the time by looking at the pictures in an atlas-sized world history. It looked incalculably ancient to me: broken-spined, dog-eared, with brilliantly coloured plates. Most of the images were familiar—*Pithecanthropus erectus,* Egyptian pharoahs and Roman emperors, King Alfred burning the cakes, Sir Francis Drake playing bowls and Napoleon looking glum on St. Helena, all the way down to the early 1900s. But one plate opened up a new world. Its title was Industry, and it was a pictorial map of Lancashire.

Not just any map; an apocalyptic vision. At its heart stood Manchester, a place of massive black castles and cathedrals, ruled by fat men in civic robes. Hellfire flames ringed a skyline of factory chimneys, and railway lines shot out in all directions, like bicycle spokes. At the end of each spoke was a worker—a man weaving silk in Macclesfield, or spinning cotton in Accrington, or digging coal in Wigan. There were also canals with barges and pit ponies; women in clogs and shawls hanging washing; and a small boy, flying a kite on a fiery hill.

Fire was everywhere, in fact. On the water, in the sky, over and under the whole working world. If I'd been older, I might have thought of Hieronymus Bosch. As it was, I was merely bewitched. Shut up in this library, rotting of plum-wax disease, I thought that nowhere on earth could be as exotic and desirable as Industria, that burning land.

THIS FIRST VISION has never faded. Manchester, for me, has always remained a swaggering town, full of flash and backhanded glamour. A sort of English Chicago, uncompromised, tough—a city of big shoulders.

In the days when industry ruled, the swagger was solidly based. Now the ground underfoot has turned treacherous and the foundations have rotted, but the flash remains, and so does the combativeness. Even when they're skating on air, Mancunians don't look down.

Manuela exemplifies this knack.

We're introduced through a mutual friend, who describes her as a diva. "She'll tell you she's Colombian and pisses Dom Perignon," he tells me. "But I remember her when she was Maxine from Bolton, and she was on the gin-and-orange."

When I first sight her, she's sitting in the lounge of the Holiday Inn Crowne Plaza, which will always be the Midlands Hotel to me, sipping a champagne cocktail and munching on black olives, a ringer for the young Bianca Jagger, only longer, leaner, more luciferous.

She wears an ankle-length dress slit to the hip, and her legs are simply not fair. Her gift from God, she calls them, and that's about par for the course, for her sense of her own grandeur knows no limits. "Aristocracy is my birthright," she tells me. "My father was a colossus."

Her history, which she says she's turning into a book, is conceived on an epic scale. She was born in Bogotá, she says, and spent her childhood travelling with her father. Her mother had died when Manuela was five and her father couldn't bear to remain in the family home. A member of the diplomatic corps, he was posted in turn to Vienna and Istanbul, Rome, Madrid and finally Geneva. Manuela herself went to finishing school in Lausanne— "a barbarian place, full of lesbians and Trotskyites." But her true passion was for music.

That was another gift from God, this time via her father, who was an expert on Clementi. His great ambition was to retire from the diplomatic corps and devote himself full-time to playing and promoting the composer's works. Unfortunately, before he had time to act on this, he was summoned home to Bogotá. Two days later, he was shot dead as he left his house.

In honour of his memory, Manuela took over Clementi. Although born in Rome, the composer spent most of his life in England, dying in Evesham in 1832, and being buried in the cloisters of Westminster Abbey.

"You must understand," Manuela says. "To me, he is

not just a musician; he is my father's living soul." So she made a Clementi pilgrimage. She visited his home and his grave; she bought herself a 1794 Walter forepiano, on which, so the salesman claimed, the Master composed *Gradus ad Parnassum,* his monumental book of etudes. She even applied to the Royal College of Music: "But the examiners there have no idea of Art."

Besides, she was the victim of certain problems. There was a man, a gambler with high connections. He promised her the moon and stars, but his only true love was cocaine. She gave him her heart and, in return, he suggested she walk the streets for him.

How did Manuela react? "I made a mistake," she confesses. "I failed to shoot him like a dog."

At this point, her story gets somewhat tangled. She left the man flat and swore on her father's memory never to be so abused again. Still, if my friend is to be believed, she didn't entirely ignore the man's suggestion. Not that she turned streetwalker. At Manuela's prices, the proper word is courtesan.

Occasionally, as she talks, old acquaintances stroll by and Manuela inclines her head, left and right, with an air of regal condescension, for all the world like Garbo in *Grand Hotel.* She crosses her legs with a snakelike slither of her black skirt and a fresh champagne cocktail appears, another serving of olives. So majestic is her bearing, it seems sacrilegious to ask what had brought her, a citizen of the universe, to the Holiday Inn Crowne Plaza. But I force myself, even so.

To her credit, she doesn't miss a beat. "I have travelled all my life," she said. And Manchester is by no means the worst place she's seen. Yes, its manners are crude; yes, she hates the rain. But the people, deep down, have big hearts. "I am appreciated here. I have many good friends, who see my soul."

In the long run, she still hopes to make her life in music. "I can never forget Clementi. He is my Master until I die." For the moment, though, she seems not dissatisfied with her lot. "If you ask my profession, I will tell you: mistress of mysteries."

When cocktail hour is finished and I walk her through the lobby, I glow to be seen beside her. Manuela is swathed in silver fox from throat to ankle but her dark head, sleek as a seal's, is bare. Out on the streets, a misty drizzle is falling, and it spoils her mood. "Where is my driver?" she fumes. For a moment, she looks fit to spit; then she remembers her breeding. "I am too good-natured. That is my fatal flaw," she says stoically, and dabs at her lips with a lace handkerchief, the perfect lady again.

Away from the pampered confines of the Plaza, her presence seems hallucinatory. Strolling the soggy, reeking streets with her, I feel as if I'm walking out with Lola Montez. At any moment, I think, she'll abandon the act, relapse into Boltonese. But that moment never comes. On the contrary, she gets even more imperious. As we amble towards Chinatown, a bad memory surges up, and she starts to fulminate. A week ago, she met a celebrated Man. United midfielder in a club and he grossly insulted her. "A hundred pounds," she seethes. "I don't clear my throat for a hundred pounds."

We're standing outside Charlie Chan's, where the featured act is Foo-foo Lamar, a drag artiste. The window is plastered with glossy photos of Foo-foo and various footballers grinning. "One hundred pounds," Manuela says. "The dirty dog." Then she bites back her bile; pats me on the hand; and promotes a tenner for her taxi home.

MARY AND I take a jaunt, west and north, through Lancashire's cities of industry: Blackburn and Bolton, Preston and Burnley, Warrington, Accrington, Oswaldtwistle. I used to visit them in the sixties, when they were still working mill towns. I saw them only on football Saturdays, from lunchtime till the last train out, but their impact was vivid and lasting.

Blame it on the picture-book in Donegal. For me, this was a land apart, whose harshness and lack of airs, perversely, only made it seem more exotic. The towns and villages cut into hillsides, black on green; the huddled row-houses; the backstreets rearing and plunging, dwarfed by the factory chimneys; the cobbles and clogs, still in evidence then; the foul-smelling canals, green and orange with chemicals; the Methodist chapels, hellfire grim; the hard-faced women who gave me one steely look and stripped my worthless soul to the bone; and, beneath it all, an odd exaltation. An almost fanatical fervour that I couldn't nail down, until one night when I went to a working men's club in Rawntenstall and swapped pints with a man who'd tried to leave. At twenty, he told me, he'd been a flying winger, a rising star in rugby league. Then an accident at work did his knee in; no more glory days. The compensation came to a decent whack, though. Enough to buy a flat in Torremolinos, which had always been his fantasy. So off he flew. And, six months later, flew back. "I missed the moral climate," he said.

That was it, exactly. Whatever else they might be short of, the mill towns had density; spiritual mass. It was in the faces, in the brick, in the dank and leaden air itself. Manchester might strut and swank, but nothing was trifling here.

Zipping up the M66 in Teal Wheels, I try to give Mary a notion of what to expect. Then we pull into Accrington, and find that it's been turned into a museum.

The mills are gone; so is the grime. The black row-houses have all been sand-blasted and are now a tasteful shade of cream. Even the monstrous viaduct, looming high above the town, no longer seems threatening. As for the moral climate, that also seems changed. When I drop into a corner pub, the girl pulling pints is wearing a halter-top, cut-offs and no bra. She tells me that it's a dead-zone here. "No work, no money, no nothing," she says. "You can't even get fucked."

What you can get is a fistful of brochures. In Accrington, as in other mill towns, the one indispensable sign these days points to the Tourist Centre. The streets are littered with tea shoppes and boutiques, any piece of worthless scrap is now a treasured antique, and there's no such thing as food, only plates of fayre.

In the name of Heritage, the brochures have invented something they call the Lancashire Hill Country and stuffed it with instant history. Any defunct mill that hasn't been razed, it seems, has been turned into an attraction—fun for all the family, with guided tours, interactive displays, gift shoppes. Even coal mines and colliers' cottages are fair game: *"Think of darkness, think of cramped conditions, think of heat and danger . . . smell the gas from the mantels . . . See the kettle on the hearth . . ."*

The effect is obscene. A complex past—impoverished, brutal, exultant—has been neatly sliced and diced, reduced to packaged product. *Become a child once more and experience the rigours of a strict Victorian education. Can you sit with backs ramrod straight and remember your twelve times table? Can you sit with your arms folded tightly and recount the countries of the Great British Empire? If the answer is yes then don't be late for the Schoolroom!*

Some of the come-ons are oddly seductive. Oswaldtwistle Mills, for example, Home of the Biggest Pear Drop in the World; or the Garden Ornaments Gallery next door, which sells John Major plaster gnomes at twenty-five quid a pop. An insidious narcosis spreads through the Muzak and the air-conditioning vents. A few minutes spent gawking at pear drops the size of fatal brain tumours and we lose all will. Next thing we know, we're wandering slack-jawed through Th'owd Calico Shop and Weavers Cottage, and vaguely regretting that, while in Southport on Orange Day, we didn't make time for the British Lawnmower Museum.

In Burnley, the theme park is called the Weavers Triangle. *Discover what it was like to live in a nineteenth-century mill town.* Luckily, I'm too late; the exhibits are shut. So I take a walk through the town. A hard desolation it is.

I remember one bitter January day here, thirty years

ago. A cup-tie, I think; at any rate, a blood match. When the game was over, I walked back through the town from Turf Moor with the local supporters. An incomer, in those days, was not at much physical risk. So we walked together, shoulder to shoulder, into the teeth of the weather. It was raw and sleeting, the footing evil with ice. Everyone was slithering and stumbling. Then an old man went down, belly up, with a fractured ankle. And the whole cavalcade stopped. Stood and waited, silently freezing, till those closest to him had picked the old man up and carried him to shelter.

Now it's six o'clock of a summer evening, and hardly a soul's about. I trudge up a long, twisting hill between rows of gutted shops. Two youths in hooded tracksuits are lounging outside a disused toy shop; I ask them, where's the action. "Action?" says one, incredulous. "In Burnley?"

Pushing on, I reach the town centre. Even here, signs of life are confined to a single Irish theme pub, full of bric-a-brac and distressed oak beams, the artifacts of instant age. Other pubs are virtually deserted; so are the betting shops. Only the Asians, running in teenage packs or strolling with their families, seem fully alive.

What happened here? For lack of any alternative, I decide to ask a policeman. "The heart's gone out," I'm told. "Nobody gives a tinker's." He is a slow-talking, ruminative man and seems to have given the matter some thought. He pinpoints the death of the mills, and how nothing has really replaced them. "There's no common cause, none. No connection," he says, and the word throws me back thirty years to that sleet-driven Saturday, tramping along with the crowd from Turf Moor: the stark black houses, the women standing watching in the door-ways, the lights coming on inside the pubs, the ice and sleet, the old man down and crying out, and the silent crush of supporters in their caps and mufflers and heavy coats, breath billowing under the street lamps, waiting till he'd been helped.

The distance seems unbridgeable. "It was another

world," the policeman says, when I mention that evening to him.

Burnley is an extreme example. Some of the towns we pass through, like Preston, are downright bustling. Even there, though, there's a sense that something essential—a sense of order, of function—has gone missing.

This is slippery thinking, of course. A little further along those lines and I'll be forgetting what the mills and mines really meant, start to glorify child labour.

As an antidote, I bury myself in a passage from *The Road to Wigan Pier*: "All round was the lunar landscape of slag-heaps, and to the north, through the passes, as it were, between the mountains of slag, you could see the factory chimneys sending out their plumes of smoke. The canal path was a mixture of cinders and frozen mud, criss-crossed by the imprint of innumerable clogs, and all round, as far as the slag-heaps in the distance, stretched the "flashes"—pools of stagnant water that has seeped into the hollows caused by the subsidence of ancient pits . . . It seemed a world from which vegetation had been banished; nothing existed except smoke, shale, ice, mud, ashes and foul water."

That was in the mid-thirties. By the time I saw these lands myself, thirty years later, the view had become less apocalyptic, though still bitter bleak. Now, another thirty years on, we roll up once more, and land in a corporate funhouse.

Welcome to Wigan Pier! ii *Sets,* 7 *Great Attractions! Available for functions, conferences, dinners, seminars, weddings . . .* Along the Leeds and Liverpool Canal, where coal trains once met the barges, there's a massive leisure complex—a shoppe full of pot-pourri and Fabergé eggs, bars, restaurants, a hotel and, of course, a heritage centre. The employees wear lapel badges that read Tradition; you can buy a clog brooch or fridge magnet.

An exhibit called "The Way We Were" serves up tidy vignettes of Wigan's past. *Imagine life in the mills! Learn about the Boer War! Experience the Maypole Colliery disaster!* A troupe of professional actors performs a promenade

play called *The Next Best Thing.* There are murder weekends, water buses, a play area, a factory shop. All this, and
live jazz at—where else?—The Orwell.

We stroll along the towpath. In George Orwell's time, a
shanty town lay along the canal banks; caravans and
canvas-covered wagons and derelict buses, a precursor
of Fraggle Rock. It's a sequence of flowerbeds now. Day-
trippers push strollers, Japanese and Germans take happy-
snaps. There's not a fleck of grime to be seen.

Even the Pier is fake. It was just a music-hall joke,
anyway; Wigan's wry gag on its own lack of glamour.
Merely an iron landing stage for off-loading coal, the real
thing was torn down for scrap in 1929. Then came
Orwell's book, and later the Heritage Centre. Come the
nineties, the old eyesore is not only famous, but finally
ripe for profit. So local students have built a replica, rust-
free, immaculate.

Across the canal, the monstrous bulk of Trencherfield
Mill has been cleaned up and refurbished, and now offers
guided tours. We stare through glazed eyes at the world's
largest mill engine, but it's no use. We've overstuffed on
Theme Pie, can't swallow another sound bite. So we start
back towards Manchester.

Orwell's lunar landscape is now bland, suburban. We
pass the scar tissue of a former slag heap, covered with
scruffy brownish grass, like a failed hair transplant. I
pick up *The Road to Wigan Pier* again and read aloud:
"Your horizon is ringed completely round by jagged grey
mountains, and underfoot is mud and ashes and overhead the steel cables where tubs of dirt travel slowly across
miles of country. Often the slag-heaps are on fire, and
at night you can see the red rivulets of fire winding this
way and that, and also the slow-moving blue flames of
sulphur . . ."

We drive through Wigan, down a mock-Tudor high
street, past a mock-Tudor shopping centre. It looks a tidy
town; spruce, cosmetic, inert. "So what d'you think?"
Mary asks. "Do you win when you lose? Or lose when
you win?"

MY DAUGHTER used to be a Trotskyite. Among the
friends Lucy made in the Socialist Workers' Party is Harry
Radcliffe, a seafarer, who lives near her in Salford, where
he was born, and works on a sewage-disposal boat in
the Irish Sea. Shit is his life, Lucy says, but his life's not
shit. If I want to know about Industria, I ought to go
see him.

He's a wiry man, fit-looking and sharp, with a trim grey
beard and a clear, straight eye. Middle-aged, he recalls a
Salford where neighbours still talked. "There was only
one TV in my street and everyone watched together. No
cars, but one man owned a motorbike, with a sidecar for
his missus; that made him a big star."

His own beginnings were rocky. There were troubles at
home, no father, and he grew up riotous. From serial tru-
ancy he progressed to burglary. By the time he was
twelve, he was in approved school, and there he stayed till
he turned fifteen. A year later, he went to sea. "One
month my life was four walls and a prayer; the next,
Savannah and New York." He had hardly been to Blackpool, but the world's lure was irresistible. "I had this
romantic vision. Like most lads who go seafaring, I suppose. It's something elemental, the defining moment in
your life. A man who's been to sea is a man who's had
adventures. A man who has lived in his work, not just
slaved."

It was seeing America—*Woodstock* in the cinemas, Vietnam War protests on the streets and campuses—that
politicised him. For the first time, he began to sense some
sort of progression. Life wasn't just random chaos; it had
a point. He got involved in his trade union, became a
shop steward, then joined the SWP. He'd been married at
twenty, had a son and daughter to provide for; now he
wanted to test his limits. "Ambition crept in. If history
has a shape, I thought, so does a man's life. I started to see
there were journeys that you didn't take on boats."

His globe-trotting days were ending, anyway. His family needed him, so he gave up long-distance voyages, looked for work close to home, and found sewage. "That was the end of the romantic phase. My own way of settling down. But a shitboat's nothing special, really. Just treated effluent; it could be anything." In his free time, he had become a voracious reader, acquiring the education he'd missed in approved school. He enrolled at university, working towards a master's in philosophy at Manchester Metro. But self-improvement came at a price. As his political horizons widened and he spent more time studying, his old life began to unravel. His children left home, his marriage broke up and he drifted apart from his friends. "Reading changes everything. You realise there's more to life than getting drunk and shagging, and you get a different viewpoint. At the same time, other people get a different view of you. You're more respected, maybe. But not better liked."

Has he doubted himself? "Who hasn't?" But he still believes in progression; in life as a journey, complete with destination. In a year or so, his job on the shitboat will finish and he'll return to dry land, moving sewage sludges around the north-west, free fertiliser for farms.

Looking back, he sees his life in two acts. "The first was pure instinct, the second based on knowledge." His existence, like any other, has been full of contradictions, wrong turns and just plain fuck-ups but he's always tried to be honest. "When you work with shit, you don't have a lot of time for pretences." He's tried to be open; to let in any light that's going. "How else will we ever learn to make sense of this barmy, beautiful world?"

I THINK OF HIM repeatedly in the days that follow, as we move around Salford, then into Moss Side and Hulme. Cruising these lost streets, where one school-leaver in three has a chance of work and only drug dealers thrive, it's hard to conceive of progress. Harry Radcliffe himself says the focus has changed. "Twenty years back, or even fifteen, people set targets; they were looking to move up. Now they're happy if they can maintain. Just hang on."

Even that much seems hardly achievable when you stand on Bonsall Street in Hulme. The whole area is one vast earthwork. The original slum terraces and tenements were razed in the fifties and sixties, to be replaced by jerry-built flats and tower blocks. Now these are being knocked down, in turn, to make way for a third set of homes, which may or may not be jerry-built as well. I notice that Pride is mentioned freely on the builders' placards, never a good sign. Perhaps, as the planners claim, this will prove a new beginning. For the moment, though, it has brought only chaos—mile upon mile of mud swamps, hundreds of families uprooted, a general sense of dislocation.

We walk into a labyrinth of condemned flats. Some have already been vacated, others are still occupied. Family homes and squats stand next to gutted shells. Some flats have lost their frontages, which have peeled away from the main structure and hang loose like tent flaps, exposing the rot and cracked concrete below. A burnt-out car has been abandoned in one of the courtyards, turds litter the walkways. On one of the balconies there's a bouquet of plastic flowers, in memory of a girl killed by dealers.

So far we could be in any ravaged city: Beirut or Sarajevo, the South Side of Chicago. But the murals are Bonsall Street's alone. A collective of graffiti artists has claimed every free patch of cement and plastered it with inner-city fantasias. Masked avengers and caped crusaders, white knights, black-power enforcers, alien invaders; battle scenes, love scenes, death scenes; revolution; Armageddon. We walk the walls as though touring a gallery, but no clean, well-lit space could be so physical. The frescoes have the impact of a last defiant yell. In another six months, a year at most, all of this will be rubble. Meanwhile, the images rise up, and roar.

Inside one of the flats, blockaded like a miniature fortress, I can hear a thud of bass, a squirl of treble. The bass line keeps repeating the same four-footed figure. Then a sampled vocal chimes in. "Undo the light," it sounds like. "Jump into the night."

It's the perfect Manchester solution. Nowhere in England is more nocturnal. As darkness blurs the damage, the city centre is transformed. Its massive blocks of stone are suddenly shot with steel, glass and neon. Cafés, bars, restaurants and, above all, dance clubs sprout in clusters, and pleasure seekers roll in mob-handed, hot and panting for action.

When in doubt, dance is the motto. As we wander from the Cool Britannia playrooms of Castlefields, under the railway bridge on Whitworth Street, along the canal to the Gay Village, the music never stops pounding. Techno, jungle, garage; straight clubs, drag clubs, unisex meat markets. There's a feeling of rising frenzy, a desperate rush for release. We pass a skateboarder, flying head-on at a brick wall. At the last split-second, he elevates; whirls up and over, miraculously intact. "I'd call that madness," Mary says. Manchester calls it flash.

I take a quick look inside Idols, where the bar staff have bared bottoms, male and female alike, and half the young nubiles in Lancashire, it seems, come to flaunt their prison-white bellies and thighs. The slithering and flopping of breasts carries me back to the piers at Grimsby, when the herring catch comes in.

NEXT DAY, I take a solitary saunter through the Gay Village. It revolves around two streets running back to back, between the bus station and the canal, and despite its name, it isn't exclusive to homosexuals. As the area's fame has grown, its original profile as a Lancastrian Christopher Street has blurred, and it has become a general haven for all those who feel overwhelmed or threatened by Manchester's prevailing machismo.

Strolling, I pass an elderly drag queen, padded and bol-
stered like Elsie Tanner; a gaggle of YMCA leatherettes,
flashing keyrings and chains; a boygirl in a fishnet body-
stocking; but also a scattering of straights, seeking refuge.
I talk to a girl who was in Idols last night. "I'm black and
blue and screaming," she tells me. "My tits are that sore,
you wouldn't believe." So she's come here to heal herself.
"At least in the Village, when they rip your knickers, they
ask you first."

It's a hot afternoon, the bars have spilled into the streets,
and there's a feeling of absolute freedom. A boy with green
hair to match his eyes explains the erotic marvels he can
perform with his big toe. Then I meet an old man, Albert
Harrick, natty in tweed jacket and cap. He started coming
to the Village, he says, because his grandson is a female
impersonator. "I never miss his shows. I'm right proud of
the lad. His Judy Garland is smashing. And as for his
Shirley Bassey, that Lily Savage has nothing on him."

Family loyalty is not the only lure. "I just like it here,"
Albert says. "Nobody bothers you, nobody cares if you're
a queer or a man from Mars." When he goes to his local
these days, or even if he's sitting in the park, some yob is
always in his face. This is the only place he can sit quiet
and know he won't be abused. "And the show is free," he
adds.

A gilded youth in running shorts, swanning by, blows
him a kiss; Albert is tickled pink. "I used to call them per-
verts but I've been taught a proper lesson," he says, looking down at the murk of the canal and the small regatta of
condoms drifting past. "They're less satanic than most."

Riene would be pleased to hear that. She has spent
most of her life trying to do herself in, precisely because
she's believed that to be gay is to be accursed.

Meeting her now, tanned and stylish, she seems in full
control. Her gaze, as direct as Harry Radcliffe's, and her
dry mill-town accent give off a no-nonsense directness.
But that's just the last few months, she says; the forty
years before were murder.

She was born in Rishton, an outpost of Blackburn; left school at fifteen; worked in a cotton mill and a paper mill; got married to a long-distance lorry driver; had a son and a daughter. She'd always known she was lesbian but she never let on, prayed that nobody would guess. "I thought, if I could keep it inside, one day it might go away, like an infection." Then her son, aged three, was stricken with cancer and died. In her heart, Riene believed that the death was a judgement. "I thought, right, I may have fooled everyone else but God's not fooled, is he? He's seen the evil in me, and this is his punishment."

The guilt was too great to stand under. She started to drink, and when she drank, she'd get involved with women, which made the guilt even worse, which in turn fired up the drinking. It was seventeen years of marriage before she could tell her husband the truth, give them both a chance to move on. By then, she'd become a chronic alcoholic. "I was totally toxic." She moved in with a lover who was also alcoholic, and violent with it. "I was always dependent. Always guilty, and looking to be punished." There were batterings, blackouts, hospitals, homes. "I kept going for cures, and she kept going for cures, but the cycle was too strong; we couldn't change." Even after she broke up with her lover, the downward spiral continued. She was drinking anything she could lay hands on—cleaning fluid, shoe polish, raw alcohol. Repeated stints in detox and rehab failed to break the pattern. One day, she woke up dying.

"I really thought I was gone. I couldn't speak, I could hardly breathe. The phone was right across the room but I couldn't walk, no way. So I started to crawl."

She ended up at a dry-house, an alcoholic last-chance Texaco. "You have to be really dire to get in." So dire that four of the eleven patients there with Riene are now dead. But she, against all odds, survived. "I just kept telling myself 'No more.'" This time she must have meant it.

Six months of treatment. Now it's been a year since she

got out. So far she has managed without drink, without batterings and almost without guilt. "I'm still crawling, really. Walking comes later on." She has a job, and she sees her daughter, now grown. In a few weeks, she's due to ride a float in the Gay Pride parade. So she sits in the afternoon sunlight, still a drink away from dying, and she watches the young at play, in their leathers and chains, their fishnet body-stockings. No curse on them; not a thought of God's burning rain. "They're free," Riene says, without envy. The corners of her eyes curl up when she smiles; she looks a beautiful woman at ease. "But the case isn't closed. It never is." It's not so much a matter of one day at a time, as one heartbeat. Still she's standing on her own. "Alone," she says, and her eyes curl up again. "What a word that is."

AT DUSK, I'm in a large and gloomy gay bar by the bus station. MTV plays silently on a giant screen, and Kylie Minogue is on the jukebox, singing "I Should Be So Lucky," and a group of leather girls are shooting pool. One wears a T-shirt saying *Get on Your Dyke.*

A small, tough-looking man approaches me. He has the squared shoulders and strutting, wide-hipped walk of a soldier, and his hair is cropped to stubble. He asks me to buy him a drink, then offers what he calls "oral service." Like a man from the *News of the World,* I make my excuses, but the soldier doesn't take offence. If anything, he seems relieved. "I only do it to hate myself," he tells me, and makes do with a Bailey's Cream.

His name is Paul; he's from Rochdale, in town for the day. When I ask him where he served, he looks at me funny. "All over the shop," he mutters. "Cyprus, the Falklands, south Antrim, you name it." A wave of anger runs through him. I can see his body go tense, a pulse start to jump in his throat. For a moment I think he might be going to whack me, but the moment passes and he sips his Bailey's Cream instead. "Twelve years in," he says.

When he first joined up, he had little choice. He was twenty, and he'd been in and out of trouble. There was a wild temper on him; he kept getting into pub brawls. "I was hurting people quite badly. Broken bottles in the face, banging heads on the floor, all that kind of stuff. I couldn't hold my rag. One wrong word and I'd just go off, up in smoke. The way I was heading, it was either end up dead or in jail, or *You're in the Army Now*."

Where the rage came from, he couldn't say. The rest of his family were all meek as lambs: "The souls of respectability, every boring one of them." But Paul himself, from childhood on, was trouble. In school, he was good at sports, running and boxing in particular, but excessively competitive. "I was always spiking people, or hitting them low; I'd kill to win." His father took him to a series of shrinks, but it didn't help. On his seventeenth birthday, when his family took him out for a curry, he almost killed his brother Michael over the last spiced papadum.

The army helped. He was able to channel some of his aggression into discipline and, when he did blow up, there were a lot tougher men than him around. "They learned me manners the hard way. The sex was good, and all." He speaks in a flat monotone, interspersed with waspish one-liners, their campness sounding odd in his dry mouth. "I fucked my way round half the world, and the world fucked me round the other half," he says. "Except in Antrim. They're very backwards about buggery in Ulster."

That wasn't the only reason why Northern Ireland finished him in the military. "I'd never killed a man. I still haven't, come to that. But I started really wanting to. I found myself getting, you know, trigger-happy. Itching to go, just looking for an excuse." He puffs out his cheeks, taps at his forehead. "Loony tunes," he says. "Time to get the fuck out."

By then it was 1989. He went back to Rochdale, opened a market garden, settled down with a sexual partner. This was his first real taste of stability. "He was a schoolmaster, Simon, like my father. A very well-respected man." Married, too, with children and a black Labrador. But he left them for Paul. They furnished a flat and exchanged vows. "I thought this was the biggie. Wedded bliss for life."

And his temper? "Not a problem." He still got twinges, but he'd found a formula for control. "Take a deep breath and think of Dame Elton dressed up as Mozart. It's better than counting to ten." Five years passed in relative tranquillity. Simon had his annoying sides but Paul could live with them. "He was very anal in every sense. He could never stand to throw anything out; he still had the collection of toy soldiers he'd had as a kid. Sometimes I thought I was one of them. But I didn't mind, not really. He could play with me any day."

Then it all just ended. They'd gone to Chester on a day trip, spent the afternoon browsing in the antique shops. Later on, they ate at a French restaurant. "Aylesbury duckling, beef Wellington, the works." They shared a baked Alaska for dessert. But something wasn't quite right. Simon looked peaky, a bit green around the gills. Paul asked him if he wasn't feeling well. And that's when Simon dropped the bomb. "He said he'd been thinking things over, and he was going back to his wife." Simple and flat as that. "No warning, no explanation; nothing."

When the waiter brought After Eights with the coffee, Simon, unbelievably, began to munch away. "I just stared at him. I was that numb, I didn't even see red." For a while, Simon just sat there, nibbling. Then he asked what Paul was thinking. "Have you ever thought of getting a penis enlargement?" Paul replied, and walked out.

He's been on his own ever since. Mostly, he keeps to himself. Every month or so, though, the pressure starts to build. He can feel he's not quite right in the head, so he takes a day off from his market garden and heads for the Gay Village. Not that he likes it here. "Too bloody cheerful by half. All these pink Pollyannas get up my nose." Unlike Riene, youth's freedom embitters him. "I'm forty-fucking-six," he tells me. "What does the future hold? Its dick in its hands, that's all."

The Gay Pride parade will find him in Rochdale, spitting bile. "I don't do floats," he tells me. Hits me up for another Bailey's Cream, then starts to move away. His eye sweeps the bar, checking for fresh targets. Half-hidden by his shirt cuff, I can see one end of a tattoo. I ask him what it says, and he turns back his cuff. SHOOT TO KILL, it reads.

OUTSIDE IN THE VILLAGE, it's night; the party is going full blast. Mary and Lucy collect me, and we start walking down Canal Street. It's like Blackpool gone pink—music blaring from the bars, drag queens shrieking "I Will Survive," lipstick lesbians voguing, tantastic musclemen in string vests and leather shorts, young and old, bent and straight, all of us made one for the night, by the night. "Look up," says Mary, and I see a firework burst high overhead. Gold and green sparks rain over the crush; for a moment the whole sky seems ablaze. Not just the city centre, but Salford and Hulme, and all those hidden miles beyond. The suburbs, the mill towns, Burnley, Wigan Pier.

Industria.

That burning land.

NOISE
POLLUTION

ONE NIGHT, in transit, I make a quick pit-stop at my home in Hertfordshire. Exhausted by the road, I wander down the orchard to take a nap but it's no use, I can't drop off. There is no sound of music.

The absence takes me by surprise. I've come to take the thud of bass, the ceaseless blasting of boom boxes, for granted. They're part and parcel of the republic, and it's only now, when they go missing, that I realise how new this is. Music in the past, even in the sixties, was always regulated by place and time. Now it never stops.

MARY HAS DISCOVERED a new master, a hardcore techno DJ called Surgeon, and we have to take a spin back to Liverpool, to hear him work out at Voodoo. The man is indeed a talent, his beats fierce and stark, alchemical. But the club is an airless black box and the heat level brutal. Sweat pours off me even when I'm still. When I dance, I go into terminal meltdown.

Stumbling, half-blinded, I finally take refuge in the chill-out zone. Rest for a few minutes, then gird myself to plunge back into the furnace. Before I can hit the floor, though, something decidedly strange occurs. Some agency within me, a rogue fusion of blood and brain, begins to rap out its own private beats. Hard and sharp as machine-gun fire, they seem to come from a half-dozen sources at once—frontal lobe, heart, lungs, gut and balls.

For a few seconds, they fill me up to bursting. Then they snap off again, as suddenly as they came on. A few more seconds pass; the beats seem lost without trace. I move back to the dance floor and take a few tentative steps. As I do so, Surgeon changes tack. His bass lines splinter, diffuse. And he starts playing my own lost beats.

Transmigration of rhythms—this is a new one to me. When I mention it to Mary, though, she isn't much impressed. "Happens all the time," she shrugs, and she's off in a flash of silver, away across the dance floor.

That glimpse of silver—a sheer glitzy strip of fabric, roughly the size of a washcloth, which shimmers like silverfish every time it moves—is the primary reason I'm here. Mary calls it her dress, but treats it more like a sacred relic. In the time we've spent on the road, I've seen it displayed, revered, but never worn. Each night it's removed ceremonially from her luggage, and each morning, just as ceremonially, repacked. Still, I've never witnessed her in anything but jeans or boy's trousers. After all these weeks, her legs remain just a rumour.

They are reserved exclusively for clubbing, as is the silver dress. Unless I sign myself on for a night of hardcore, I'll never have the chance to see them united in action. So I follow her into Voodoo, into the darkness and swelter, the strobe lights swirling, the strangers whacked out on E who keep slinging their arms round my neck and slobbering about love, the sweat-sopping bodies, and these skull-splitting beats that never settle or reach resolution, never seem to end. "Paradise," Mary yells in my ear, flitting past. But her legs? All I can make out, by the flickering of the strobes, are two bony Derry kneecaps and her purple boots, stomping rump.

I have spent other nights in Electronica, many of them, dating back to raves in the early eighties, and the promised magic has never worked. The rapture has always seemed too easily won, too self-adoring. Those blissed-out eyes, the waving arms and upraised palms—in no time flat, I'm looking for cats to kick. But tonight is different. Age and damage are forgotten; so is all thought of dignity. Heart pounding, lungs bursting, a dancing fool, I give myself up.

This, of course, is the gospel according to Mary; the message she's been pounding me with since first we met: "In techno, truth." For her, the music is redemptive, a form of salvation.

Soon after that first meeting, she took me down to Brighton to meet a DJ friend of hers. Dundee-born and raised, his whole pre-techno life had been one long catalogue of excess. He'd grown up sniffing glue, butane gas, Potter's Asthma Mix; anything that could get him wrecked. Then he gulped down an entire packet of Marzine, travel-sickness pills. The result was black-death paranoia. He saw a man come crawling in through his letter box, and they started fighting. Rolling over the settee, hand-to-hand combat, one of them must die. The next thing he knew, he was in the psycho ward.

That was twelve years ago but he still couldn't sleep right at nights, he kept thinking that someone was breaking through his door. He'd tried everything to keep them out. Steel plates, prison bars; nothing worked. Only techno. "Electronic body music," the DJ called it. "That's my shield. It's anything you want to make it, and it'll take you any place you need to go. Whatever your secret desire, techno can give it you. Everything but fear; it knows no fear. And when the fear goes, there's only love."

It could have been Timothy Leary or John Lennon talking. So much rhetoric, from Elvis on, has revolved around this same need to freeze the moment, give permanence to a passion that is, by its nature, not built to last. Rock & Roll Will Never Die, All You Need Is Love, Punk for Ever—the basic message is always the same: *Don't say that this will end. Don't, for pity's sake, say that one day we won't be young, our music won't be new, and someone else, our children, will be saying these same things about another trip, another noise.*

Looking across the dance floor now, I catch a flash of

these bodies in twenty or thirty years, the bared belly-buttons now sagging over the bands of the lycra tights, the tattoos and piercings encrusted, still flailing their arms and blissing out, while Surgeon feeds them another of the good old good ones, just one more once.

But that's not the proper spirit. When I try to slink back to the chill-out zone, a girl I've never met grabs my hand and drags me on to the floor again. "Believe!" she screams in my ear. And I picture the city outside. The shattered streets; the rage and helplessness. A killing floor of the soul. But not in here. In this black box, for this one night, there's victory.

SURGEON HIMSELF is a slight, unimposing figure. Expressionless in his glass box, he looks like a trainee lab technician. Give him a white coat and a Bunsen burner, and he could be mixing combustibles.

The day after Voodoo, we track him to his home in Birmingham. Over the last few years, that city has forged a style of hardcore techno all its own—raw, underproduced, even clumsy, but full of energy and funk. The House of God is its Mecca, Downwards Records its prime source and Surgeon its champion.

Before confronting the baby-faced killer in person, we stop off at the Custard Factory, where Downwards Records has its office. The factory, once owned by Bird's Eye, is now an arts complex, full of dance studios and galleries and PR firms. Its restaurant serves quiche and designer coffees, and Rollerbladers perform acrobatics in the forecourt, turning somersaults and back-flips. PVC and phat pants, orange dreadlocks and diamond tongue-studs—it's not what I think of as Birmingham. Then again, what is?

Karl O'Connor, a mainspring of Downwards who doubles as DJ Regis, bristles at the question. "Birmingham?" he says. "It can be crap, but it's my crap." He's a beefy man in an anorak, Birmingham to the bone, which means no airs, no graces. His defining passions are the West Bromwich Albion football team, beats, a hatred of glitz.

The Downwards office is a bright bare room, entirely without furnishings, so we sit on the floor, while he tells me how the scene began. Electronica, in the eighties, was a cabal. "We all knew each other, we were in and out of each other's houses, scheming to blow up the world." All they had was attitude—a shared scorn for mainstream pop. Instead of limos and bodyguards, their fantasy was a club to call their own. Just one room, any room, where they could let the music blast, no holds barred.

"It was a very Birmingham situation," Karl says. The art of living and surviving in this city has always been to feed off the negatives. On the one hand, you develop a fierce loyalty, because it's your home town, and outsiders love to slag it off, and you're sick of being sneered at by a bunch of London trendoids; on the other, you're driven half-mad by the drabness. "In the end, you build up a siege mentality," Karl says. "Inferiority complex, paranoia, rage, you can pick your own adjectives, but that's what drives us, that's where we get our hunger."

Karl runs Downwards with a couple of childhood friends. "It's still a cottage industry." In Germany or Scandinavia, where techno is huge, a DJ like Surgeon can play for crowds of twenty thousand or more. Over here, as often as not, he plays for a few hundred. Clubbing is a luxury, and techno fans, at least in the provinces, are usually skint. "There just isn't the necessary." So hardcore, the real stuff, remains underground. "I call it a mass secret."

SURGEON'S REAL name is Tony Child. He says he's twenty-four but he could pass for seventeen, and he lives and works amid schoolboy disorder, cooped up in a bedsit in Moseley. There's virtually no furniture, just studio equipment—mixing board, assorted keyboards and bass machines, computer programmes, enough levers and knobs to launch an Apollo moonshot.

A graffito on a nearby railway bridge reads MUGGER-SCUM OUT! a phrase that Child annexed as the title for one of his records. The basic tone of the area, however, is casual, shabby-genteel, and his own street is largely Asian. Housewives with shopping bags and full shalwar-kameez; white-bearded and white-robed elders discoursing at their front doors—it seems an odd setting for techno. "That's the attraction," Surgeon says in his flat Midlands drone, just above a mumble. "I like to come from outside." He fumbles for a more vivid description. "Sort of like an alien," he offers.

There is a curious sense of detachment about him. He answers our questions carefully, with every effort at completeness. Still, I sense a lack of engagement. It's as if words aren't his natural medium and everything outside music is somehow an intrusion. What was his childhood like? He can't really remember. What did his father do? He isn't sure; maybe an accountant. Where did he grow up? Different villages; he can't recall their names.

All he can tell us for certain is that his family was South African, and he himself was born there. Everything else is wrapped up in sound.

Where did it begin? "It was always there." But not the music that most people heard. "I was never exposed to mainstream pop, the Beatles, none of that. The sounds that affected me were the things my father liked—space stuff, soundtracks from old sci-fi films, Japanese electronics."

That was where the alien connection came in, the feeling of being apart. Right from the outset, he didn't respond to songs and never much cared for performers. What obsessed him, quite simply, was sound. "I liked racket. When I was six or five or whatever, I used to mess about with tape recorders, trying different tricks and distortions. Or I'd play about with records, say a Pinky and Perky forty-five, I'd play it at sixteen rpm and realise that the singing was only two men talking, then speeded up. Shattering the illusion, I liked that, it gave me a feeling like power."

The problem was how to harness this power. "For a long time, I hadn't a clue what I was doing. I knew, whatever I did with my life, it had to be around music, but I didn't want it to be like a career choice, all about money, I thought that was prostitution. I didn't want to study music at college, I didn't want to be part of the industry. I was floundering, sort of. Just washing about."

It took techno to anchor him. At home-brewed sessions in the back rooms of pubs, he began to realise that he wasn't on his own. There were others like him; electronic aliens all. Not many of them, not at first. But a nucleus.

A friend in Kidderminster set up a studio, and Tony began to tinker. At the same time, he was working with a band that went in for fancy dress, so he donned rubber gloves and a surgical mask, renamed himself Surgeon.

Those were the bare bones. What really mattered, though, was not dates and factoids, but the evolution of sound inside his head. "I kept hearing different textures, new tones and beats, but I couldn't seem to give them form. When I tried to make demos, they had no bite." Then he came to Birmingham and met Mick Harris, one-time drummer with Napalm Death, who had built a makeshift studio in his toilet. He was a hard taskmaster and wouldn't stand for any half-measures. Weary of Tony's waffling, he simply threw him in the can and turned the lock. "Don't stop to think, just do it, push it. Whatever's in you, get it out," Mick Harris told him, and wouldn't release him till he'd obeyed.

What did Tony emerge with? "Rhythms and riffs," he says. "It was never melody in my head, just noise, the manipulation of sound. Emotion through noise—that's what techno is. How you can change moods and feelings just by switching beats, lightening a pulse or making it darker, reworking a phrase, or even a single tone."

I picture Mick Harris's toilet, in years to come, done up as a tourist shrine, a hardcore Graceland with incense and candles and 3-D postcards of the throne. But Surgeon has no time for such levity. Sitting in his bedroom, hemmed in by gadgets and gizmos, he could be manning a spaceship. "You can change everything," he tells us, dreaming. "Build a world in a beat."

I'M SITTING in my daughter's living room and the TV is on. A man with prodigious pink ears is talking and talking. His voice is pious and mournful, a vicar's bleat, and his ears seem to glow with reverence. "Elvis is everywhere," he says.

This is true. Mary and I have been on the road for over a month, have already covered two thousand miles, and the King has been with us constantly. His pictures, young and old; his voice in pubs and supermarkets; his songs in karaoke bars—if I were a visiting Martian, with nothing to go on but pictures in shop windows, I'd guess that Elvis and Princess Diana are married, and together they rule the republic, with Gazza as Prime Minister, the Spice Girls for spawn.

The name alone is an open sesame. Whenever conversation bogs down or storytellers lose their way, I've learned to flush Elvis from my sleeve like a buried ace, then sit back and wait for the reflex response—a curled upper lip, a few bars of "Jailhouse Rock," a karate pose, a blimp joke, a scrap of reminiscence. He is, above all, a key to memory.

This isn't confined to the old-timers who grew up on Presley in the fifties. One day in King's Cross, when my journey was just beginning, I got talking to a lad off a building site, who came into McGlynn's after work, stripped to the waist, with a bulging tattoo of Elvis on either biceps. He'd had them done for his mother, he said. She suffered from Alzheimer's, was confined to the house, and Elvis was one of the few things she still reacted to; the sight of him always cheered her up.

For me, the concept of Elvis as healer isn't easy to grasp. The figure I fell in love with, aged ten, was dangerous, sexually ambivalent, a force of destruction and righteous chaos; a murdering son. Now he's become a hallowed father. "My mum gets him mixed up with God sometimes," the bricklayer told me. They often played the gospel albums together. His mother always wept at "Crying in the Chapel"; occasionally, so did he. "I've prayed to that man in my time," he said.

I ponder this as we drive south again. The anniversary of the King's death is coming up and London is the only place to be. I've read that there are over three hundred Presley impersonators at loose in south London alone. By my estimate, that works out at ten tons of mortal Elvis, a mile and a half of sequinned jumpsuits.

As soon as we reach Kentish Town, Mary takes to her bed and sleeps for forty-eight hours. In her absence, I am turned over to a friend of hers, Larry, for whom Elvis is a household deity.

He's a man of parts, Larry: haircutter, bass player, street chronicler, wide-boy, would-be priest. Small and trim and serious, every detail of him immaculate, he reminds me of a sixties' Mod—the same obsessive neatness, the same inwardness and the same style of anger, tightly battened down.

Both his brothers, Michael and Pat, are frontmen with post-punk bands, and Larry's in and around the music business, too. At any given moment, he might be a manager, a booking agent or even a musician. Most of the time, though, he simply hangs out at the Fortress, formerly a tax office but now a labyrinth of recording studios and cut-rate rehearsal rooms, off the City Road.

The first day we meet, I'm still road-lagged. "You look like you've seen a ghost," Larry tells me, and in a sense I have. The spectre of the North still looms, dark and ravaged, in my mind. London, by contrast, seems vast but bland.

To jar me back into sync, Larry takes me walking round Kentish Town. He wants to tell me his story, which is also, indirectly, a story about Elvis. But first, as background, he needs me to witness the housing estate and the streets where he grew up.

Kentish Town these days is a curious hybrid. Parts of the area have become gentrified, now harbour journalists and luvvies, but the route Larry takes me—the Mathews Estate, Caley Street, the dark end of Queen's Crescent—remains unredeemed. He points out crackhouses, villains' pubs, armed-robbery scenes. After Granby and Hulme, however, it all looks like Ideal Homes to me. The houses are still standing, only a few of the windows are iron-clad, and none of the cars are burnt-out shells. Even so, Larry sees it as hell. "This is rock-bottom," he tells me, not without satisfaction. "The living end."

The neighbourhood was never soft, even in his childhood. But the violence was controllable then, the drugs mostly speed and smoke. Besides, his father had it sorted. "Never mind Elvis," Larry says. "My dad was the King in these parts."

His father is the centre of the story. He came to London at sixteen, a big, handsome lad from Clonmel in Tipperary, and took up with Larry's mother, a Catholic girl raised in Brixton, extremely devout. He had loads of charm, a sharp intelligence, all the wit and gab in the world. But he was also cursed. "There was something wrong in his head, a chemical imbalance, but nobody called it that. People didn't talk about manic-depressive disorders back then. As far as we knew, he just had moods."

These moods were exacerbated by alcohol. There was a lot of hard drinking, day by day, and that led to terrible rages. Each of his three sons suffered brutal beatings. "He could have killed the lot of us; it was just chance we survived." Sometimes he thrashed them with his fists, sometimes he used a snooker cue. Their mother got walloped, too. "There were days she could hardly move." But she never walked out. "It was against her religious beliefs." Besides, she loved the man.

They all did. Hated him and feared him both, but the love was always strongest. "He has this incredible presence, my father. If he was a film star, you'd call it charisma. It's like a seduction, almost. You keep thinking, This is wrong, this is sick. But you can't walk away."

He was an avenging god in his house. But the father's own god was Elvis. "Our living room was a shrine," Larry says. "Pictures and records everywhere, calendars, the lot. When I think about growing up, I tend to picture the madness on one side and Elvis on the other, a little pocket of strength and calm. He was the one thing my father never wanted to destroy. A symbol of everything good."

And the three sons, raised in this church of Presley? The way that Larry describes them, they sound like the Karamazov brothers of Kentish Town. Michael, the eldest, who bore the greatest weight of the father's rages, emerged both tortured and torturing; Pat, the youngest but also the toughest, brawled and boozed and drugged his way through his teens to something approaching sanity; and Larry, like his mother, took shelter in God.

"I don't know where the call came from," he says. "I've just always had this compulsion, whenever I see someone hurting, to try and cure it, take it away."

In his time, he's logged his fair share of excesses, but he can't walk past any waif or stray. His brother Pat calls him Mother Teresa; Mary says he has a martyr complex. For Larry himself, however, it's a matter of perspective. "I'm not bothered by surfaces, only what's inside. If a person has beauty or potential, deep down, I can't turn my back on that."

If he was a priest, as he's often thought of becoming, the situation might be easier. He has done missionary work in Portugal and feels he may have a vocation. For the moment, though, all he can do to give solace is cut hair.

For Larry, this is a form of sacrament. "Anyone who thinks that it's all just a matter of rinses and perms knows nothing. A serious haircut is a very spiritual thing." Every part of the ritual has its own significance: the washing and soaping and rinsing and drying; the cutter's hands massaging, shaping; the position of the cuttee, head bowed, neck bared, as if surrendering; the whole idea of regeneration through loss. "It's definitely a healing," Larry says.

All this, in some way he can't describe, is tied up with the figure of Elvis. His home life is a little easier now. His father is on pills; the mood swings are less extreme. Even so, as Larry talks about love and respect, he keeps returning to his childhood. Small and solemn, soft-voiced, he summons up a memory of his father, wild-eyed and raging. The father's after Michael, his eldest, for some real or imagined crime. "You can't get away from me, boy," he keeps saying, pool cue in hand. Michael's running and yelling, Pat has done a bunk, their mother is praying. And Larry himself? He's watching; eternally watching. The crucifix on the wall. And Elvis, looking down.

WHEN MARY emerges from her sleep, we take a slow ride through south London, the living heart of Presleyland. Every high street seems to have its own Elvis shrine. Reunions, tributes, memorabilia shows; an impersonator who advertises himself as the King of Kings. There's even a talent contest for Junior Hound Dogs, ten or under.

Somewhere near Streatham, stuck in traffic, we are visited by an apparition: a man in late middle age, decked out in a full Vegas suit of lights, complete with pompadour and wraparound shades. He's sitting in a laundromat, serenely watching his wash.

Then we come to Graceland.

It's the end of a long quest. Many months ago, before I began this journey, I was walking near the Pantiles in Tunbridge Wells, when I passed a Chinese restaurant. The windows were plastered with action glossies of a Chinese Presley: Paul "Elvis" Chan. But the restaurant was shut. A passer-by told me that it was open only at weekends; the rest of the time, Chan travelled.

Further enquiries, phone messages, even letters brought no response. Then I learned that Chan's head-quarters are in the Old Kent Road. Finding ourselves in the neighbourhood, Mary rings on the off chance, and Chan picks up. "I not sing tonight," he warns her, decid-edly gruff. "Talk, maybe, a little. But if you expecting Elvis, he not be here."

Graceland lies beyond a maze of tower blocks, in the shadow of a railway bridge. The restaurant is dimly lit, almost deserted; the kitchen closed. There's nothing but empty tables, and the reek of disinfectant. Paul Chan, sit-ting alone, surrounded by Elvis photos and movie posters, does not look a happy man.

Slim, neatly made, with longish hair swept back at the sides and a jet-black forelock trained to flop loose across his forehead, he doesn't take after Elvis so much as the King's first English disciples: Billy Fury, the young Cliff Richard. "Why you here?" he demands, his upper lip curling with just the right surly twist. "If you want to write about Elvis, you better think deep. You don't do this for fun, understand? Only if you have need."

His eyes are red-rimmed; he looks spent. When he starts to talk, it's grudgingly, in fits and starts: "I am born in Hong Kong, that's where it begins. It is 1956, I think, and I'm hearing 'Teddy Bear.'" From that moment, the pursuit of Presley consumed him. "At school when I start my education, I am not really concentrate or work hard on my study, my only care is Elvis. I take money from my mother, I go to the cinema, *Love Me Tender, King Creole,* this is my whole life, understand, this is all I am."

He came to England in 1970. By this time, he was mar-ried. "We get income, we have house, we have everything. Two children, first daughter, second son. We work; we work and sing. We are the one happy family."

But now a strange pattern began to take shape. More and more, Chan's life echoed his idol's. "Our marriage, similar, not too much different. My wife, she not respect me truly, never listen to my deep wishes. At the end she leave me, gone. Bring me a divorce, and she give me my broken heart."

After the split, his wife kept the house and children, while Chan restarted from scratch. "I work in Chinese restaurant, also living there. Year goes, then one day I say, 'Chinese restaurants, too many, too much boring, they need a song.' So I'm saving three years more, four years, and I open here. For Elvis, understand? To bring us together, same place, same time."

Eight years after launching his first Graceland, he now owns three. Each weekend, he starts off his evenings by appearing at the one in Tunbridge Wells, then moves on to Sevenoaks, before finishing up at Elvisworld Central on the Old Kent Road.

The rest of the time, he lives alone in a big house in Bexleyheath, also named Graceland, with a one-acre garden, a Cobra in the garage that he never drives and gates decorated with clef notes, just like the original in Memphis. "Same as Elvis, I did all right. I only small, he so big, but not all different inside. We make it, fine, but everything is not all right. In our heart, understand, we both lonesome tonight. Sometime when I sing, I feel upset, I cry. In my opinion Elvis, he was not a happy guy. He have money but he can't go to restaurant, get Chan's good food. I just think he sad to be alone, all the time alone."

As he talks, he stares. His dark eyes are velvety, sombre with awe. "Is Elvis in me? His spirit living?" he asks. "Sometimes I think so, yes. I feel him inside. Sometimes, yes, I can feel him move."

Chan jumps up from his seat and ducks behind the bar. Fumbles with a cassette, then vanishes, leaving us alone with the Dettox and the hundred faces of Elvis on the walls. Ghostly faces stare in through the windows. There's a leaking tap somewhere.

Suddenly, the silence breaks: "And now, the moment

you've all been waiting for," a canned voice intones. "Ladies and gentlemen, please put your hands together for . . . Mr. Paul . . . Elvis . . . CHAN!!" Taped multitudes roar, and Chan erupts from behind the bar, resplendent in a tight white jumpsuit with rhinestones and fringed flares. This dark, troubled room lights up: *Well, it's one for the money, two for the show . . ."*

THIS IS Bobby Friction's time: Saturday morning in Hounslow, the streets thronged with young Asian girls showing skin, smells of spice and fresh sweat in the air and Sunrise Radio blasting bhangra through the open windows of his beat-up Sierra. In front of the Bulstrode, the drinkers stop talking and stare as he swings into the car park. His great moon-face, framed in the driver's window, has the rapt, ecstatic look of an overgrown baby who's stumbled on a brand-new trick. People smile just to see him.

The Bulstrode is a large, brash, rambling pub, where Asians and whites mix freely. For Bobby, it's office and bar and playpen combined, his second home. When he strolls into its shadowy back garden, he takes it over, a lord in his manor.

With his spiked black hair piled high with gel, his glittery black shirt that his mum brought home from India, his nose ring, his scimitar-shaped sideburns and his glossy dark eyes, he's a non-stop show. Not remotely hip—he's constitutionally incapable of understatement—but loud and flash, full of juice. Words rocket out of him; jokes and stories, meditations, remembered dreams, political diatribes. Swaying back on his seat, one pint already downed, he turns his face to the dappled light, as though inviting pot-shots. All around him, people are watching, waiting. "I'm the Anti-Cool," Bobby crows. "It's the only way to be."

Away from Hounslow, he's a DJ, part of the Asian

Underground. It's a loose-knit collection of writers, artists, filmmakers and musicians, British-born and made, sometimes called second generation. Essentially non-sectarian—Muslims, Sikhs and Hindus contribute equally—its communal voice is full of anger and pride, mystical yearnings and back-alley hungers. From what I've heard so far, its lung-power is ferocious.

Hounslow doesn't care about that. At the Bulstrode, Bobby's just another Sikh homeboy, an *apana,* born Paramdeep Singh Sehdev. Another pint slips down; his gut, already spreading nicely beneath his black shirt, gives a gentle rumble at the memory of his mother's pilau rice; and he loses himself in a romantic reverie about the girl he dated last night, how she looked him dead in the eyes and how she crept up behind him in a phone box. The windows were plastered with prostitutes' pictures and she slipped a calling card for *Young Asian Model, 18, Awaits Your Pleasure* inside his breast pocket. "We really connected; it's on. I think this could be the one," Bobby says. Then he jumps back into his Sierra, and takes a quick whirl round his world.

Hounslow life is built around an optical illusion. At first glance, it seems a changeless English suburb, eternally stuck in the fifties. The tidy little shops, the streets upon streets of semi-detacheds, the rose bushes and lilacs, the rising suns above the front doors: for a moment, spotting a radio inside an open window, you half expect it to be tuned to *Mrs. Dale's Diary.* Then you catch sight of the saris and the turbans, the shalwar-kameez.

One reason Bobby treasures the place is that it once was lost to him. "I got booted out of the garden, aged five." Until then, his only memories are of feeling total safety. His father, who'd come to England from Lahore, was a street trader in Indian clothing. Then he saved enough to open a shop. Business thrived, and soon he had a string of five stores. The family, riding the wave, moved to Farnborough. "We joined the middle classes," Bobby says. "Bigger house, a better school. But the other kids used to call me an African. From being surrounded by love, I felt like a freak."

His father's business got caught in the recession and ended up bankrupt. Instead of the smart house in Farnborough, there was now a housing estate in Camberley, routine bullying at school. "Nothing life-threatening, just aggro and name-calling. I was a dirty Paki, I stank. I was scum." And scum he remained till he reached thirteen and his family returned to Hounslow.

"You can't imagine the buzz. All those years, growing up, I'd been cast out, and now I belonged again. It was like coming in from the cold, back into the womb. I kept walking round the streets with my eyes on stalks, drinking in the warmth. Young, free and Asian, what more could anyone want?" And all the Asian girls, dangling like ripe fruit. "I couldn't believe the beauty." He started going to daytime dances, sneaking kisses and more. "I was into some serious paradise."

Whipping round Hounslow now, and over the narrow bridge that leads into Southall, he conducts a guided tour of his history. Southall High Street looks like a bazaar. The pavements throng with stalls selling bright silks, spices, Bollywood videos, and every block seems to carry its own tale. Here's Lady Margaret Road, where the riots went off in 1979 and here's where the rioters threw vats of curry at the cops; here the patch of pavement where his father had his first stall; and here the side street where the police pulled him out of his car on the night of Vaishaki, the Sikh religious holiday, three years ago, and clobbered him for giving them lip.

With his wild look and wilder mouth, he's always tackled confrontation head first. Last August, for example, he was in Gerrard Street late one night, leaving a club called the Clinic, when he saw a gang of Triads beating up some Southall *apanas*. Some of the Chinese boys were pounding a fallen Asian with a City of London dustbin lid, and Bobby went to the rescue. The fight broke up, but the Asian failed to move. Bobby was heading for a nearby phone booth, meaning to call an ambulance, when two police vans came screaming into view. One glance at Friction, the nose ring and the spiked hair, and cops swarmed all over him. When he tried to resist, out came the cuffs. At the station, and later in court, he gave his name as Mohandas K. Gandhi. So now he's on probation: "Bound over for keeping the peace," as he puts it.

The way that trouble follows him is the reason he's called Friction. "I'm always pushing and stirring, asking awkward questions. Shoving my big nose in where it's not wanted, according to some people, but I think that's healthy, don't you? So many things need shaking up. Well, I'm the man to do it."

He often thinks of the *Godfather* films. Not because of the gang wars or the bloodshed so much, but because of the closeness, the immigrant family bonds. There are times when he sees himself as a Don, taking care of business. "I look out for my own; all my Asian brothers and sisters," he says. In part, that's why he still wears combat gear, even though it's long out of fashion. "It's not aggression, really; more protection. A statement to say I'm here, I've got your backs."

AT FIVE O'CLOCK sharp on a Monday evening, he groans. By day, he and his friend Davinder run a computer sales business, and now he's sitting in the office, under the tacked-up card of *Young Asian Model, 18, Awaits Your Pleasure,* quietly chatting up a prospect on the phone, when a sudden stab of gas kicks in and his stomach clenches like a fist. This is the night when he plays at Swaraj, the Asian Underground's weekly club night. Time for him to turn DJ. He thinks he might throw up.

The fact that he lives to perform doesn't mean it comes easy to him. Every show is an ordeal by fire. The Indian word for nerves, for butterflies in the gut, is *khabrat.* Bobby Friction is the *khabrat* king.

The only way to find calm is to stare himself down in

the mirror. It's a trick he learned in the Camberley years, when he was the butt of every school yard kicking and his face, perhaps in response, broke out in a plague of spots. One day, skulking out of sight, he started fooling around with his mother's make-up. Her foundation looked to him like brown sludge, but at least it offered cover.

Powder was even better. And then there was skin cream, eye shadow; a whole world of camouflage. By the time his mother found him out, half of her prized supply of Helena Rubinstein was gone. She screamed and yelled, she gave him two slaps. Then she quieted down and bought him some Rimmel instead.

That, in spirit, was Bobby's debut as a rock star. Around the same time, he fell in love with Prince and realised that weird-looking aliens in make-up and ruffled shirts, wielding spaceship guitars, were not necessarily freaks—they might be gods in disguise. So he stopped running, both from himself and others; turned his strangeness into a weapon.

When he got back to Hounslow, he started wearing six pairs of braces at once, looped and criss-crossed like bandoliers. Then came the piercings and plucked eyebrows. He was a Sikh warrior, and a Goth, and an old-style Rock & Roller, all rolled into one. He made a poster of Gandhi with a machine-gun, in front of a Union Jack. His mother had conniptions and his father lapsed into long, dead silences, more terrible than any rage. But what did that matter? Out on the streets, there was sex without end. Girls who kissed, and girls who lay down. Girls who would give their souls for a shot at a hand-me-down Prince.

By the time Bobby left for university, up in Nottingham, he knew that he'd been put on earth to perform. He broadened his tastes to Jimi Hendrix and the Beatles, studied graphic art, became politicised and played Benvolio, the peacemaker, in *Romeo and Juliet*: "Madam, an hour before the worshipp'd sun / Peer'd forth the golden window of the east, / A troubled mind drave me to walk abroad . . ."

He liked the restlessness of that. He himself was living in several worlds at once—academic, artistic, street, Asian, white—but the feeling of being fragmented was not unpleasant. On the contrary, the more he explored, and the more selves he unearthed, the more he could sense his own latent powers, just waiting for the signal to ignite.

The Asian Underground gave him his chance. It's a mad mixture of styles—Indian classicism, breakbeat, drum 'n' bass, Bollywood, and sitardelia, all flung together in a stew—and when it's done up right, nothing I've heard in recent years sounds better.

Two years ago, the Underground was confined to a couple of club nights—Outcaste and Anokha. Bobby, fresh down from Nottingham with a BA in Contemporary Arts, went to one of the first Outcaste gigs. He was dressed in full Don mode, at least the Hounslow version: Indian pyjamas in screaming orange, Armageddon boots, a combat-print waistcoat. Most of the audience assumed he was one of the acts. Then the music kicked in. It was the sound he had been waiting for all his life.

Before then, he'd played guitar, a little drums, but DJing was new territory and his initial attempts were bumbling, all thumbs. Success came only when he stopped imitating and trusted in his own ears. At heart, he's still a rocker, in love with blowing things up. To that extent, his present incarnation as DJ Friction is just a way station. Somewhere down the line, he can picture himself creating a total show—a rock Ramayana, full of mythological Indian culture, ancient, gaudy, outrageously tacky, with bits of Prince and Hendrix slung in for luck, not forgetting Sly and the Family Stone. Right at this moment, though, his main worry is keeping his lunch down.

The shakiness is all his own fault. Last night he was out at the Calcutta Cyber Café. It's meant to be an evening of rest and decorum: Indian classical sounds, sofas and big chairs to lounge on, a few quiet drinks. The prevalent tone is typified by the sumptuous Sweety Kapoor, all elegance and poise. But Bobby Friction and poise have never been an easy fit. In the small hours of the morning, he found himself in a room above Brick Lane, trapped with a bunch of spliffheads, musicians and girls of bad intentions. He tried to escape, of course. The trembling in his hands is proof that he didn't succeed.

One pickle is following another, his father always says. The more he tries to straighten up and fly right, the more he's shot down in flames. There are nights when he finds the second-generation mob too self-conscious. Compared to his friends back in Hounslow, they seem unrooted. That's why he keeps one foot in either world, and never cuts the cord.

TIME TO SHIFT. It's taken him two hours to get his spikes just right, perfect the two crescents of bindhis around his eyes. His face in the mirror, larded and powdered, is still puffy, but the *khabrat* has calmed; he's ready for action.

Make-up is scattered all over the floor and bed. Gandhi's autobiography and *Brave New World*, the prophecies of Nostradamus and *Prince* by Dave Hill are on his bookshelf, and his combat gear is hanging on the back of the door. Downstairs, a Bollywood movie soundtrack blares on Z-TV, and his mother is cooking up the food for tonight's gig at Swaraj. She's shrieking and storming, as ever, and his father, as ever, answers not a word. On Argyle Avenue, a young girl is standing in her doorway, fiddling with her hair. Along Hounslow High Street, the local teen gangs, derisively known as In'its, are revving for the night ahead. And Bobby starts down the stairs.

His father is distinctly dubious. "What is your opinion? Can this foolishness bring success?" he asks. But his eyes, as he takes in Bobby's get-up, are not hostile; merely concerned. The night's food stands wrapped and waiting. At the front door, by a painting of a robed Sikh housewife brandishing a sewing needle, Bobby pauses to kiss his mother goodbye. From the intensity of the parting, he might be off on a great journey.

IT'S MIDNIGHT when his set ends and his friend Imran Khan, who edits *Second Generation* magazine, takes over. There is a rogue chemistry between the two, which invariably leads them into dust-ups. The other day, invited by Baroness Flather to a House of Lords cocktail party for Asian movers and shakers, they wound up in the cellars, crazed drunk, planning to do a Guy Fawkes. A guard collared them in time, and they did no major damage, but not for lack of anarchic intent.

Their taste for renegade excess sits oddly here. *Swaraj* is Hindi for self-rule, and the crowd seems resolutely solemn. Half the early punters are white. They cluster in the upstairs bar, sniffing Mrs. Sehdev's curries and watching a masseuse dispense back-rubs. Meanwhile, down in the basement, Bobby Friction plays for a half-dozen listless shufflers.

Little by little, he reels them in. Stuck behind a gauze curtain, he stomps and rages, pounds the bass, makes the night happen by pure force of will. Bollywood stills flash and whirl on a screen, and Asian anthems rock the house. State of Bengal's "Flight IC408" comes on, the walls start to sweat and white boys fling themselves face-down on the stage. Bobby is leaping and twisting behind his decks. Big beat stings the soles of the feet, creeps up the calves and thighs, then buries itself in the groin. One of the speakers is smoking; the floor is dripping wet. Sweety Kapoor, regal in a kurta, smiles approval, and Mary, arms pumping, sees God.

Later on, in an upstairs office, Bobby sits splay-legged on the floor, his back against a wall. Spent, he looks shell-shocked, and only half-listens as his friend Farooq, aka DJ Pathaan, holds forth on the second generation. The dissertation is solemn and stern. "We are fighting to eclipse the old stereotypes," says Farooq at one point. And that's when Bobby perks up. Eclipses are right up his alley. They even fill his dreams.

The fascination goes back to a former girlfriend. After they broke up, he was visited by a series of three dreams, over three successive nights. In the first, he and the girl were talking in a Greek temple, which looked like something in an aftershave ad, and the eclipse was in the background. In the second, the girl was gone, Bobby found himself on a lost planet with a few nuclear survivors and the eclipse was centre stage. And in the last, he was alone. Just him and the eclipse, which seemed to him both god and devil.

The dreams impressed him so deeply that, when the next solar eclipse came round, he travelled to India to view it. He went to Fatehpur Sikri, near Agra, where he could enjoy a perfect view. There was a 500-year-old mosque there, perched on top of a hollow hill. The stones of the hill had cracked into vents, which let out a drum-like booming, and it sounded to Bobby like the breathing of the world's core.

At sunrise, he and other watchers sat on the mosque steps, blankly staring. Nothing moved but cats and stray dogs and a whirling flight of ravens. Then the sun came up. For 500 years, it had been turning east-west. Now its motion was reversed. And Bobby, transfixed, felt himself fuse with it.

Remembering now, with the drum 'n' bass thundering below, he forces his eyes wide open, as if to outstare the light. "For that instant, I am the sun," he says. He pauses to let the image sink in, then slowly lets out his breath. "So what will become of me? Am I going to be eclipsed? Or do I shine?"

THERE ARE DAYS when just the sight of Mary fills me with such envy, it feels like a creeping poison. Nothing in her has staled; she has never learned how to patronise.

My feeling of being spoiled goods weighs particularly heavily when we dive into karaoke. Before we started this journey together, I was a reflex sneerer. Karaoke was cheesy; drunken yahoos bawling "My Way." But Mary won't stand for that. "It's people making music," she says. "It gives them hope."

South London is karaoke heaven; it booms from every second pub. Near the Thomas A Beckett one day, I pass a sign advertising Stormin' Norman and Anita, with a phone number underneath. When I call, a glad voice answers. "Are you storming?" I ask. "I most certainly am," the voice replies, and asks me round for tea.

Norman lives in Camberwell, in a semi-detached with fruit trees in the back garden. "It's just like living in the country," he tells me. A glib, bouncy man, full of bon-homie, he sits in an overstuffed armchair, surrounded by songbooks and backing tracks. "Let's talk karaoke," he says.

In his view, it's a virtual life-saver. "You should have seen it round here ten years ago; before karaoke came in, there wasn't nothing shaking but the leaves on the trees. I was born on the Old Kent Road, down the New Cross end, and I can remember, as a child, when the whole area was jumping. There was cinemas and fancy shops, the

Bermondsey market, singsongs in all the pubs. Then everything went down. They did away with the cinemas and the pubs fell into ruin. Everyone that could afford it was moving off to the suburbs." Then some of the pubs, in desperation, started karaoke nights. "The Gin Palace was the first, I'd say, and then the Frog and Nightgown, and then the others followed. You had these rough old pubs, half-empty, rotting away, and suddenly they've got a new lease on life. You rip all the old stuff out and start again. New carpets, new seating, disco lights. Next thing you know, the place is packed. It's like a resurrection, almost—when the pubs come back to life, so do people. You have a party spirit again, everyone mucking in together, just like the old days, only with a new twist, and that ain't bad, not bad at all."

His own involvement goes back five years. He comes from a musical background; his father played the guitar and the family had an amateur band—drums, piano, electric guitar, mouth organ—in the late sixties. Norman became a truck driver but the musical itch never left him. When karaoke first reared its head, he laughed at it. Then he started wandering into pubs and hearing it live, and gradually he changed his mind. "I saw all the people who never did much of anything, never been in the spotlight, and here they was, getting up and having a go, performing. And you could see the effect on them, the way it brought them to life. Everyday people, y'know, but when they got on that stage, there was a bit of magic."

Anita, his daughter, was also musical. As a child, she'd spent a year playing one of the children in *The King and I,* up in the West End. So Norman conscripted her, and they started an act together. "Cost us a bomb; about two and a half grand, just to get off the ground," the stormer says. "First off, your karaoke machine. Then your amplifier and your telescreen for the lyrics, plus a back-up tele, in case the first does a wobbly on you, and then, of course, your discs. Your basic library alone, that comes to thousands of songs, and you have to keep updating.

Can't afford to fall behind, or you're done for. We're talking heavy investment here. And that's without the refinements. The competition's so cut-throat these days, you've got to have your own angles. We do different kinds of lighting, according to the performer. Flashing disco lights for the youngsters who think they're God's gift; soft spots for the old dears. And suits, of course. We have to dress up smart, look our best. Can't afford to look like cowboys, can we? You gotta give 'em the old pizzazz."

Anita, demure in a high-buttoned white blouse, is a qualified paralegal, contemplating a career in law. About eighteen nights a month, she turns karaoke presenter. "I never would have believed it," she says. "The stigma! But everything changes in life."

A few nights later, I take Mary to the Windmill, one of the pubs they appear at. It's an old-fashioned local, with no frills or pretensions, stuck beneath a railway bridge.

Stormin' Norman and Anita are transfigured: he resplendent in a twenties gangster suit and fedora, she a vision in cream silks. He crouches behind his karaoke machine, shuffling the discs, while she handles the introductions and most of the vocals. Her style is cool and understated; all the barnstorming is left to the punters. And barnstorm they do, with a vengeance. Young and old, white and black, drunk and sober, they cluster round the bar, awaiting their crack at the mic, and once they get it, they take no prisoners. A swag-bellied man past sixty turns pleading teenage lover. A young pool shark morphs into Jimi Hendrix, and a greengrocer becomes a drifting cowboy. In the course of the night, we witness the second comings of Tom Jones and Helen Shapiro, Thin Lizzy, Madonna, even Frank Sinatra. Some are in good voice, some not, but all of them give it body and soul. Up on stage, with the disco lights bouncing off their skulls, they seem to swell; catch light. "We're all stars here," a woman shouts in my ear. She's only half-joking.

A bit later, the same woman belts out "I Need a Hero." She isn't young, and her voice isn't smooth; much of the time, she veers off-key. But none of that matters. Her sheer passion blows all quibbles away. Head thrown back, bare arms striking the dead air, she hurls herself on the song like a starving wolf and rips it into shreds. *"Give me a hero. Someone who'll love me till the end of the night,"* she roars, and the whole pub roars back.

THIS KARAOKE LIFE, it can make you, it can break you. Another night and another pub, I get talking to a girl in a chartreuse-green dress. "I'm a smash-up," she tells me. "A total car-wreck."

If that's the case, she wears it well. The chartreuse dress sets off shimmers and sparks every time she moves, and she sports a bubble-cut blonde wig. The effect is such high glamour, I assume she must be part of the show, but she shakes her head. "I'm just a babe," she confides.

A drag queen with a hairy chest and legs to match is shrieking his way through "You'll Never Walk Alone," and the pub is heaving, a swill of smoke and slopped beer. No chance of a conversation, so we make our way outdoors into the beer garden.

I fetch her a Moscow Mule. "I shouldn't," she says, but she does. An overhead lamp shows the join at the base of her neck where the wig meets her own dark hair, and also a deep arm bruise, brown and mottled-yellow. "You're not meant to notice that," she says, following my eyes. "Nosy bastard." Still, she doesn't make much show of outrage. "I've got another one on my arse. Want to check that out as well?"

The business strikes me as forced. Though her lips have the right suggestive pout, there's something brittle and unfocused behind the eyes. "I'm dead shy," she admits.

I ask her name; she says Barbette.

It isn't what she was christened, of course. The label on her passport is Pamela Susan, but she hates and despises that. "It was never really me, even as a child; just a tag I got lumbered with." All her life, she's seen Pamela Susan as dead weight: dowdy, grey, the antithesis of glamour. "In school, when they asked me what I wanted to be when I grew up, I said wild." But how could a Pamela Susan achieve that? "I was jinxed before I got started."

In her fantasies, she's always been a rock star. Showbiz is in her blood, after all. Her mother worked as a model in the sixties; was one of the nudes on the cover of *Electric Ladyland,* and almost pulled Jimi Hendrix, while her older sister Vi used to be a back-up singer. But neither of them was committed. It was a living to them, nothing more. "'Beats working,' you know the attitude." Not like Pamela Susan. For her, the word *performance* has always been sacred. To be an act. Any act.

The only thing stopping her is nerves. All her life, she's been dogged by the feeling that she is doing wrong. "I don't know where it came from. I didn't have an unhappy childhood; I wasn't abused or anything. I just had this feeling of shame. My mother and sister always seemed in such total control. They're both really strong in themselves, they know how to get what they want. And I'm the family fuck-up."

Growing up, her efforts to perform were always sabotaged by the shakes. So she went to work in a travel agency. And the rest of her life has proved equally frustrating. The one bright spot is her daughter, Jasmine, aged three. But Martin, her current boyfriend, is a total loss. A lying, thieving waste of space, and he hits her. Most of her boyfriends have.

"I don't mean to sing the blues," she says. It's just that she doesn't get many chances to talk. Martin turns up the telly every time she opens her mouth. And Pamela Susan pipes down.

But Barbette, that's another matter. Barbette kicks ass. One wrong look, or a word out of place, and Barbette will clean your clock.

She first came into existence two summers ago, when Pamela Susan was holidaying on the Costa del Sol. She was in a disco near Torremolinos with a group of her girlfriends, and they spotted this hunk across the dance floor. A drop-dead Spanish fly, tight black pants, black eyes burning.

How to catch his attention? Normally, she'd just have stood there like a lemon and suffered. But this was Torremolinos rules; nothing normal applied. Krissy, her best friend, bet her the whole night's bar bill that she wouldn't dance across to the Spanish stud and flash him. So what was a girl to do? She danced, she flashed, she took the boy back to her hotel, and it was the best, most abandoned sex of her life. No guilt, and no leftovers. "When I woke up the next morning and looked at myself in the mirror, I saw a different woman."

That woman, born of a bar bet, is now enshrined as Barbette, karaoke temptress. "She's done wonders for my self-image. Really taught me to get my tits out." Not that Pamela Susan is dead and buried. In daily life, she still walks into doors. "I got a right battering the other night. Police, the hospital and all." But now there's an escape. Once or twice a week, she gives Pamela Susan the night off, and lets Barbette out to play.

Karaoke is a godsend. The crowd is always so friendly, people don't judge you, and nobody cares if you're pissed. A bit of Dutch courage is par for the course, and just as well. A few fast drinks are Barbette's medicine. She calls them starter fluids.

Sometimes they work, sometimes not. There are nights when she manages the alcohol just right, achieves the perfect buzz, and then she's unstoppable. She has a big voice by nature, belter's pipes, ideal for disco anthems—"I Love the Night Life," "I Feel Love," "I Will Survive": "Anything that starts with *I*," she says.

If only the right person could hear her, an agent, say, or a record producer, she wouldn't be surprised if they signed her up. She knows she has a gift. With a bit of luck, she might be the next Donna Summer. Just a little luck.

Then again, luck has never been her strong point. And there are other nights, she has to admit, when things don't go so well. Either she drinks too much, or no amount of alcohol can unfreeze her. At times like that, she may be dressed as Barbette, but she's still Pamela Susan inside. "Stupid cow, I hate her." But the woman won't leave her be. "I'm stuck with the sorry bitch."

Which one is she tonight? "I'd like to tell you Barbette, but I'm never really sure. Until I get up on stage, and I feel the mic in my hand, I'm basically just guessing."

By now, she's three Moscow Mules down the road, and it's time for her to face the music. Back inside the pub, the noise and smoke levels are approaching blitzkrieg. An aged redhead in a leopardskin leotard is doing a Shirley Bassey on "Goldfinger," and a girl with a diamond stud through her tongue keeps taking her top off. "Are we karaoke yet?" the presenter shouts.

Some of Barbette's girlfriends have shown up while we were out in the beer garden. I'm introduced to Krissy, whose disco dare gave birth to the whole fantasy. She works as a computer analyst, and has a burning belief in Barbette's singing talent. "If they put her on TV, she'd blow their arseholes away," she predicts, and starts pushing Barbette towards the stage. Krissy wants her to sing "All I Wanna Do," but Barbette balks. "I forget the words," she claims.

"All I wanna do," Krissy prompts, "is have some fun." This Barbette remembers. Her chartreuse sheath sparks and dazzles like struck steel. Strutting, she sets her shoulders and climbs on stage. Krissy, below her, is mouthing the words. "Have some fun." And Barbette nods, radiant.

ONE LUNCHTIME, I'm walking towards Chiswick High Road when I hear a man singing "Don't Blame Me." He has a light, jaunty voice, a wartime voice, so evocative of gallantry and lost romance that it stops me in my tracks.

Turning the corner, I see a white-haired man in his seventies, rake-thin, a touch fragile, but fierce with energy. The motto on his guitar case says, "Peter Vincent—There Goes That Song Again."

Once started talking, he isn't easily stopped. "Am I having a good day? Well, not exactly, I wouldn't say *good*, that wouldn't be what you'd call the *mot juste*, in fact I'd be outright lying, which is a sin, of course, though very tempting sometimes, and temptation has always been a problem with me, I'm afraid. But anyhow, no, not good, more like mediocre, poor, paltry, or actually lousy would be closer to the truth, yes, on the whole, I think lousy."

He's never still. He jumps up to emphasise one point, spins on his heel to demonstrate the contrary, does little walkabouts, cocks his head like a bird, acts out each change of mood. "I can't help it, what's the use, I'm just an old ham," he explains.

These are mean days for buskers; he's never known worse. He plays here in Chiswick, in Harrow and Kingston and Richmond, all good-class areas, but even the rich are tightwads today. "I'll give you my theory, and I think you'll find this correct: the busker is the perfect barometer of society. Never mind the feel-good factor, that's just publicity, a lot of hooey. No, if you really want to know the country's state, ask a street entertainer, we see it all. Not only the financial side but the moral as well, what you'd call the spirituality. Which is pretty much up the spout today, if you ask me, pretty much on life-support. In bygone days, I once had a fifty-pound note handed to me. I've had twenties and tens many times. Not out of sympathy, I don't want that, but because I touched a chord. And now that cord has almost been cut, it's hanging by a thread."

He finds himself plagued by alcoholics, thieves, degenerates of all descriptions. That's why he's packing up early today, because it's a Saturday, football day, and he wants to get home before the tough stuff starts.

Perhaps I'll come and visit him? He'd be pleased to speak at greater length, either in his house or at the corner pub, "though I don't really drink, no, well, only a little, if I'm performing at a party or a restaurant sometimes, I take a touch of savoir faire to steady the old nerves. Just a nip; well, maybe two. But no, I don't really drink."

His home is a tiny backstreet cottage, lost in the wilds of Uxbridge, that he shares with two dogs, an ancient black cat, a rabbit, a Trappist parrot, and his second wife, a placid Russian lady named Irina.

I arrive to a feast—pastries and bonbons, sticky chocolate confections: "We don't get a lot of visitors here. As a matter of fact, I don't think much of *Homo sapiens* as a rule; not a patch on animals," Vincent tells me. "Of course, I come from Norfolk, where animals rule the roost pretty much, and sometimes, d'you know, I yearn to go back.

"My father was an actor. His stage name was Vincent Young, and I was born in Great Yarmouth; that's where he was appearing. He ran a concert party in those days, he was an educated man and he could charm the birds off the trees but, like a lot of actors, of course, penniless. Before the Great War, he had a lead part in *Hello Tango* at the Lyceum, but then the Spanish flu came along, knocked him for six, and out he went, no mercy in those days, out he went on his rear end. So he became a broken-down actor, which was rather sad in a way. He always had the monocle and the manner but he hadn't any money and, quite frankly, he was drummed out of many places because he got along through, well, through little cons. Very much to my poor mother's grief, I might say, because she was a piano teacher, a most respectable Baptist lady."

Vincent himself became a ballroom dancer, and gave lessons till Hitler's war. Then he met Josie, a young girl of seventeen, and she couldn't dance a step, but he loved her anyway. They were married, a child on the way, so he was forced to turn civilian. For years, he laboured on building sites: "My dancing days were over. Oh, I gave a few lessons on the side, but I couldn't go out and dance at night, could I? Too much of a good thing—you dance, then you meet some pretty young thing, then your marriage is on the rocks, and that's the way of the world, sad to say."

Even so, he itched to entertain; it was the family curse. His daughter grew up an actress—"Katy Butler, you may have seen her on TV"—and he himself, when he got too old for building sites, decided to turn songster. He took the old tunes he'd once danced to—"Pennies from Heaven," "Mister Sandman," "Fools Rush In"—and taught himself to busk them. Built up a repertoire of eighty songs, bought an ancient guitar and then he hit the streets. "I was nervous at first, scared witless in fact, but they can only lynch you once. Besides, I had the mortgage to pay."

So far, telling me all this, he hasn't sat down for a moment. Every tale provokes its own little pantomime. Irina, watching him in silence, has the slightly punch-drunk look of an indulgent parent at a child's birthday party. Whenever there's a moment's lull, which isn't often, she pushes another cake or chocolate éclair at me.

"What a treasure," Vincent says, absent-mindedly, then hurries back to his story.

Josie's death almost destroyed him. "We fought like cats and dogs; I absolutely adored her. We were living here together, crammed in with all these animals and, when Josie got sick, I thought I'd build an extension for her. Well, I had certain skills from the building trade, so I worked away, worked away, nine months, till it was all done. Just the last bit of skirting board to finish, so I tacked up a strip of ornamental ribbon, and I told Josie to come down and cut it. She didn't feel up to it, though. She was in the bathroom upstairs; she wouldn't come out. And when I went up to fetch her, she'd died. Sat down to take a rest, you know, and she just expired."

This extension is where we're sitting now. It's a neat-looking piece of work, chock-full of Staffordshire pottery and theatrical mementoes. The last bit of skirting board, however, remains for ever unfinished.

"Well, I'm a romantic. A silly old sausage," Vincent says. "At seventy-plus, you'd think I might know better, but that's the way I was fashioned. And just as well, in a way, or I'd never have found Irina. I had this dog, you see, it had an insatiable appetite for golf balls. Every time we walked by the course, it stole another ball, and Irina, as it happened, was just learning the game. So this is the point I'm making," Vincent says, and raises a gaunt fore-finger for dramatic underlining. "Fate."

I ask him to sum up his own career. "Not a bad life, all in all," he judges. "Successfully married and properly papered, companionship, a *soupçon* of harmony. Perhaps I should tart myself up a bit, invest in a better amplifier or a new guitar, but if I did, I might pop my clogs tomorrow, so why bother? Just keep going, that's the spirit." He raises the warning forefinger again. "Of course, it isn't always easy, the powers that be are not exactly on my side. Everywhere I go these days, there are notices forbid-ding certain activities, you might call them, of which I'm very fond. No Smoking, No Cycling, No Busking, No

Dogs; Don't Feed the Pigeons. And I do them all!" He flashes me a bandit grin. "I am Dillinger," he says.

His livelihood is constantly under threat. At different times, he has been labelled a fire hazard and a noise pollutant. Nothing keeps him down, however. "P.C. Plod showed up one day and ordered me to move on. 'I'm an entertainer, not a criminal,' I told him, but I'm afraid he wasn't impressed. 'It's all the same to me. Just move on,' he said. And I thought to myself, righty-ho, I thought, that's it. That's what I'll put on my tombstone." Dramatic pause; then a vicar's pious bray. "Here Lies Peter Vincent—Finally Moved On."

CIVIL
DISOBEDIENCE

THE PAPERS KEEP talking of bloodless revolution. In place of the old ruling class, the English are now asked to defer to a self-enshrined meritocracy: rock stars, fashion designers, spin doctors, PR persons, TV presenters, Sunday columnists, footballers, chefs.

Every morning, I interrupt the whirl long enough to grab the *Evening Standard* and read more about this brave new world. London is now the hottest and most happening city in creation, I'm told; a creative crucible. And maybe this is true. If I started trolling the media, haunting the anointed bistros, hanging out at openings and receptions, I might get swept up. The view from the corner pub, however, is less euphoric.

I have been staying with an old friend. For present purposes, I'll call him Robin Banks, because that's how, over the years, he's earned the best part of his living.

I first met him in the late seventies, when he walked into a friend's Manhattan apartment. A winter storm was raging outdoors, the streets were blanketed thigh-deep with snow, and Banks, who had just flown in from Canada, looked considerably the worse for wear. Not only was he frozen, he also had a painful limp. Even so, he cut a dashing figure, massively built in shoulder and chest, with a head of curly, steel-wire hair, a nose that had once been flattened by an iron bar, a lopsided grin, a brigand's glinting eye and the dirtiest of dirty laughs, the whole package resplendent in a fur-lined overcoat, fur hat and gloves, armadillo-skin kneeboots.

Parking himself in the best armchair, he let himself thaw out for a minute, then started to strip. Off came the overcoat, the hat and gloves, and finally, after painful struggle, the kneeboots. Wincing with relief, Banks held the boots in mid-air, one in each mighty fist, as though weighing them. Then he turned them upside down, and shook. A thick wad of sodden banknotes tumbled out. "Let it snow, let it snow, let it snow," said Banks, his dirty laugh snaking down to his stocking feet. And a lasting friendship was born.

He has always approached life as a pirate, grabbing what he wants, burning and wrecking what he doesn't. In his time, he has done a deal of damage. Just the same, he has his own code.

By his own lights, Banks is a man of morals, and the fact that he's a lifetime villain in no way contradicts that. Crime, to him, is adventure, a series of punitive raids in which the targets are always institutions, not humans. Not that he's averse to flashing the spoils. He revels in living large, the gaudier the better. But loot is not his addiction. What he's after, first and last, is action: the rush he gets, every nerve and cell wired, when he goes charging into a big one and the pieces start falling into place.

The way he explains it, each new job is a testing ground of discipline and nerve. Success depends not just on planning but on a complex equation of attitude and luck. In his world view, you crash and burn for one reason only, because your number's up. Which is how he sees England now.

Our days together tend to follow a set pattern. Rising late, we loiter over morning tea by his living-room window and watch the undercover cops patrolling the street. Banks, these days, is under constant surveillance. Just the other day, he passed a middle-aged woman at the corner. Something about her didn't smell right, so he gave her a quick backhander, knocked her sprawling. Then he made a grab for her handbag, and a walkie-talkie fell out.

Banks sees this as flattering attention; confirmation of his high status. "I have a reputation in the highest criminal circles," he's fond of saying. So he gives his shadows a cheery wave, and we set forth to parade his manor.

The manor in question is Chiswick. It isn't where he started, or where he mastered his trade, but his former stamping grounds—Paddington, Maida Vale, Fulham—have grown a bit ripe for him, and Chiswick, he finds, has a pleasing anonymity.

At least it's west London. To Banks, the East End is full of the wrong sort. "Gangsters," he says. "I've got no time for them." As far as he's concerned, the Krays and their like are no more than school bullies, sick in the head and cowards to boot. "A gangster is an evil bastard, who rules by fear and never even pulls his own jobs." A proper criminal, on the other hand, is a pro. He does all his own work, and never sheds blood without cause.

This sense of righteousness colours his whole vision. As he strides along Chiswick High Road, as imposing and unstoppable as a full-rigged galleon under sail, he delivers a non-stop diatribe on England and its fall. "The structure's gone," he explains. "The way this country was put together, everyone had a certain function, a place. You knew what you'd come from, and where you'd got to, and most likely where you'd end up. There were rules; even villains had them. Now all that's gone. There's no moral fibre."

This talk of moral turpitude is delivered poker-faced, without a trace of self-mockery. Banks is a smart man, and often a funny one, but irony is not his style. As far as he's concerned, the trail of blown safes and broken bones he's left behind him are merely accidents of war. True immorality is lack of self-pride and lack of balls, and he's never been guilty of either one.

The ruin of England, he thinks, has been cowardice. "This whole country's choking on fear," he says. "Everybody's terrified of losing what they have. The aristocracy's on the run, the middle class has its head up its arse, and the working class has no work. The only ones who're in clover are the bullshit artists."

According to Banks, they are the new ruling class. "They feed off the fear, then tell you how to feel safe again." What cars to buy, what clothes to buy, what restaurants to stuff your face in. "The emperor's new clothes never had it so good."

Almost everything he casts his glinting eye on fills him with disgust: the Hooray Henrys with their beepers and Beamers; the scared-rabbit wage-slaves, slowly choking on their mortgages and bank loans; the corner boys who go howling by, threatening to beat up the world, yet turn piss-yellow the moment he looks at them sideways; the social-benefit skivers, demoralised and feckless; and, worst of the lot, the new breed of villains, who have no skills, no values, no concept of hierarchy.

"It's all gone ape-shit," he says. Forty years ago, before he turned villain, Banks mastered a series of other trades—plumbing, wiring, floor-laying. Now there'd be no point. "The average British working man starts his day with nine inches hard stuck up his arse, and every move he makes just gives it an extra twist, to remind him he's being royally fucked." Playing by the old rules is a waste of time. Workmen cheat their mates, criminals rat out their partners, bent cops go back on their deals. "Honour is dead," Banks says.

We duck into his local. The clientele there is mixed— small-time crims, old gays, bikers—and Banks is un-crowned ruler. He downs a large vodka tonic and mops at his brow. "You can't trust anyone," he mutters darkly. "And the dead ones are the worst."

When I mention Tony Blair's New Britain, he laughs in my face. "Act your age," he tells me. "It's all a scam. A bunch of licensed wankers swapping porky-pies over lunch." He wrinkles the remains of his splattered nose and calls for a fresh vodka tonic. "Just take a blimp at Blair's teeth, for fuck's sake, that shit-eating girl's grin," he says. "Nobody gets a face like that by accident."

Every year he feels more isolated; a man out of time.

Many of his old comrades are dead, in jail or retired to Marbella; a few, even worse, have turned grass. The Firm, for which Banks did some of his finest work, is ancient history, and his recent plans for coups have all come to bad ends, bolloxed by the fuck-ups and rank amateurs he's forced to work with these days.

Of late, he's spent much of his time with a different crowd—Hell's Angels, and the bikers who haunt his local. They may not be major players, not quite the stars he's used to, but at least they know how to laugh, and they don't rat out their friends.

This coming weekend, two of the bikers, New Zealanders named Lee and Leigh, are getting married at the Angels' chapter-house in Hackney. Banks is among the guests, and he asks me to tag along.

The wedding party departs Chiswick High Road at lunchtime in a hired coach. There's already been a fierce celebration the night before, and most of the guests are barely crawling. Restorative flasks are handed up and down the aisle. Groans and whimpers rise up in their wake, but are quickly drowned out by pounding soul tapes. Banks himself, white and shaking, clutches at his stomach. "I've been unwise," he confesses.

The majority of the guests, like the bridal couple themselves, are Kiwis. Though not full-fledged Angels, they are devout bikers, and this sedate coach trip across London is not their speed. "Most hearses go faster than this," my neighbour complains. His arms and chest, beneath a leather vest, are covered with tattoos of devils. "This one's Lucifer," he says, pointing to one shaved pap, where a horned and bearded gent with flaming eyes is snacking on a virgin. "And this here," he adds, pointing to the other, which sports a hissing virago, a dead ringer for Posh Spice, nude except for a scaly silver tail, "is the serpent of Lust."

By the time the coach arrives in Hackney, the medicinal flasks have done their work and the bikers are back in stride. The Angels' crib sits down a side street. Previously derelict, it's in the process of being done up. Ranks of

Yamahas and Harley-Davidsons are stacked outside the door, and the bar is already open upstairs. A black-bearded Angel sends bottles skimming in all directions. A mountain of a man, he makes even Banks look petite, but his manner is oddly gentle. "Not drinking? I don't blame you," he says to me. "I've got bleeding ulcers myself."

For a total stranger, I'm greeted with rare indulgence. Banks's good word is a help, of course, but there's also a spirit of real, if sardonic, welcome. Angels slap my back and gut, and ask me what I ride myself. "Raleigh three-speed," I reply. For a moment, there's stunned silence, then the bartender snorts with laughter. "Sure it's not a trike?" he enquires.

The marriage ceremony takes place in the basement, a brick-walled grotto, dark and dank. Lee and Leigh, still woozy from last night, take up position beside the Angel-in-chief. His bare belly is prodigious, and so is his fierce stare. "Do you, Lee, take this woman to be your righteous old lady?" he demands.

"I do."

"And do you, Leigh, take this drunk sod to be your righteous old man?"

"I do."

"Then I pronounce you wed," the Angel says. "And may God help you both."

Afterwards, there are more soul tapes, and more evil potions, and the happy couple shoots pool. Banks wanders round the scuffed and beer-stained table, dispensing tips, and sometimes wielding a cue himself. His earlier dyspepsia has passed; he now looks like a genial gargoyle. Observing the newly-weds, the tribe of Kiwis and the massed Angels, his smile is almost avuncular, and his steel-wire hair shows a renewed spring. "They've got standards, this lot," he tells me, chalking his stick. "We could do with a few more like them."

The comradeship round this table, and the sense of freedom it engenders, is catching. "You can do anything you want here, so long as you don't shoot heroin," the chief Angel informs me.

"Why not smack?" I ask.

"It's dirty," he replies.

Banks, overhearing this, can't help but laugh. "Standards," he says again, and pots the black, corner pocket.

I HAVE ALWAYS been besotted with boxers. As a child, I fixated on Billy "Spider" Kelly, the idol of Catholic Derry, who held the British featherweight title for a spell in the mid-fifties. He was one of the city's most honoured martyrs.

His martyrdom involved a single bout. Early in 1956, as British champion, he had travelled to Glasgow to defend his title against Charlie Hill. The first rounds were close, then Kelly got on top. Though not normally known as a puncher, he knocked Hill down and gave him a thorough beating. At the final bell, he was chasing his man pell-mell round the ring. The referee, however, raised Charlie Hill's hand.

It was a bare-faced robbery; no Irish eyewitness has ever doubted that. Kelly was Derry Catholic, Hill supported Glasgow Rangers. In the Bogside, you need say nothing more.

"That ref had my heart broke," Spider said in later years. And he certainly broke mine. The night of the fight, aged ten, I sat up at my bedroom window, staring fixedly at the dark. I had heard, if Kelly won, there'd be bonfires in the Bog. Each time a car's headlights gleamed along the Lone Moor Road, or someone flashed a torch in Brandywell, my heart began to pound. Hour upon hour of false alarms dragged by. Then, sometime after midnight, I jerked out of a restless doze to see a fire for real. A hard orange blaze, leaping high. And another. And another, till the whole darkness was lit, and I could go satisfied to my bed, watching the flames dance and flicker across the wall.

Only next day did I discover the truth. The bonfires had been struck in defiance, not triumph; Billy Kelly was betrayed. Hiding behind my hymn book at school prayers, I blubbed.

Like most of my childhood obsessions, I never outgrew it. At thirty and forty, I was still a hopeless groupie. A boozy picture taken in some nightclub with Esteban de Jesus or Bobby "Schoolboy" Chacon meant more to me than any good review.

One thing that has always impressed me, among the fighters I've known, is their innate honesty. My friend Willie Pastrano, once the world light-heavyweight champ, used to tell me that this was because they'd been robbed of their natural defences. From childhood on, they were flaunted half-naked in front of crowds of drunken, braying morons. They bled and hurt, got knocked senseless, all in public. "We're like strippers, out there in our bones," Willie said. Modesty and evasiveness, all sense of privacy, were rendered meaningless. "You can't lie to a left hook."

There is a certain moment before every fight, big or small, just after a boxer steps into the ring, when he seems utterly alone. An instant earlier, parading down the aisle, he's protected by handlers; an instant later, he'll be leaping around the canvas, fists flashing, drumming up his adrenaline. But here, for this one beat, the rituals fall away. As he ducks through the ropes, the fighter is forced to stoop awkwardly, face down. And when he straightens up, the awkwardness remains. His silk robe is stripped away, and he's left exposed. In that moment, as his hands, reflexively, come up to cover his chest, there is always a sense of invasion. Something startled, oddly feminine, like a girl surprised at her bath.

FIGHT NIGHT at the York Hall in Bethnal Green is like a works outing. Almost everyone you see there—boxers, trainers, managers, backers and the women who go with them—is in the trade, and the fighters in the audience, as often as not, are higher class than those in the ring.

The night's card is a typical republican mishmash. The bill includes a Ukrainian, a Bulgarian, a Nigerian, a black Canadian, an Islington Italian, assorted south London Jamaicans and an Indian heavyweight from East Ham named Sugar Raj Kumar Sangwan. Thirty years ago, when I watched similar fights at Shoreditch Town Hall, even one West Indian was considered a novelty. Now it's the English faces, pinched and sun-starved, that look out of place.

The hall itself is a fine high-Victorian folly, all pomp and circumstance, with sweeping marble stairways and built-in echoes. Standing outside on the steps, waiting for the doors to open, I feel like I'm hanging about a magistrate's court. The evening's fighters, kitbags in hand, speak in mumbles. Everyone is wary, self-consciously cool. Everyone, that is, except for Abdul Mannan.

It's impossible to miss him. A slight and mercurial figure, resplendent in a flash Italian suit, he has a jet-black, shoulder-length ponytail, and he never stops moving, never stops making noise. Buzzing around these big, stolid men with their kitbags, he seems raw and fevered—a boy burning up with hungers.

When I introduce myself, it's like flipping an On switch. A writer, eh? Good, right, he's in the media himself, or he's going to be. At the minute he's going to college, learning to be an actor, but one of the teachers, well, they don't see eye to eye, and this is a big frustration, because he's so ambitious, determined to get on, it's just killing him inside.

Does he box as well? "Of course I do, I'm Abdul," he says. His voice is high-pitched, his accent strong Lancashire. "I've been on TV." He had thirty-three fights as an amateur, won twenty-six or twenty-seven, and now he's turned pro, a super-bantamweight. "So far I've only had twelve contests—won three, lost seven, drawn two—but that's deceiving, it doesn't paint a true picture. I've had management problems, licence problems, but that's all behind me now. Plain sailing from now on, the sky's the limit. This is the Year of Abdul."

His dark eyes bore into and through me, and his legs keep jiggling; he seems to be running on the spot. "Come and talk to me where I train," Abdul says, beginning to move away. "Whatever you want to know, I'll tell you the truth. No bullshit, I don't know how. Ask anyone and they'll say the same: 'Abdul Mannan, God help him, he's an honest man.'"

The journey to see him train takes me back to south London, an area that has always seemed foreign to me. George Melly used to quote Henry Mayhew, the Victorian sociologist, who wrote of crossing Westminster Bridge to visit "a transpontine brothel," and this seemed to sum up the place's peculiar flavour. Transpontium—not just a gaggle of boroughs, but a whole separate kingdom, complete with its own set of rules and rituals, none of which I've ever managed to master.

The moment I cross the border, I lose all sense of bearings. Everything seems interchangeable—the faceless brick terraces, the mile after mile of housing estates, the scrubby back gardens glimpsed from train windows, the traffic-choked high streets, and the general air of death-like apathy, interspersed with furious bouts of bother, exploding out of nowhere. "You can disappear here, no sweat," says Abdul. That's what I am afraid of.

Abdul trains at the Thomas A Beckett. Years ago, when the Old Kent Road was a boulevard, the gym above the pub used to be a house of champions. Muhammad Ali trained there; so did Henry Cooper and Rocky Marciano. Even in the early seventies, when I went there to watch a Welsh heavyweight named Carl Gizzi, the place was always packed and cacophonous, a fistic foundry. Gizzi, a mild and meditative man who once had lost an open-air fight in Johannesburg when he paused to admire a passing moth, used to call it The Works.

In recent years, the Beckett has fallen on mean times. It has been closed, reopened and is about to close again. On the morning I show up, Abdul has the run of the place, apart from one middle-aged shadow boxer and two pre-teens from the housing estate up the road.

Stripped, Abdul has a blocky, sawn-off look, much more heavily muscled than he seems in street clothes. Since the night at York Hall, he has had his ponytail shorn, and this, combined with his three-day stubble and slightly flattened nose, gives him a surface toughness. Even so, he looks like an overgrown kid playing fight-games, not a professional hard man. When the pre-teens give him lip, he laughs and pretends to lunge at them, then buys them Coca-Colas in the bar downstairs. "I'm soft," he says, but sounds happy to be so. "Never grow old; it's bad for your health."

At my first question, words spill out in a gusher. He doesn't just part his lips when he speaks—his whole mouth splits open, wet and wide, and his shrill voice is hoarse with urgency.

He's from Accrington, he says, the fifth of seven children; his parents, Bangladeshis, run a restaurant there. "I was meant to go in the business myself, but I had this dream, yeah? When I was a child, I was like Forrest Gump, I couldn't walk till I was eight. My bones weren't coming in properly, and I couldn't talk, either. I was sent to a special school at weekends, they gave me a book and a tape recorder, and it told me how to colour in. Then I started to talk, and it was like I couldn't stop, I had no brakes. Same with walking, too. Soon as I could run a yard, I just took off. Ran for miles and miles, they thought I'd never come back, yeah? In a way, I never did."

Being slow to learn, he was an easy target for bullies. "They crucified me, right. I got battered every day of my life, but I'd just see red and go at them. I took on guys twice my size. I used to come home in pieces, bloody nose, my eyes smashed shut. So my older brother, he got me into boxing. The art of self-defence; I heard that someone called it the sweet science. Well, I thought it was just beautiful. Still do."

Boxing saved him, really; without its discipline, he would have imploded long ago. "There's too much inside me, yeah? Too many feelings, too much hurt, and then the anger. Past a certain point, I can't control myself, I totally lose it. One time I almost got done for GBH. I was working in this restaurant and this guy tried to put his hand in the till. When I wouldn't let him, he started mouthing off, but when I offered to fight him, he changed his tune. 'We don't have to fight,' he said, and I said, 'No, of course not, no need to fight.' Put my arm round his shoulders, right friendly like. Then, when I felt him relax, I smashed him. Broke his nose in two places, boom, just like that."

The two lads from the housing estate are greatly taken with this tale. One of them gets the other in a headlock and pantomimes a nutting. Abdul fakes a left jab at them, then slaps them instead, pretending rage. Three boys in a playground, horsing around. "These are my mates," Abdul says. He still has anger and hatred in him, but these days, he claims, he keeps them chained. "I would rather live my life quiet; I don't snap. My ex-girlfriend has another man now, and that breaks me up, to think I've lost five years to a stupid, childish, heartless person that wasn't worthy. But I just smile, like a tiger smiles: my time will come."

When the pressure grows too fierce, he runs. "Long distance, I do marathons, and when I come back, I'm myself again." Still, his wrists and forearms are razor-scarred. "I used to try and damage myself, right? But not now, I learned better." He stares me down, daring me to disbelieve. "But I'm cool now, I'm sorted. Dead to rights."

A FEW DAYS LATER, I visit him at his home, a one-room council flat in Lavender Hill. The night streets behind Battersea are dark and dead, and I keep getting lost. When at last I find his street, I'm almost knocked flying by a passing car. Abdul is at the wheel, eyes blazing. He looks fit to kill.

"I can't stand to wait," he explains, coming back to

scoop up my remains. All trace of anger has vanished; he's grinning hugely. "You move fast for a slow man," he says. Punches me on the upper arm, then looks abashed. "Watch yourself, Abdul," he tells himself. "You might be heading for the danger line."

We share a curry at the local Taj Mahal, and Abdul insists on ordering. "My parents have a restaurant, remember; I know the shit they put in this stuff." Expansive, on a roll, he snags a fly in his clenched fist, then lets it go. "Never kill," he says, "unless you mean it."

Death is much on his mind these days. He has a new girlfriend, a Sikh named Parminder, who's studying pharmacology. She's lovely, voluptuous, wise, and Abdul is nuts about her, but they're always rowing. So far she has knocked him out with a well-aimed bottle of baby oil, bloodied his toe and given him a thick lip. Abdul, in return, has hit her only once. That was after he'd been reading an article about serial killers and Parminder came in unexpectedly. She made a snarky remark, and he pushed her down on the bed. She slapped him; he slapped her back. "Then I wanted to die," he says.

The trouble is, he's lacking about five layers of skin. "I can protect myself in the ring, but outside it, I'm defenceless." He needs to stop feeling so intensely. If only he could shut out his emotions, he would be invincible. "I might rule the world—why not?" His eyes dart around the curry house, calculating infinity. "I don't recognise any limits. Prince Naseem and everything he has, the stardom, all that glory, it could be me. The only thing that's holding me back is fate. That's the sad part of boxing: it's such a beautiful sport, but the business stinks. The people I'm involved with, they're handling me all wrong. They keep trying to make me change my style, turn me into a brawler. But violence isn't me," he says. "Abdul is all about style."

When we finish eating, he takes me back to his flat. Before he lets me inside, he does a hasty clean-up. So I sit on a wall in the walkway, listening to the dull throb of Transpontium by night.

Abdul's room is minimal: kitchen chair, TV, stereo and a bed built into an alcove. The duvet and sheets are a deep blue, and above them is a mural—a vivid blue sea, with a black palm tree and small golden swirls for the sun and moon and stars, painted on a dark-red background. "I call it my art," Abdul says, and perches on the kitchen chair, the scars on his arms and wrists exposed. His eyes, by the bare overhead light, are scrunched and panicky, and the wet rift of his mouth is flecked with spittle. "This world isn't meant for people who wear their hearts on their sleeve," he tells me. "I did that, but I've learned. From now on, the real Abdul stays in the closet."

He shows me a video of his only televised fight. The tape is rough and jumpy, a blur, and the bout itself unimpressive. Abdul keeps rushing his opponent, throwing punches in furious flurries, but most of them miss. The long baggy trunks and tasselled boots on his stubby little legs make him look more than ever like a schoolkid in fancy dress. "I'm a little bit nervous here. Trying to make a good impression," Abdul says. Maybe that's why his balance is wrong, his footwork out of sync. Every time he throws a big punch, he lurches sideways, wide open to a counterpunch, but his opponent is too rattled to take advantage, and Abdul wins the decision. "I murdered him," he exults, rocking back and forth on his chair.

His eagerness is painful. I'd like to reassure him, but we are meant to be men, and there are no words. "So what d'you think?" he demands.

"Very nice," I say.

Hitting people for cash is an odd line of work; not everyone is suited. But when I broach the subject, he brushes it off. "It isn't hitting people; it's self-defence," he insists. "The noble art."

He talks about his grandmother, back in Accrington. They were very close, and when she died, Abdul was distraught, till one night she appeared to him in a dream. She took him out of his bedroom, high into the sky. Together they flew south to London, where he'd never been. His grandmother showed him the whole city from above; it was teeming, a madhouse, but marvellous. "I'd never imagined so much life. So much action and drama, such passion." It was as though he was being shown his own future, a preview of the possibilities. Then he was back in his bedroom. His gran touched his eyes one last time, and left. "I had such a feeling of peace inside," Abdul says. "The whole world was mine."

That's the vision that drives him on. Something inside him, despite his record to date, keeps insisting that he was born for greatness, or at least for something wild. "I'm so many different people," he says. His hands, with their swollen fighter's knuckles, grip the back of the kitchen chair, clenching and flexing. "Strange people. Some of them, to be honest, I don't even know myself." He flashes a sheepish grin, then cuts it short. "Who's to say where I'll end up?"

Thinking hard, Abdul raises his face to the light. The skin round his eyes is dotted with tiny scars, his eyebrows ridged and hooded. "Well, I'm going to end up dead, of course, but that doesn't bother me. It's a beautiful subject, death."

MARY WANTS US to take up squatting. Ever since Fraggle Rock, the day we met George and Gilles, she's been hankering after a purer existence, freed of possessions and bills. To this end, she mounts a flat-out assault on the clutter that fills her basement flat. Underwear, old newspapers, interview tapes, snapshots, tin boxes, yellowed letters, scribbled addresses, tea bags and age-encrusted sweets go flying in all directions, only to reassemble, by some mysterious process of transmigration, across the room. "I don't love possessions, but possessions must dearly love me," Mary concludes, slamming her door on the whole mess, and we take off in search of the simple life.

It isn't easy to find. Since the seventies, when squats were almost everywhere in London, local councils have been waging a steady war of attrition, and they've gradually gained the upper hand. Whole boroughs are now virtually desquatted. Hackney's the last citadel, and even that is under threat.

A shapeless sprawl, covering much of the East End, Hackney is in many ways a microcosm of the whole republic. According to the press, it's the poorest borough in England, as well as the most racially diverse. Some of its many detractors have dubbed it Heinzland, a snide reference to the fifty-seven varieties it's supposed to contain, but this is actually a gross underestimate. Depending on whose figures you follow, there are either 108 nationalities at large here, or 122.

The advertised poverty is not immediately obvious. Time and again, circuiting London, I'm struck by how survivable even the harshest neighbourhoods seem, compared to the worst of the North. A lot of Hackney is grim—crumbling tower blocks and jerry-built estates, rubbish-strewn backstreets, sweatshops—but it doesn't look like a bombsite. On the contrary, it's full of action and display. Even on a rainy Tuesday morning, the array of Muslim robes and African silks and baggy Turkish pants on Mare Street, the main drag, is a global kaleidoscope.

The keynote is shambles, not affliction. For the past twenty years or more, Hackney has been a prime magnet for the young and feckless, the terminally dodgy. Its politics have been a byword for corruption, its social services a farce. Apologists like to call this laid-back. Critics call it criminal.

The grandiose town hall is known locally as Fawlty Towers, and its shenanigans are never-ending. Back in the early eighties, power was annexed by hardline left-wingers, and there's been a constant stream of scandals and government inquiries ever since. By 1991, the situation was so dire that a squad of fraud investigators was set up under the direction of Bernard Crofton, the head of the housing department. The local paper called them the Untouchables, but the love affair didn't last. Soon Crofton himself was being branded a liar and a fraud.

Things were different once. Back in the forties and fifties, when the area was largely Jewish, it was an intellectual hotbed. Harold Pinter and Arnold Goodman went to school at Hackney Downs, bright East End boys on the make. Now the school has failed, like almost everything else. "Diversity? It's just a fancy way of saying there's more ways to fuck up," I'm told.

At least the place is welcoming. Or it was until recently. In the eighties, it took in all-comers, no questions asked. Apart from the 108 (or 122) nationalities, there was a mass influx of drop-outs, runaways and would-be artists from all over Britain. They set up communes and collectives, and nobody bothered them. "It was a bit like that film *Field of Dreams*," one veteran recalls. "Squat it, and they shall come."

Not lately, though. The nineties version of the council may still be corrupt and incompetent, but the old liberality is gone. Rent-paying artists are still encouraged, and Hoxton, the area around Old Street, once a bastion of the National Front, has recently become the new centre of the fashionable Underground—London's answer to Manhattan's East Village, full of clubs and galleries, hip hang-outs. But freeloaders are out.

Evictions have become commonplace. The council smashes up the toilets and baths in empty houses to render them uninhabitable, or breaks into squatted properties with duplicate keys. Many of the squatters, as a result, have cleared out. Others, toughened by attrition, have simply tightened ranks.

The heart of the resistance is around London Lane, in two back-to-back streets of nineteenth-century workers' cottages. Handsome rows of terraced brick dwellings, they don't fit in with the workshops and manufactories that have sprung up around them, and so, the council has decreed, they must be torn down.

Fi has a room in one of the threatened squats. A girl with wide eyes, gentle and dreaming, she comes from Norfolk, and still speaks with a soft country burr. When not tripping off to India or sequestering herself in a meditation retreat, she does work as a publicist. She used to be a mouthpiece for a children's hospital and once trod the wards with Princess Diana. Currently, with fine irony, she's debating whether or not to take a PR job with Hackney Council.

The house she occupies is an Ideal Home among squats. Kitchen and bathroom are fully functional, the bedrooms swept and dusted; there's even a phone. The real focal point, however, is the ratty sofa that's parked outside the front door in a scrofulous scrap of garden, ringed around by buddleias and blown dandelions.

A whole treatise could be written on the role of the outdoor sofa in the republican age. It has replaced the doorstep as the centre of local gossip. Just as the doorstep, scrubbed spotless, reflected the spirit of its time, so now the sofa—springs broken, guts spilling, a ringing slap in the face of sanitation departments everywhere—reflects its own. The very act of plopping down, feet up, is to give the cosmic finger to any and all pretensions. Now God stands up for slobs.

One night, Fi takes us on a guided tour of the squats. The people we meet, in general, are articulate, decorous, not young. Most might be called middle class, but Mary won't allow that term. "Too broad, too nebulous, too damn patronising," she calls it. So let's just say they come from comfort.

Their homes, like Fi's, mix function with whimsy. A lot of hard work has gone into them—reconfiguring the plumbing and wiring, plugging up the leaks, driving out the rats—but they still have a ramshackle feel. The living rooms share a common post-hippie love of the East: throw pillows, kilims, ethnic drapes; mementoes of Lompoc and Goa. In one place, I sit facing the terra-cotta figure of a Chinese devil. It seems to be winking at me.

Many of the squatters have day jobs. There's Siobhan, who has a degree in Turkish and wants to be a social worker; Martin, who's a cycle courier and silversmith; and Mike, who works in a gallery. Others dabble in writing or art.

Sitting on these floors, I feel half a lifetime replaying. The clothes and props and faces have hardly changed since the sixties, and neither has the rhetoric. As the joints and mugs of tea do the rounds, I listen again to the time-honoured riffs on freedom and self-discovery. Their smugness used to enrage me, but now they seem pleasantly familiar, almost reassuring, like hymns I once suffered at school prayers. "The universe is inside our minds," I hear. Or again, "Better to drop out than to destroy." And I'm lulled. Jimi Hendrix is still alive, and

Jagger looks good, and the times they are a-changin'. Across a rug-strewn mattress, I watch Mary's rapt face. "The fusion of cosmic energies makes magic," somebody says.

Why does London Lane feel so different from Fraggle Rock? The absence of necessity, that's all. I remember Gilles telling me that no one stayed in a travellers' site unless they'd lost everything else. "The ones who endure have no choice," he said. But here, in this picturesque disarray, everyone has a choice. If the bailiffs come knocking tomorrow at dawn, there are other boltholes waiting, and, should those fail, safe houses back home. Families and jobs; made beds. "We won't go hungry," says Martin, the cycle courier. "It isn't life and death."

This note of realism is the one real change. Compared to the hippie communes of the sixties, or even the squats of the early eighties, the prevailing tone is battle-frayed, a little weary. No one claims that revolution is just around the corner, or that love is all you need, or even passes the acid. True, there's a silk-robed transvestite in one kitchen, and a woman wrapped in a tie-dyed shawl is still mulling over a deck of tarot cards. On the whole, though, the millennial squatter seems almost down to earth. "We know the score," says Siobhan, the Turkish graduate. "When you squat, you expect to be shat on."

So this is how the squatting world draws to an end. Not on the barricades, with trumpets blaring and banners waving, but in near-resignation, quietly awaiting the bailiff's knock. A few still plan to resist; there is talk of a petition, perhaps a fund-raiser. But most sound ready to take the count. "Nomads move. That's what we do," Siobhan says. Inside this room, though, not a soul stirs.

ON A CHURCH wall in Mare Street, I pass a sign that reads: IF WE COVER OUR LIVES WITH EVERYBODY'S FLAG WE WILL CREATE HEAVEN ON EARTH AND PEACE FOR ALL. But that's not the way it plays. When the nice white artists and dreamers put on a music social at the Lady Eve, a squat-turned-club near London Fields, a gang of black youths descends and makes off with the sound equipment. They don't even bother to operate with stealth—simply come barging in the front door, swagger round the dance floor a few times, then start to help themselves. There's a prolonged pitched battle, first inside the Lady Eve itself, then spilling into the streets and over the park. Some of the blacks wield straight-edged razors, and they start to slice and dice. After a long delay, a few police show up, but they don't seem greatly bothered. Between black hooligans and a bunch of over-aged hippies, they're hard-pressed to choose sides.

The bit of bother at the Lady Eve, according to Fi, is by no means untypical. Hackney Council keeps putting out glossy brochures with titles like *Succeeding Together*, but the feel-good factor does not translate to the streets. "Togeth-erness?" says Fi. "There's not a lot of it around."

A black friend of mine confirms this. Jamaican by background, but Hackney-raised and crazed, I met him originally in the pubs of Portobello. Tall, loose-limbed and athletic, with high cheekbones and pillow lips, he was trying to become a writer, while earning the rent as a night guard for an Arab millionaire. On first sight, he looked formidable—a swaggering street-tough—but his eyes were soft and full of self-doubt. "He isn't what you'd call a brave boy," his then-girlfriend told me. He tended to panic when off his own turf, and he was forever doing runners. Just the same, he had style; a lazy charm. "I slide by," he said himself.

One afternoon, he told me his story. He didn't want his real name to be used in print. So what would he sug-gest? He thought a moment; then he burst out laughing. "Call me Caf," he said. "C-A-F, Cool as Fuck. I used to know a guy on the Sandringham Road who called himself that. I always fancied it for myself."

The heart of the story was how he'd grown up in Hack-ney, run with the street gangs and ended up selling urine for a living.

This wasn't what he'd intended. "It was the last thing on my mind, believe me," Caf said. He talked as if to himself, his big hands splayed on his spread knees and his heels drumming restively on the latticed steel roof where we sat.

His first real memories of Hackney were of coming back from Jamaica. "I was ten, and I'd been away five years, living with my grandmother in St. Anne's Parish, the same parish where Robert Marley was born. Chickens and cowshit, very rural. Then I arrived in London, and my mother was living in a dive. The windows were gone, there wasn't any carpet. But what I remember most was the brackish sweet smell. That weird reek of London, you never can pin it down."

To begin with, he didn't fit in. He talked in a thick Jamaican patois, and he did too well at school. "English, drama, anything to do with words, I was a teacher's pet. But three years into comprehensive I started to change. Started to gamble, smoke dope, and I bunked off school for weeks at a time. There was this friend of mine, Jeff, he seemed like glamour personified. Loads of jewellery, a shitload of attitude. To me, he was the Man."

Caf had three older brothers, but all of them had left home, and he felt like an only child. "Mother couldn't hold me, forget it. I was into shoplifting, breaking into cars. Left school the first day I was legal, 1981, just as the old bottlesnatcher was getting her feet under the table in Downing Street. Of course, she was an inspiration, Ma Thatcher was, she changed the whole climate. *Get the money,* she said. So we did. Mugging and scamming, taking-and-driving-away, with just a smidgen of burglary thrown in. Fifteen to eighteen, those were the most exciting years in my life. We had a posse thirty or forty strong, the Cromer Posse, with Jeff on top. A whole street of squats, Cecilia Road, it was like an Aladdin's cave of stolen goods. I had seven thousand pounds in the bank, maybe more. I owned cars, even though I couldn't drive. A Triumph PI, an ex–police car, you could hear it coming by its whistle. Fuel injection, understand? And a ratchet.

Ratchet with rings, imported from Jamaica. A ratchet in my waist, "Johnny Too Bad," cool as fuck. Then I got arrested."

He got three months in a youth custody centre in Sussex, known to its inmates as Holiday Bay. "One of Ma Thatcher's 'short, sharp shocks,' and it certainly shocked me." He cried a lot, which he'd never done before, and thought about the waste. "I'd been smart in school, I could have been a writer. That's what I kept repeating in my mind—I'm not just a nothing, I have something to say." So he decided to start out fresh. "Get a job, fly right." At the end of eight weeks, released, he went back to Hackney and his new life. "So what did I do? Sold dope."

Jeff used to tell him that work was white man's talk, designed to suck out your spunk. Dealing dope was a real man's work. And Caf was always precocious.

For the next three years, he was out on the frontline, seven days a week. The Yardies had come in by then, and Jeff's gang were Yardies, London-style: Clark's suede boots and baggy pants, a flannel in the back pocket, string vest, a silk shirt, a cap. "We owned Sandringham Road, nobody could mess with us. What I'm saying, we were a political force. Hurled bricks at the police station, Stoke Newington Station, and if the cops came down to raid us, we sent them home with a bloody good hiding."

When he was twenty-one, however, he started sampling his own supplies. Up till then, he had only smoked a little weed, occasionally dabbled in coke, but now he got caught up on crack. "I used to hang out in this pool hall," Caf told me. "There was a little office downstairs, full of broken pool cues, broken-down tables, a naked lightbulb with moths flitting. And then, this guy—we called him Killer. He was a serious crackhead, and he had a total ritual when he smoked. He used an empty bottle of Evian, with a hollowed-out biro stuck into the side, baking foil stretched over the top, a ratchet to stab smoke-holes in the foil, and he always said the Lord's Prayer just before he took a lick. So I did, too." At first, he couldn't get it right. "Then it hit me, and it was everything. I stretched out my legs, my hands, I could feel every vein in my body."

The problem with crack was, you were always chasing the virgin lick, that first wild rush. You couldn't ever catch it, but you'd kill yourself trying, you couldn't give up. "I just fell apart, let everything go. I didn't wash or eat or sleep, I couldn't piss for shitting. Killer was my smoking partner, a dark, dark man with big red eyes. A most aggressive personality, he'd stab you just for fun. But he had a wisdom, too. Sort of Merlinish, a supernatural ability, he could read your mind. Although, to be honest, I had no mind left to read."

On the last night, he and Killer were in Caf's Hackney flat, smoking, and the flat was like a graveyard. Filthy, broken glass, no light but candles. Killer had this big stash of rocks, and he kept hogging it, feeding Caf crumbs, so that when he finally got a full hit, he took too much and flipped. "I was looking at Killer in the flicker of the candles, and he turned into a duppy. Something out of *Alien*, a total monstrosity. I tried to jump out the window, but he held me back. Then I started screaming, fighting him, and he threw me down. I ran through the door. My mother was downstairs, and I flew to her. I was shaking, cold-sweating, next to dying. Didn't move from bed for the next nine days."

It gave him time to think and give himself a good kicking. He thought about the lost way he was, and it seemed to him he was split. There was this tough, street-smart shell, and this whole other self inside. A being that could write and think and feel. Jeff would call that soft shit. But playing at Johnny Too Bad had almost put him in the graveyard. A little soft shit sounded fine.

"I went into rehab, fifteen months straight, and stayed clean the whole time. Lots of others didn't, though." And that's when he became a urine salesman.

You had to give random specimens, two, three times a

week, and there were all these stone junkies, their piss thick with dope. If their tests came back dirty, of course, they were kicked out. So Caf sold them substitutes. They'd walk into the khazi to take a whiz with his clean urine in a rubber tube, taped to the inside of their belts. All they had to do was syphon it off into the sample bottle, and Bingo! Clean as a whistle.

Payment, though useful, was not the point. The real reward lay in beating the system; fucking with authority's head. You were not free in this place. Not a prisoner exactly, but under orders; out of your own control. "Each time you took a leak, it was like saying you had no secrets, no private self." But switching samples defused the insult. "Instead of giving the piss, you took it."

When his fifteen months were up, Caf went off to college in Harlow. "I took a course in journalism. Graduated with honours and brass bands, the works. But did it get me any work? Did it shit?"

So now he just wrote. He was working on a novel, and it looked good so far. On nights when his guard duties didn't keep him busy, he sat up in the Arab millionaire's house, in a kitchen filled with science-fiction gadgetry, all the latest in electronic toys, and let his mind roam free. It wasn't cool as fuck, exactly. But it beat the graveyard any day.

HE'S BACK IN Hackney now, Caf. It's over a year since he told me his tale, and he has turned thirty. For some reason he can't explain, this milestone has devastated him. All he can do is keep thinking how old he is, how many wasted years have passed. The more he broods on lost time, of course, the more time gets lost, but he feels powerless to break loose. He has stopped writing, quit the fast tracks of Portobello, and moved into a council flat in Dalston. Some days he sits indoors and reads. Most often, though, he just vegetates.

"It's the Hackney disease," he tells me. We're having a

drink at a pub in London Fields, and I'm doing my ritual best to buck him up, but Caf stays resolutely glum. "It's over," he keeps saying. No more passions, no more adventures. So what remains? He thinks for a moment, his big hands still splayed on his spread knees but his heels no longer drumming.

"Passive resistance," he decides.

It could be Hackney's motto. Leaving Caf to moulder, I take an amble back to London Lane. On Mare Street, I pass Turks and Somalis and Sikhs, Bangladeshis and Serbs, expat Americans in sandals, robed Arabs, black-suited Russians. WE ARE HACKNEY! a poster outside the public library brags. But I get no sense of interaction. Each nationality seems to walk by itself, airtight in its own bubble.

When my buttocks sink into Fi's sofa, a small cloud of dust puffs up. The day is warm and muggy, an afternoon made for idling, and Mary is already ensconced. Envying our sofaed splendour, passers-by are lured to stop and soliloquise. A Scot moans about rising rents, a drinker remembers old footballers, a neighbour rhapsodises on the virtues of bean curd. Turkish workers from the manu-factory across the lane are lounging in the doorway, sur-reptitiously sharing a smoke. Mary is pondering our future—to squat, or not to squat. And I ponder a remark that Martin, the cycle courier, made, the night we toured the squats. "In a world where glorious revolution seems not to be realistic," he said, "the most you can do is try and live as decently as possible."

Tea and biscuits appear. One of the Turks across the street blows a smoke-ring; a stray dog rambles by. "I could murder a custard cream," sighs Mary.

ONE MAN WE meet in Hackney doesn't share in the general languor. He's known as Andy Signtist, and also as Andrew Nominus—an all-purpose artist (gallery, graffiti and murals) who occupies a squat near the Lady Eve and breathes blue flame.

A global traveller, born and raised in Australia, honed on the American road, he makes squatting seem like an act of philanthropy. Not only did he rescue his house from dereliction, put a roof on it, rewire it and paint it throughout, he turned it into a place of rescue. He's sheltered the homeless, mental cases, thieves. Some have stolen from him, others have damaged the house. "That's not important," he says. "Just a part of the learning curve."

Wiry and hard-muscled, all edges, Signtist has never drawn the dole, conducts free workshops for local street kids, cleans up the cigarette butts in the park. Nonetheless, there's a sense of danger about him; a tension, barely tethered, suggestive of inner furies.

The morning we call on him, he sits coiled on a kitchen chair, his tight body drawn up like a gathered spring, and rants at such runaway speed that Mary can't keep up with her notes and stray wads of shorthand end up scattered about the floor like so many exploded white gunshells.

His central theme is the need for public art; its function in bringing light. "Art has got to be a weapon to change reality," he says, "to jolt people's consciences awake."

He has mounted two exhibitions at the Alba Café on Mare Street, with the paintings priced according to the buyers' means. He has also spawned graffiti, legal and illegal, around the world. But his most visible achievement, at least in London, is the giant mural of a screaming black woman that covers an exterior wall of the Hackney Empire theatre.

He found the image by chance, on a leaflet campaigning to free a jailed woman in Deptford. "It was a face I seemed to have seen before, a face of universal pain. Plus, I liked the thought of it being stolen art. So I rappelled down the building in the night and went to work. Next morning, when people woke up, there it was. A statement you couldn't ignore."

The council appeared to welcome it at first. Social conscience was still in fashion then, and the mural made them seem like masked activists. More recently, though, the climate has started to shift. "It's like squatting, really. What was acceptable before is now a royal pain." Sometimes he gets discouraged. His instincts tell him to throw up his hands, get the fuck out of the city, but he can't swallow defeat; surrender won't go down. "I'm in for the long march," he tells us. "I'm here. Doing it."

What baffles him is the red rage that public art provokes. People sit in front of their TVs and confront the worst atrocities without a blink: wars and famines, wholesale slaughters. But let them take the dog for a walk and find a bit of graffiti, a stray splash of paint on some concrete slab, and they're reduced to spitting fury. It's as if they've been personally threatened. Yet what is graffiti, in the end? Just your mark; a way of saying you exist. "We've been doing that since caveman days," Andy Signtist says, coiling tighter, then slowly unfurling. "Is it a crime to say *I am*?"

The case of Fista suggests it is.

Twenty-three years old, real name Simon Sunderland, he comes from South Yorkshire, and he's been sentenced to five years in jail for graffiti banditry.

Before his capture, he worked the Sheffield-Barnsley

area, daubing his tag—sometimes Fista, sometimes Fisto—in red, black and silver letters, ten feet high, and signing it with a clenched fist. He sprayed walls, abandoned houses, motorway bridges, a broken-down bus, a town hall. Local councils launched a massive hunt for him but Fista, a spray-can Zorro, kept eluding capture.

When at last he was collared, there were alleluias. The trial judge, passing sentence, wished to "give people hope that Britain would one day be graffiti-free." And the *Sheffield Star,* wrapping up the case, mused that "graffiti yob Simon Sunderland once said the only way to stop him vandalising South Yorkshire would be to cut his hands off. Many will think it a shame that such a penalty is not available in British law . . ."

SIMON SUNDERLAND has been jailed in North Yorkshire. I write to him there, but his reply is tentative. He doesn't want to stir things until his appeal has been heard. Perhaps I could talk to his mother.

Angela Noble, the mother in question, is a social worker in south London. Her home is neat and impersonal, except for the piles of books, many of them academic tomes on sociology and politics, and a number of her son's paintings, tucked away in the spare bedroom.

The paintings are schoolboy efforts—a couple of abstracts, a self-portrait, strongly drawn but rudimentary in technique. "He's been highly praised. Commended," Mrs. Noble says. She is a nervous woman, somewhat scattered, and her remarks tend to fade in and out. "Some agents say . . . talent . . . represent him, maybe . . . when he comes out . . . a show."

Her credentials are impressive. When she was pushing forty, she started going to college in Sheffield and got a degree in applied social sciences. Since then, divorced from Simon's father, she's worked on a project supporting families in need, and in a respite home.

Where does Fista, *graffiti yob,* fit in with this? He

doesn't, his mother says. The boy she knows is a quiet sort, obsessively curious. "Growing up, he was always . . . enquiring . . ." Someone gave him a clock, and he took it to pieces. Then the phone went missing. "He had it hid in a cupboard . . . all its guts taken out." She sketches a smile, but her mouth is tremulous, her eyes aren't right. "He just wanted to know how things worked," she says. "He's not robbed a bank, not killed anyone." One hand, fluttering, goes to her lips. "He painted on walls," she says.

A few days later, Simon Sunderland agrees to let us visit him in jail.

We meet him in a large, open space like an outsized classroom, with no divides between inmates and guests. Children race freely round the tables, shrieking and buzzing, playing aeroplanes, while wives and girlfriends pass sweets and cakes, fruit, drugs, scarcely bothering to dissemble. The air is thick with smoke.

Sunderland is shy.

Six foot, strongly built, he could pass, at first glance, for a builder's mate, but not at second. He lacks the brickie's machismo; there is no sense of strut. Instead of the cartoon character who so outraged the *Sheffield Star,* I'm faced by an overgrown schoolboy, studiously polite, who avoids eye contact and swallows his words.

Prison-pale, with his hair cropped to a fuzz, he sits stiff and unsmiling, beetle-browed. Only when our meeting is half-over, and I'm reduced to telling him tales of downtown Manhattan, where graffiti artists like Jean-Michel Basquiat have now been raised to godheads, does he begin to ease. He's been to New York himself; the memory starts him talking. "It's mad there," he says. "I liked it."

I ask how he started in graffiti. "There were nothing else," he replies. He had a portfolio full of drawings, but no one was interested, he had no outlets. His parents were breaking up; his mother was moving to London; he saw no hope. Graffiti art was in all the magazines, and he hoarded them in his room. There was a wall in Barnsley he had his eye on. A derelict property; nobody was using it. He saw it as his big chance. The perfect platform to show what he could do. He went to the authorities about painting it, to help brighten up the town, but they turned him down. They said he might fall off his ladder and injure himself. So there was no wall; nothing. That's when Fista was born.

Talking of street art, his language is less high-flown than Andy Signtist's. He simply says that he used graffiti as a protest, and also a release. "There was so much inside me, bottled up, it had to get out somehow." Mostly he worked late at night, in relative safety, but there were also times when he took silly risks, playing games with capture. More than once he got caught, spray-can in hand. He was hauled into court and convicted in Barnsley, Rotherham, Mansfield. Even so, he never got really nailed. The more chances he took, the more he seemed unstoppable. A Fista cult began to develop. In graffiti circles, he was an outlaw hero. Someone compared him to Che Guevara and his story got into the papers. The writers called him a street-art fiend. Then Francis Butler, a Liberal Democrat councillor, made it his mission to bring the evil-doer to heel. That pushed Simon to redouble his efforts. He was working every night now. Walls and houses, street signs, even a police van. He lived on a continual high—excitement mixed with paint fumes and fear. Councillor Butler was at his wit's end. One last ploy remained. There was an appeal for informers. And Fista was grassed up.

The law came knocking at six a.m. Two plain-clothes detectives, a uniformed bobby, a cameraman and a forensic expert: "Everyone but Inspector Morse," Simon says. In his bedroom, they found four hundred cans of spray-paint, street maps, pamphlets, a library of graffiti art, spraying gloves and a vent mask to prevent inhalation of fumes: "Enough gear to equip a car-body shop," one police spokesman claimed. Simon sat downstairs, under guard. The street outside was full of police cars. *The Day of the Jackal* had nothing on this.

Remembering the massive forces deployed to bring him in, the graffiti desperado allows himself a wry smile. A small boy from a nearby table keeps running at walls and butting them head-on. "Anything for attention," Simon shrugs.

His days in jail are focused on his appeal. He spends as much time as possible in his cell, reading or drawing. The other inmates don't give him too much grief, but many are career villains and he can't afford to be caught up in a criminal mindset. He steers clear of the drugs and home-made alcohol, the war-story sessions. His art work has been developing; he has filled a whole new portfolio. Mark Ticktum, an agent who wants to sign him up, calls him "a Picasso of the urban art world." But Simon him-self is less bombastic. "I only want to be seen," he says.

We make our goodbyes awkwardly, not knowing quite how to break off. "Give my best to New York," Simon says. His broad pasty body seems to waver, amorphous, in the fluorescent light. Then he's swallowed up in the stream of men returning to their cells. It's as if he has been snuffed out, and I go back to the fresh air feeling guilty. The late afternoon has turned dirty grey. The air smells laden with rain.

We head back south. The horizon is lined with outsize industrial vats like space-age ovens. Then night comes on. The motorway speeds past Doncaster, Rotherham, Hoy-land Nether. Nearing Barnsley we flash under a bridge. And there by the roadside, in huge, ornate letters, we glimpse the tag:

FISTO

A glimpse is all. An instant later, we're away down the road, headed for the next Little Chef. "I only want to be seen," Simon said. But it's come up too fast and sudden for that. Before I can focus cleanly, his mark is already erased.

NEXT DAY we travel Fista's turf, zigzagging from Barnsley to Sheffield, via Worsborough, Wombwell, Ecclesfield,

Jump. Most of them used to be mining towns before Maggie Thatcher killed the pits. Now they're deadlands, bereft of function.

The towns are a series of shells. Eerily preserved, with pubs and schools and chapels intact, even the stark skeletons of the collieries still in place, they don't look much changed from afar, but when you come up close, there's nothing left save the bones.

I plod round the housing estate where Fista gestated. Last night's scattered rain has set in solidly, streaming down with the stubbornness peculiar to Northern wet, a grim pleasure in its own wretchedness. I pass men in sodden pit jackets, dragging beagles or Jack Russells through the puddles. They look at me like drowning men. But their sons, hanging round the pub doorways in their trainers and Top Shop tracksuits, seem even more lost. The fathers have had lives, however raw. These lads have nothing but vacant time.

I think of Ralph Ellison's *Invisible Man*. In England now, it's these white boys, even more than blacks or Asians, who are the true invisibles. No jobs, no prospects, no leaders, no voice. Just this endless waiting.

One night in Barnsley, we drop into a pub where there's a function for the Free Fista campaign. The crowd is a broad mixture—fellow graffiti artists, neo-Goths, neighbours, a Morticia Addams lookalike in black-and-white warpaint, a table of old ladies drinking stout, and two of Simon's aunts.

Handsome women, Yorkshire-toughened, the aunts sell T-shirts, collect signatures, call down a few choice plagues on the judge's head. Then a band comes on. The room is hot and airless, packed solid, and the music murderous—a rapid series of two-chord punk thrashes, all more or less alike. The lyrics are lost in feedback; all that gets through are screamed curses. But the crowd is delighted. The orange-haired lead singer, all chains and tattoos, keeps screaming "Fuck off" in their faces, so close they get splattered by his spittle, and they just laugh. The old ladies with their stouts, the neighbours, Morticia, the two aunts—they're all caught up in the same spasm. Some of them merely look on and smile, it's true, but others are up and cheering, screaming back. It's a moment of purging, pure release. Because there's nothing else to do, in the end, and nothing else to be said.

Sweet. Fuck. All.

I've been reading a book on the man who's been called the devil incarnate. The book is *The Enemy Within,* and it's all about Arthur Scargill.

He is the man in England I most want to meet. From the first time I saw him on TV, way back in 1972, he's seemed an epic figure to me. I remember how his flying pickets descended on the Saltley coke depot in Birmingham then, an avenging army from South Yorks, bearing down in cars and minicabs and beat-up old jalopies, and how they forced the depot to close, and how that won the strike. The miners seemed invincible. In sober fact, they almost were. Two years later, when Edward Heath tried to break them, he got slung out on his ear. Such was the power of the unions, of the working class as a whole, only twenty-five years ago.

My fascination with Scargill is essentially apolitical. I'm not a Marxist, his faith is not my own; but I treasure him as a performer. King Arthur of the Red Hand, battered, betrayed, never beaten: like all great mythic self-creations, he's skirted farce, but he has never been mundane. His resilience, his wit, his bloody-mindedness, his follies of grandeur, his essential aloneness—everything about the man has been scaled to the heroic.

Travelling his territories now, I keep flashing back to the great wars of 1984–5, when Mrs. Thatcher determined to succeed where Heath had failed and reduce the National Union of Mineworkers to rubble. I remember Scargill on the march, and the riot police with their helmets and shields, the mass arrests, the running battles, day after bloody day, and the look on the miners' faces, their clenched fury at Orgreave, when pickets were charged and cudgelled and felled, and Scargill himself was knocked unconscious. Nothing was going to defeat those men, you'd have said; no power on earth. But they had lost, just the same. The mines were closed down, and the redundancies went through, and King Coal was slain.

In *The Enemy Within,* I find a quote about the strike, and the pitmen who fought in it: "Many said they would do it all again and many had clearly enjoyed the experience: they had lived at a pitch, physically, intellectually, morally even, which they could not expect to again, and which most who have not undergone war would never emulate."

The quote is borrowed from *The Miners' Strike,* a severely anti-Scargill account, which makes the imagery even more striking. The miners were indeed at war. When the strike collapsed, they became a defeated army.

On the streets, and in the half-empty pubs, Scargill's name now rouses mixed reactions. Some are embittered— men and women who lost their houses and their furniture, stood and watched their TVs and fridges and even their bedding hauled away, while Arthur kept his job, his home, his Ford Scorpio. Others say he fought the good fight and refuse to parcel out blame. Almost all, mistrustful of an outsider, make haste to change the subject.

When I penetrate upstairs into living rooms and kitchens, though, I find that the fires of combat have not all died. A few of Scargill's old-time followers still keep the faith intact. "I'd lay down my life for that man," one veteran tells me, wet-eyed.

"You already did," says his wife.

But that's an old man talking, after all; a man now racked by coughing, with shaking hands, who can't face the thought that his life's struggle might have been for nothing, his dying irrelevant. "It were all necessary," he insists.

Not if you judge by his inheritors. None of the youths I talk to shows the smallest interest in going down the mines. It's less than fifteen years since the strike, but it might be another age. "You'd have to be an idiot," says one lad, dole-smug, lounging in the open market at Dewsbury.

The figures could hardly be starker. When Scargill took over as NUM president in 1981, membership stood at over 350,000; now it's down below 10,000. In Yorkshire alone, where there were once two or three hundred working mines, ten are left, and only four in South Yorks. "A search and destroy mission," Tony Benn has called this purge, but an ex-miner I talked to near Skipton, a man who'd put in twenty-two years, pitched it even higher. "Scorched earth," he said. "Industrial bloody genocide."

That's been the price of resistance. But what was the reward for appeasement? We take a side trip south to Notts, where most miners kept working through the strike. They'd never been as militant as their Yorkshire brethren, and they'd been guaranteed a long-term future by the Coal Board, or at least they believed they had. So they rejected Scargill's rule, formed a breakaway union and tried to negotiate on their own. At the fiercest stage of the conflict, when the government faced capitulation, it was the Nottingham mines that saved Mrs. Thatcher's bacon.

The pay-off has not been tremendous. As soon as the strike was done, the Coal Board forgot all promises. Mines continued to be shut down or sold off at a rate of between ten and twenty a year, roughly the same pace as before the strike, and Notts suffered with the rest. The pits that survive have been privatised and are now run by Richard Budge, a man identified in a 1994 report for the Trade and Industry Department as "unfit to be concerned in the management of a company."

We come to rest at Warsop, a town that's had its share of bad publicity. A couple of years ago, the *Telegraph* magazine singled it out as a symbol of Yob Power. Hooligans, the writer claimed, were terrorising the place. Teenage and pre-teen gangs, up to three hundred strong, got boozed up every Friday and Saturday night, then went out burning and looting. They'd torched the headquarters of the Army Cadet Force, the bowls pavilion down the road and the sports ground changing-rooms. Hard cider and harder drugs ruled, especially among the ten-year-olds. "It could be almost anywhere in Britain," the writer concluded.

The country roundabouts is dotted with mining villages, mostly defunct—Warsop Vale, Meden Vale, Spion Kop—but Warsop itself is not a pit town. On the contrary, it's making strenuous efforts to distance itself from all things grimy. It prefers to call itself Market Warsop, its streets are a riot of floral displays and its brochures emphasise the local prowess in campanology—the noble art of bell-ringing. The only remaining signs of coal are the three refurbished pit trucks at the town's centre, enthroned on a plinth and filled with flowers, with a sign announcing that Warsop won the East Midlands in Bloom competition in 1993.

The heart of the town's trouble, according to the *Telegraph*, has been the Old End, an area of run-down pit cottages, backed by wasteland and scrub. We make our way through a patchwork quilt of allotments, past rows of cabbages and runner beans, to Alexandra Street, where the worst delinquents are said to lurk. The late-afternoon sun is still hot and people are gathered in clusters outside their front doors. Many of the men have the square-shouldered, stiff-legged gait of former squaddies. They watch us stone-faced, trained to indifference. A woman with pillar-box red hair is saying she needs a good shagging. "Any volunteers?" she asks. A young boy on a bike does wheelies.

Not a drug-crazed vandal in sight. We ask three schoolgirls where to find the gangs. "What gangs?" they reply. They've lived here from birth but have never come across the advertised carnage. Instead of three hundred hard-core terrorisers, their own estimate is twenty. "They get bored.

We all do," one of the girls says. If you're old, you can play bowls or hang out at the working men's club. For the young, there's nothing. "Just finish school and get out."

Older heads disagree. A retired policeman, lounging on a bench overlooking the bowling green, reels off a laundry list of possible diversions. "Sports centre, swimming pool, sand bowl. A lad could have joined the cadet force, before they burned down the clubhouse, or used the disco, only that got trashed. Or books." He glares at me; false teeth flashing, daring me to argue. "They could read a bloody book."

That is his best offer, and apparently it's not enough. In the car park behind the police station, there's a graffito that reads, WARSOP IS THE BEST PLACE ON EARTH IF YOU LIKE TRAINSPOTTING, 'COS IT'S THAT WANK. Another simply says, DOES ANYONE KNOW A DECENT DRUG DEALER? I'M DYING HERE.

At twilight, we sit by the sluggish stream that runs through the Carrs, Warsop's public park, and watch a few boys get legless on White Lightning. Slumped on the river bank, the grass worn bald by their nightly sit-ins, they move only to pass the bottle, hardly speak except to say "Fuck."

Only one among them meets my eye—a sharp-faced youth, his fuzz-cut hair bleached blond, in baggy canvas pants and a paint-smeared white T-shirt with rips and rolled sleeves. It's an arty look, and it sets him apart from his mates. So does the sky-blue falcon tattooed on his left biceps.

One of his ears sticks out, while the other lies flat to his skull. The imbalance gives him a mongrel air, raffish and eager; a sense of perpetual enquiry.

He gives his name as Grady. "First name or last?" I ask. "Suit yourself," he replies, and lets the White Lightning pass by him untouched, to show his independence.

The *Telegraph* story was crap, he says. Or, worse than crap, it missed the whole point. The thing about Warsop is not the violence: "What does my head in is the deadness."

Not that Warsop's unique. Grady has travelled quite a

bit. His father used to sell fresh produce from his allotment at markets all around the East Midlands and Grady liked to go with him. During school holidays, they'd be on the road almost every day, and he built up an overview. "It's one big void," he says. "Not only coal towns, but anywhere there used to be physical work, an industry, and now there's none. It's like a spinal cord, reaching down the years. Then the cord gets cut. Paralysis."

His fellow drinkers, eavesdropping, pull faces and say "Fuck" to such fancy talk, but Grady isn't bothered. "They're sad. A lot of sad wankers," he tells me, rogue ear cocked. He's only with them for old times' sake. A few last nights getting bladdered, and then he's away. He has won prizes for drawing, been offered places at art schools, but his first love is music. He's in a band, playing bass and writing a few songs, and now he wants to test himself on the market. "Nottingham, or maybe Leicester," Grady says. "Any place that isn't here."

What would await him if he stayed? He shudders. "Half-bricks and liver disease." A gluttonous reader, he's proud of his turn of phrase. "I went through the library like a one-man hunger march." But it didn't stock many books that challenged him, nothing on the edge, and he hasn't the money to buy. "That's what I mean by a void." Frustration, testosterone, boredom, all thrown back on itself. "I've started fires myself. Not recently, but when I was young. They kept telling us to use the swimming pool, use the sand bowl, but what the fuck good is that? When your bollocks are blowing up, you can't just drown them in chlorine or bury them in sand."

Behind our backs, the good people of Warsop are taking the evening air. Pensioners walking dogs, young mothers pushing prams, couples holding hands. Grady, having recently read *The Stranger,* watches their passage with ironic distance. "D'you think they play bowls in limbo?" he asks.

We spend the night in Sherwood Forest. Not under the greenwood tree, precisely, but in a B&B at Edwinstowe, down the road from the Visitors Centre. I sit by the window and watch the headlights of the passing cars on the great oaks that flank the churchyard across the road, and in between cars I read *The Enemy Within*.

Back at the Carrs, when I finished talking to Grady, I asked his views on Arthur Scargill. He thought a beat, then fed me his mongrel grin: "He thinks he's Robin fucking Hood, doesn't he?"

Sleepless in my B&B, I keep replaying that flip dismissal in my mind. It sets off a train of thought that leads me back to the late sixties, when I visited Russia with a tour group. The only person among them that I made any connection with was an American studio musician, a Los Angeles session man, who played mostly on movie soundtracks. He was grizzled and disillusioned, deeply sour; I liked him enormously. Everything he saw or tasted or smelled in Russia displeased him, and our visit to Lenin's tomb was the last straw. The humanoid guards, the eternal flame, the other-worldly glow, and the incredibly tiny hands of the little man under the glass—when we plodded back into the daylight, I asked the session man what he'd thought. "One man's revolution," he answered, "is another man's Disneyland."

As soon as morning comes, therefore, we hit the Robin Hood trail. First we go marauding in Sherwood Forest. What little remains of it is flush with car parks and souvenir shops, but that doesn't damp our ardour. We play the Automatic Outlaw machine and I draw the Sheriff of Nottingham. We buy a plastic bow, three arrows and a dagger for 99p at the Magical Medieval Shopping Experience. Friar Tuck's Cafe is closed, to let, but there's a week-long festival coming up soon, replete with banquets, skirmishing and jousting, Outlaw Antics and Medieval Maniax. Mary sticks her head through the hollow trunk of a thousand-year-old oak, and I take her picture, and then it's off to Robin Hood World, where a well-upholstered lady done up as a character called Winnie Scarlett, complete with fringed tunic and overstuffed leggings, takes us on a guided tour of Merrie England. There are dioramas of evil Norman barons and terrified Saxon serfs, lashings of gore all around. We are asked repeatedly to be brave. We do our best.

Only when we're back on the road, heading north again, and we see the slag heaps looming through the trees, do I mention Grady's one-liner. The images it summons—Scargill resplendent in tunic and tights, winging arrows, bedevilling the barons and from time to time letting rip with a gay roundelay—keep us mindlessly amused all the way to Yorkshire.

I've acquired a brochure for the Caphouse Adventure. This is ad-speak for the Yorkshire Mining Museum, a few miles south of Dewsbury. "Historic Caphouse Colliery," says the bumpf. "In this country built on coal, discover for yourself the hidden secrets of a real mine."

About a dozen of us, adults and children, are equipped with helmets and lamps, ushered into the metal cage and dropped 450 feet underground. It's a dreadful fall, slow and choking. I picture the lamps failing, the cage thrown into pitch blackness, lurching and clattering, down, down, down.

Once safely at the bottom and out into the workings, the terror recedes. The first tunnel is wide and high-ceilinged, clearly lit, and the subterranean coolness is refreshing. The children press forward eagerly, poking at the walls. Our guide, an ex-miner himself, says we're going to have fun.

The tour takes about an hour, designed to take us through mining history. There's a reconstruction of early pits, a stall for pit ponies, a long progression of trolleys and diggers, beams and cables and various mighty machines, ever more complicated—a trepanner, a dint-header, a dosco roadheader. At one point, the ceiling drops to about four feet, and all of us except for Mary and infants have to double over for a few yards. One woman, cramped for space, stumbles against the pit wall, but no dirt rubs off on her coat. Then we're restored to light and space, and shortly afterwards we're excused.

So now I've been down a mine. Rising to the light, the cage no longer threatens me. It's just a lift, after all; transportation, not a steel coffin. By the time I sniff fresh air, I'm full of self-congratulation. It's only when I'm safely at lunch in the Miner's Pantry, stuffing myself with pies and pints, that the penny drops: I might as well be in Robin Hood World.

Belatedly, I dig out my copy of *The Road to Wigan Pier*, and reread George Orwell's account of the mines. And it's nothing remotely akin to what I've just sauntered through. The cage drops 400 yards, not 450 feet, and plummets at sixty miles an hour. Then he starts off, stooping, down a dimly lit gallery. "It is bad going underfoot—thick dust or jagged chunks of shale, and in some mines where there is water it is as mucky as a farmyard." Soon he has to drop to a half-squat, then down on all fours. It's a mile to the coal-face, or sometimes three miles, and every yard tweaks a different muscle. He gets a crick in his neck, cramps in his knees and thighs, scabs like buttons on his spine. But pains aren't the worst of it. "There is the heat," Orwell writes, "and the coal dust that stuffs up your throat and nostrils and collects along your eyelids, and the unending rattle of the conveyor belt, which in that confined space is rather like the rattle of a machine gun." And all around him the miners: "the line of bowed, kneeling figures, sooty black all over, driving their huge shovels under the coal with stupendous force and speed . . ."

In other words, I've not been down a mine at all.

As we drive away, past the nature trail and the picnic area, the pit ponies out to grass, I'm troubled by a vision of England's future: a vast, interlocking grid of theme parks; hundreds upon thousands of family attractions (kiddies half-price) endlessly recycling the past, till every last aspect of living, great and small, old and new, has been reduced to souvenirs. Who then will still know the difference, or care, among a renovated colliery, a souped-up steelworks and Medieval Maniax?

"You are in error," says Arthur Scargill. "If you will forgive me, and I say this with due respect, you are articulating opinions that are total balderdash."

We are sitting in his office at the new NUM headquarters. As the union has shrunk, it's been forced to move from its £2 million stronghold in Sheffield to smaller premises in Barnsley—a nineteenth-century red-brick mansion known locally as Camelot. Smaller it may be, but Scargill's own office remains palatial, wood-panelled, with an ocean of plush carpeting, a private bathroom and shower, a desk the size of a paddling pool. Scargill and I luxuriate in sumptuous armchairs, while Mary wallows on the sofa, sunk so deep in its depths that she seems nothing but head and boots.

"Let me endeavour to set you straight," Scargill says. Close to sixty, scrubbed and fit and sharp-suited, he looks superb. He's lost much of his hair, and with it his quiff, that gingery plume of combat he used to flaunt. But his eye is still steely, his glow intact. Energy comes off him in waves.

These are flush times for him. In the early nineties, he seemed done for. The strike had been smashed, mines were closing, the NUM was shrivelling and the *Daily Mirror* was calling him a crook. He was accused of having sticky-fingered the hardship funds meant for the striking miners, of having used handouts from Libya to pay off his mortgage, of having made dirty millions on the back of his own men's sufferings. There were calls for a public inquiry, and for a while, it looked at though he might end up in jail. But all of this was smoke without fire. *The Mirror's* accusations proved a frame-up. The Tory government and MI5 were exposed as co-conspirators, and Scargill wholly exonerated. By 1992, when John Major's government tried to close thirty-one of the remaining fifty British coal mines and sack 30,000 men at a shot, public opinion had swung back in the NUM's favour. Ninety per cent of the public supported the miners then, and Major was forced to back down. Arthur Scargill, against all conceivable odds, had survived.

Not only survived, but flourished. Tony Blair, having

broken up the old Labour Party, abandoned the pursuit of common ownership and in general treated socialism as a dirty word. King Arthur has leaped boldly into the breach. In a vintage flight of invective—"if the church to which you went decided to stop worshipping God and started worshipping the devil, you would have second thoughts"—he's turned his back on Blair, and set up a counterblast, the Socialist Labour Party.

How's the new party faring? "Our early progress has been more than edifying, thank you," Scargill tells me. The SLP, built on a platform of nationalisation, full employment, a four-day week and retirement on full pay at fifty-five, has so far done little in public elections, but that is not the point. Too canny to stand for parliament, Scargill's been quietly rebuilding his support. In the months that follow our meeting, one of his cohorts will take charge of ASLEF, the train drivers' union, and raise the prospect of a militant super-union, SLP-controlled, encompassing not only ASLEF and the NUM but the Rail Maritime and Transport Union. If that comes to pass, Scargill will wield more real power than he ever did, even before the miners' strike.

The prospect has him purring. He tells us a long story about meeting Billy Graham in 1985, soon after the strike collapsed. At that bleak moment, the evangelist asked Scargill how he kept going. "I just looked at him, and I said, 'It's called faith, Billy.' And he looked at me and he said, 'I unnerstand.'"

I know he's told this story to writers before, virtually word for word, but that only serves to solidify its status as holy writ. From the moment we enter his presence, he keeps us primed with a steady flow of such anecdotes, all delivered with a conspiratorial air, a sense of leaking mighty secrets. "I cannot mention names," he says, or, "I have never told this to anyone." The effect is to flatter the arse off me, and leave me helpless to face him down.

Not that confrontation is really an option; he's far too wily for that. The moment I try to frame a tough question, I'm made to feel like a novice boxer, rushing forward in crude frenzy, punching at air, while the old pro calmly slips away and leaves me floundering.

At one point, a secretary serves tea and biscuits. Scargill strips to his shirtsleeves, but that doesn't mean he goes native. The shirt in question is an immaculate blue pinstripe, its collar crisp and unsoiled. It isn't the shirt of a man prone to stains or unseemly sweats. Like everything else here—the carpet, the desk, Arthur's own patient smile—it speaks a language of statesmanship. Call it presidential.

He tells us everything he wishes us to hear, and not a word more. He has surprisingly warm eyes and a mobile mouth, he is unfailingly courteous, he listens to my weak objections and Mary's Derry rants with equal sufferance. But he is never touched; nothing has been destroyed irrevocably, he insists. The mines still have a future. "The logic is blindingly obvious," Arthur says. "In the attempt to break the miners' union, various alternatives have been tried: nuclear power, North Sea gas and oil, imported coal, even open-cast mining. All have failed. They are uneconomic, they are anti-social, they are unnecessary. And politically they are so short-sighted that they may be termed stupid."

And so on, and so forth. As the measured sentences unfurl, I try to picture his life away from the podium. I know he lives in Worsborough, a nearby pit village, in a house with a goldfish pond in the garden; and he has a daughter, Margaret, who is a GP. After he stopped mining, he used to keep himself fit with judo, became a green belt, but his back gave out. Now he has two schnauzers called Chloe and Che, who weigh eighteen stone between them, and he walks them four miles each morning. He goes to bed at two a.m. and rises at six-thirty. Sometimes he watches TV. *Inspector Morse* is a favourite, and he also enjoyed *The Two Ronnies,* though he reads the papers while the set is on. For the rest, the private Scargill is a blank.

Occasionally, there have been distant rumours of discord—a story that he blocked his daughter's marriage because he didn't think her intended was good enough, for instance. "People don't realise what a terrible snob he is," the rejected suitor told the press. A nice backhander, that. But there seems little point in raising the matter. "I never speak about my family. I think it is proper that I should not do so," Scargill's on record as saying. So I try him on Tony Blair, but this goes nowhere, too. The only facet of Low Tone he thinks worth mentioning is that once, when Blair was a young MP, they shared a stage, and Blair said it was one of the proudest moments of his life.

The more that Scargill runs rings around me, the more I'm dazzled by his footwork. The casual scorn with which he greets my arguments remind me of Mr. Schneider, an actor-manager in Los Angeles, who used to grace a tiny theatre off Sunset Strip. The first time I was in Hollywood, he was performing an hour-long distillation of Coriolanus, with himself in the title role and a total cast of three. The other two, having done their various bits as Volumnia and Virgilia and Menenius Agrippa, also had to play the mob. At the climax, they set on Coriolanus with rough and violent words, but the great general would not be cowed. "Do you think with your puny breaths to put out the mighty fires of Rome?" he demanded with a shrug. "Don't make me laugh. . . ."

Compared to Arthur Scargill, Mr. Schneider was humility itself. "It stands to reason," Scargill says. Hope, belief, a future bright with promise—it's as if the country we have travelled through, and all the people we've been talking to, have magically ceased to exist. South Yorks is not maimed, merely resting. The final victory is yet to come.

From the depths of the sofa, I hear Mary protest. "Look on the streets out there," she begins. But what's the point? Scargill does not go on streets. He may drive them in his Granada Scorpio K-registration, on his £20-a-week fuel subsidy, or view them from the back of a taxi, but his walking is done across green fields, with Chloe and Che at his heels.

By the time he ushers us out, his victory is absolute. "I'll make the tea this time," he tells his secretary, to show he's still a common man at root, whatever the cut of his shirt. The secretary looks as dubious as if he'd promised to make gold. "Kettle's in the sink," she mutters. But King Arthur requires no clues. "I will find it myself," he tells her airily.

Afterwards, we trundle downhill to the car park and Teal Wheels. Slung out into the fug and stale-beer sourness of Barnsley on a thundery, airless afternoon, it's as if we've been banished from the garden. Suddenly, in place of rectitude and infallibility, we're back in a land of chaos—dirt, stink and gridlock. A man in torn clothes comes reeling towards us, shouting words I can't make out. Somewhere behind us, a car backfires, and we wheel like scattered pigeons, looking back up the hill.

The Victorian brick splendour of the NUM headquarters, turreted, impregnable, stands clear against the sky. Not exactly Camelot, I think. More like Scargill World.

SOME BOYS WERE playing football in Bradford. That much is agreed, but little else. A few Asian teenagers were kicking a football up against a row of blue-painted garage doors in a cul-de-sac near Oak Lane. It was about nine on Friday evening, and the boys were simply boys, playing in the street. Or else they were delinquents kicking up a racket, causing a disturbance. At any rate, a neighbour complained to the police, and a squad car arrived. Of the two officers inside, one was known locally as Steroid Man. On the street he had a reputation as a virulent racist, given to irrational rages, but his superiors denied this. There were, they said, no racists on the Bradford force.

When the policemen broke up the football game, they were firm but fair. Or they were gratuitously abusive. One of the Asian boys, Shahid Majid, aimed a kick at the squad car. Or he did no such thing. Then the squad car ran over his foot.

According to *Trends*, a Muslim magazine, "the two policemen got out of the car and, with intense amusement at what they had done, began laughing, eyewitnesses said. They began harassing the youth and, whilst his foot was still caught under their car, they decided to arrest him." But another eyewitness, a white photographer, saw it differently. His first impression was simply of din and confusion, a patternless milling, and two teenagers being dragged across the pavement and bundled inside the squad car.

All of this was happening in the heart of Manningham, which is ninety per cent Asian, and by now a crowd had gathered. Women were pouring out of their houses, screaming and trying to intervene. More squad cars were called in. Some say fifteen cars appeared, others two. Police swarmed the street in body armour, brandishing their chain batons and yelling at the Asians to get back in their houses. Or they were models of restraint. One unleashed a guard dog, which tangled with a youth named Hafeez Bashir. Bashir's injuries sent him to Accident and Emergency. "He will be permanently scarred and may have to have plastic surgery," *Trends* reported. Or he was unharmed.

A youth named Imran Masjid, meanwhile, passing on his way to pray *salat-ul-malgrib* at a nearby mosque, had paused to protest at the police aggression and was promptly arrested as well. Another youth, Javed Iqbal, ran into his house to escape. Officers followed him; there was a struggle. Iqbal's sister, who was carrying her eight-month-old daughter, had her dress ripped, and the baby was struck. Or the dress was torn accidently, and the baby was merely scared by the commotion.

At last the prisoners, four in all, were gathered up and removed to Lawcroft House, the new police station at the top of Oak Lane. This station was designed as a fortress, impregnable. Its stark and windowless bulk hung over Manningham like a boast of strength. Some 20,000 Asians lived under its walls, most of them Kashmiri Muslims.

About sixty of these now gathered outside the citadel, clamouring for the boys' release. Street youths mixed with community leaders; there were chants and impassioned speeches. Scuffles broke out, and five more arrests were made.

Among those detained was a teacher, Mahommed Taj. A round-faced young man in glasses, he'd always been a peacemaker. Or he was a firebrand, a militant troublemaker. "The police told him not to interfere, pushing him to the ground," said *Trends*. "They then proceeded to arrest him, handcuffing him so tightly that his circulation slowed and his hands turned blue." Or he was merely persuaded to cease and desist. Outside the station, the cry of *Taj, Taj, Taj* spread through the crowd. Fires were set on Oak Lane, and four Asian city councillors entered Lawcroft House to negotiate. The police were persuaded to let five prisoners go. Or they agreed to release all nine. Or no such bargain was ever struck.

Shop windows on Oak Lane were smashed and cars set afire. The chanting and speeches went on all night. Only at first light did the crowd begin to disperse. Sullen but passive, the Asians drifted back to their homes. Their rage had played itself out. Or the trouble was just beginning.

It proved to be the latter. Throughout Saturday, Asian leaders negotiated with the police, but the charges against the nine were not dropped, and by evening patience was exhausted. Older heads in Manningham still pleaded for restraint; some form of peaceful demonstration. But the street youths were no longer listening. Unlike the first night, the TV cameras and the national press were on hand. So were carloads of outsiders, ferried in from Dewsbury and Doncaster, Manchester, even Birmingham. Everything was set fair for riot and the youths obliged. They swept through Manningham towards the city centre. A helicopter circled overhead and the police set up barricades. But they did not attempt to intervene, though petrol bombs were thrown, and more cars torched, and hundreds of shop windows shattered.

Most of the businesses that suffered were white-owned—Morrison's Supermarket, Barclay's Bank, Appleyard's Citroëns—but not all. A number of Indian and Bangladeshi stores were attacked, as well as a couple of Kashmiri restaurants. Total damage was estimated at a million pounds and three of the police suffered minor injuries.

On TV and in the press, this played as a holocaust. But the truth, according to onlookers, was less bloodcurdling. Even when the rampage was at its most furious, crowds of sightseers assembled, competing for the best vantage points. At the foot of Oak Lane, on the terrace of the Cartwright Hotel, drinkers raised their pints as the gangs swept by. This might have been a riot, but it was also a spectacle.

TWO IMAGES have dominated the press coverage. One is a picture of an Asian youth, his face fanatical with hatred, in the instant after heaving a brick at some unseen cops; the other is of Oak Lane in the aftermath, littered with refuse and guttering fires. So I arrive in Bradford, the city of J. B. Priestley and Delius, expecting a burnt-out ghetto. And find myself in a strange land.

First of all, there are the smells. Curries simmering, whiffs of cardamon and ginger wafting out of corner shops, and an odd, brackish scent I can't identify, a sweet-sour tang that clings to my hair and skin. When I sniff my own hands, I feel I've left England behind.

The physical setting is extraordinary in itself. Oak Lane, like much of Bradford, is built on a semi-precipice. At its foot, behind ornate wrought-iron gates, is a park full of formal flower gardens, surrounded by Victorian homes. Farther up, stateliness gives way to rows of huddled terraces, back-to-backs intercut by cobblestone alleys; while right at the top, opposite Fort Lawcroft, is the Lister Mill, a monumental structure with a 250-foot chimney done up as an Italian Renaissance *campanile*.

To stroll through the side streets in the freak heat wave that grips Yorkshire all week is to walk two cultures at once. The houses are archetypal Northern working class, squat and black with grime, each with a little concrete yard in back, where washing hangs on the lines. But the washing in question consists of long tops and baggy trousers, and children's bright orange bodysuits, vividly embroidered at the throat and cuffs. Through open doorways I glimpse veiled women and men in white smocks, their long beards fierce under round white caps. Garish pictures of Mecca overhang the TV sets, and the peeling walls are covered with inscriptions from the Quran.

Here is poverty, no question, but few signs of third-world squalor, and still less of defeat. The streets are clean, no broken glass underfoot, and many patches of pavement have been newly swept and scrubbed. There are roses round some of the doorways, geraniums in flower-pots. The sense of communal pride is all-pervasive.

That pride is clearly the key to much that had happened here. From Oak Lane, I make my way to Lumb Lane; *notorious* Lumb Lane, the tabloids call it, as if it's an off-shoot of King's Cross. This is the strip where the city's prostitutes have always worked, where the Yorkshire Ripper prowled and where, in the weeks and months before the riots, Muslim residents lashed out. Sick of finding used condoms and hypos in their front gardens, and even sicker of hearing the police saying they could do nothing to clean things up, they took matters into their own hands. Fathers and sons set up pickets and started shadowing the hookers wherever they moved. For the elders, the major issue was moving trade away from the three mosques and five schools nearby. But some of the youths went further. Prostitutes complained of being sworn at, jostled and worse. One of the girls claimed to have been set on by a gang of eight, two of whom twisted a length of steel wire around her throat while another slashed at her face and hands with a machete. In retaliation, a pimp pulled a shotgun. There were reports that Muslim graves had been desecrated. Then Ricki's Café, where prostitutes gathered, was firebombed. After that, the girls moved on.

Most of them have relocated in an industrial wasteland far away from the pickets, but also from their clientele. Business is so desperate, I hear, that one or two diehards still prefer to risk Lumb Lane. But none are in view when I walk the strip, late on this broiling afternoon.

The Lane is a microcosm of Bradford's history. I pass a fine Victorian square and the looming mass of Drummond's Mill. A few elegant terraced houses, built of mill-stone grit, are interspersed with burnt-out shops, council houses, patches of scrub. Many of the stores and pubs have their windows boarded up, an aftermath of the riots.

I seek shelter from the heat in a corner pub. The only other drinker is Asian, supping deep on a pint of best bit-ter. A gangling scrawn of a man, with his Western clothes hanging off his bones like bunting, he has a twist to one corner of his upper lip. At first I think he's affecting an Elvis-style sneer, but it's simply a scar. "Went through a windscreen," he explains. His accent is hard Yorkshire, flat as flat. "Bloody daft I am."

He seems happy to chat, but wary of being pinned down, in case his family and peers don't like what he says. "You can't give my name," he says. Yet total anonymity doesn't satisfy him either. "Well, you could call me Ish-tiaq," he decides at last. "That way I'll know who I am."

I ask him about Manningham. "That's a long story, is that," says Ishtiaq. So I buy him another pint, and a packet of crisps. Salt and vinegar. "I'm addicted to them buggers, I am," he says.

It all started in the fifties, he says. Bradford was still a wool town, as it always had been. Worstedopolis, they used to call it, the biggest wool town in the world. But the trade was going down, other countries had started to take over. To compete, the Bradford mills had to bring in new machinery. And to make that new machinery cost-effective, they needed to work extra shifts. Women couldn't work night shifts by law, and white men wouldn't. So the mills had to find cheap labour else-where. The cheapest possible. And they had the notion of looking in Pakistan. In Kashmir, to be exact; in the Mir-pur area, which was dirt poor. The lowest wage in England, by comparison, seemed like a fortune. So the mills brought a few men over, gave them a trial. Then a few more, and then a floodtide.

At first the men thought they were in England for a few years, just long enough to get rich. To save money, they

lived in group houses, fifteen and twenty to a small terraced kip, eating, sleeping and working in shifts. There
were no Asian shops or cafés, only work. The biggest
diversion was to have their photograph taken, holding
some symbol of Western affluence—a radio, say, or just a
fistful of banknotes—and send the picture back to Mirpur.

In reality, they weren't doing well at all. The more
hours they put in at the mills, the further away their freedom seemed. By the middle sixties, they started to realise
that Plan A wasn't working. So they sent for their wives
and children, and settled in for the long haul.

Bradford liked them then. They still had novelty value,
they weren't yet a threat. Ishtiaq himself arrived in '66,
when he was five, and he can remember white women
giving him sweets, petting him in the street. But that
didn't last long. The city was going through a terminal
slump. The wool trade was dying, cheap Asian labour or
not. Workers were being laid off in droves, white and
black alike. Worstedopolis was done for and Pakistanis
became the scapegoats.

The first time that Ishtiaq got beaten up after school,
he was eight. *Your mother fucks dogs,* they said. Asians
weren't strangers any more, but intruders. "Aliens," says
Ishtiaq. "A bunch of bloody gatecrashers."

His own father never understood this. Just couldn't get
it. And most of that first generation was the same. They'd
grown up with this set picture of England as being so
strong and fair, Rule Britannia and all that kind of thing,
and they couldn't shake it. They thought the problem
must be something in themselves. So they never fought
back. But Ishtiaq, and the other people his age, they
weren't so easy. If they were exploited at work, they
responded in kind. "My best mate out of school, his first
job, he went to work on a building site," says Ishtiaq.
"The foreman called him a black bastard, so my mate
knocked him kicking. And there you had it—racial harmony."

Bit by bit, the Asians won concessions. Grudgingly,

they were given jobs on public transport, in local government, in schools. Then they got into politics. By the eighties, there were Asian councillors, even an Asian mayor. Bradford built a reputation for successful race relations. It was called a blueprint for a multiracial England.

"Window-dressing, that's all," Ishtiaq says. A few Asians had got rich, and a few more almost famous. For the great majority, though, the reality was lousy living conditions, broken-down schools, no jobs. Plus, the racism was getting worse. In these same eighties that were meant to be so harmonious, Paki-bashing became a sport of choice. The National Front had a stronghold in north Bradford, and even when they were driven out, council-estate thugs remained. There were III attacks on Asians in one year alone, seventy-nine in just three months. The favourite tactic was to call a taxi to some remote spot, then jump the driver and pulp him.

From time to time, some hint of trouble reached the national press. But any sympathy the Asians might have won was wiped out by the public burnings of *The Satanic Verses* by Muslim fundamentalists. "That were the killer. We never got over that," says Ishtiaq, and he polishes off the last of his crisps, bursts the plastic bag.

Worse than all the bad publicity, or even the Paki-bashing, has been the creeping paralysis. Overall unemployment in Bradford runs at eighteen per cent; for young Asians it's almost sixty per cent. For most school-leavers, there's nowhere to go but the mosque, and nothing to do but fester.

Ishtiaq doesn't approve of the rioting. Bad behaviour can't be condoned. But he can understand the rage. The youths involved are the third generation. The first was passive, and the second, Ishtiaq's own, believed in peaceful protest. But these kids look at their fathers, or at someone like himself, who worked fifteen years on the buses, then got chucked on the scrap heap, and they think *No, not us, we're not falling for that.* So either they go backwards into

Muslim fundamentalism, or they just cut their losses. Hang out on the streets, do drugs, break into cars, whatever: "Fuck up for the sake of fucking up," says Ishtiaq, and he starts to say something more. But there seems nothing left, he's said his full piece, so he just sighs and orders another packet of crisps. "Bloody addicted I am," he says again, his lip twisting in that false sneer. "Bloody mad."

I've been studying a brochure called *Brilliant Bradford,* a ripe piece of boosterism. "Ten years ago, the City of Bradford and the townships along the Aire Valley through to Keighley were on the verge of becoming an industrial wasteland," the text begins. "Today the District is a thriving metropolis of successful businesses and new initiatives, planning for the future."

So far the Bradford Breakthrough, as it calls itself, has gone widely unrecognised. In the early nineties, a survey rated Bradford the worst place to live in England, and the insult was nothing new. Even J. B. Priestley, perhaps its most celebrated son, looked at the city askance. "The dark ugly place," he called it, though he loved it anyway. "What it has not got, either in its people or its stones, is charm—not a glimmer of it."

That verdict baffles me. Priestley's Bradford, of course, was a mill town, full of belching chimneys and soot. But the city I travel is full of grace. A barbaric town planner in the early sixties razed much of its late-Victorian architecture and replaced it with jerry-built crap, yet enough survives to convey a sense of former glories. The public buildings are superbly overwrought, all pilasters and balustrades, gargoyles and turrets. Then there's the Alhambra Theatre, an *Arabian Nights* fantasia, with its silhouette etched in lightbulbs; and St. George's Hall, still featuring the likes of the Syd Lawrence Orchestra in "Moonlight Serenade." True, they're hemmed in by Burger Kings and Pizza Huts, but the city still has a swagger, a sense of pomp and mighty weight of stone.

As for Manningham itself, I'm warned repeatedly that it's a no-go area after dark, but my experience fails to bear this out. I take leisurely strolls at ten, at eleven, even after midnight, and never encounter anything more threatening than a stray cat or a couple of schoolboys, lounging under a lamp-post, who ask me for a light. One night, on Lumb Lane, I pass a lone prostitute, with not a picket in sight. Fat knees and a microskirt, a ratty blonde wig. Even she declines to harass me.

A spot of bother might come in handy; at least it would be contact. As it is, I know no one in the Asian community, and I can't seem to bridge the gap. Passersby on the street are open to idle chatter, but the moment I try to probe deeper, the shutters go up. And why wouldn't they? After a glut of tabloid headlines like *Flame Mobs Battle Police*, a certain wariness is to be expected.

The breakthrough comes by accident. Discarded in a litter bin along Carlisle Road, I find a copy of a Muslim magazine and carry it away. Within minutes, catching sight of its cover in my hand, youths begin to approach me. Am I a Muslim myself? No, I say, just interested. And that's all it takes. I am invited into homes, given cups of tea. Fathers and grandfathers sit me down, and tell me their stories. The basic narratives echo Ishtiaq's account, but the emphasis varies with the teller. Some believe that England betrayed them, some blame the youth gangs. Some think the answer lies in a return to stricter Islamic discipline, while others talk up the need for assimilation. The only theory that nobody seconds is the police version.

In the aftermath of the riots, the Assistant Chief Constable of West Yorkshire blamed them on generic teen angst. "I see a community tearing itself apart," he pronounced. "The youth seem to be rising up as much against society and elders as against the police."

In his view, the youths, being Bradford-born, no longer feel a part of Muslim traditions. But this turns out to be nonsense. I watch Asian boys rushing home from school, doing their ablutions, then heading straight out to the mosque. If anything, the swing is towards militance. Every morning I see HAMAS chalked on walls, though they're always scrubbed clean by night.

Aurangzeb Iqbal, the lawyer for the first two boys arrested, says that even the street gangs remain devout. "I've had lads up for multiple murders that still had to fast for Ramadan," he tells me. A breezy, buttonholing sort, Iqbal has raised eyebrows with the giant billboard he's put at the Bradford City football ground. KAMA SUTRA–WE GET YOU OUT OF DIFFICULT POSITIONS, it reads, and that sums up his style. He invites me to his annual barbecue for his clients, held in the car park beside his office. A DJ plays ragga, not bhangra, while the clients in question stand around in huddled groups, wolfing down kebabs and samosas. "I just got out fooking yesterday. Fooking screw took my Quran," says one. "I'll fooking kill him when I get back in."

The car park is full of men laughing and eating, men bragging, men feeling good. And the women? They're all back at home, safely confined. Every time I enter a Muslim household, young girls are immediately shooed out of sight. The older women, meanwhile, bring me tea and cakes, clear space for me to sit, but never meet my eye. I am a stranger; to look on me isn't permitted.

Many young women are less complaisant. In particular, there's a growing resistance to arranged marriages. Aurangzeb Iqbal has written a poem about it from the male angle: "I told them in no uncertain terms / That the idea of arranged marriages gives me the worms." But it is women who risk vengeance. The same week I'm in Bradford, the body of one such bride, heavily pregnant, is found just over the Lancashire border. Her dismembered head and sundry other body parts have been incinerated. She had tried to run away from her chosen husband.

In Lister Park, I come upon five Asian schoolgirls, scarfed and veiled, in full shalwar-kameez. Though they giggle a lot when I speak to them, they don't hesitate to give opinions. Most of the boys in the riots, they say, were just showing off for the TV cameras. "It wasn't serious politics," says one. But they themselves, they're serious. When they finish school, they are going on to Bradford University. Get an education, qualifications— that's the way to bring real change. Of course, their parents don't agree. Girls aren't meant to make waves. So what's the better way? To burn down the world, or to make yourself free through knowledge?

LISTER PARK is also the site of the Mela, the annual two-day Asian festival. There was talk of scrapping it this year, but sanity prevailed, and the fiesta goes off as planned.

J. B. Priestley grew up listening to brass bands on Sunday afternoons here. "There the youth . . . congregated densely, some of the lads and girls parked along the rails, looking down the blue haze of smoke and catching what came to them of Coppelia or 'Les Deux Pigeons,'" he wrote. The order of this weekend, however, is tablas and sitars, bejewelled native dancers, bhangra at night.

The crowd on Saturday is watchful. Whispers that the National Front is planning a raid have been going the rounds, but the day passes off without a hitch. Asians and whites move peaceably through the fair in their separate groups. Though few interact, they seem content to share the same funfair rides, sprawl on the same lawns. At one moment, a white boy appears hand-in-hand with an Asian girl. Muslim youths nearby begin to glare and mutter; one picks up a fistful of gravel. Then the lovers have passed, and the moment is gone.

That evening, the bhangra group Golden Star performs before a hillside filled with Muslims of every age. Though the beats are apocalyptic, the lyrics often angry, the crowd's mood is beatific. While teens dance in front of the stage, white-bearded patriarchs hold their grandchildren up to see, and dreaming women lay out feasts for their families.

At dusk I wander out of the park. Across the road is a pub called the Spotted House; inside, a band is playing country music. Half the crowd wear cowboy hats, line dancing in formation to "Stand By Your Man," and I sit down on a bench outside. As I sip my pint, a whip-thin man sporting a black stetson, chaps and a bandolier filled with silver bullets emerges from the bar for a breath of air. Hearing the bhangra drifting down from the park, and watching the dancers in their bright robes, he sucks his teeth. "What a fooking shower," he says, and ducks back indoors.

I turn down a side street towards the canal. From across the road come sounds of arythmic thumping, and I look to see what it is. Some boys are playing football.

JOY RIDING 2

Now the whirl spins us faster and faster. Almost every day brings another town, a new combustion.

EVERY NIGHT A RIOT!

That's what the poster on the Gazza Strip says, anyhow, and it isn't far from the literal truth. The Newcastle streets are bedlam, the whole city about to implode. Every bar in Bigg Market is crammed with half-naked flesh—thousands of young bodies crushed together, hot, drunk and dripping, so tightly intertwined that they seem one mass fuck.

It's thirty-five years since I lived here, fresh off the boat from Derry, and twenty since my last visit. The city I knew then was a stern Northern fastness: hard-working, thrifty; above all, dark. As soon as daylight faded, it was as if a blackout had descended, and you groped your way through the gloom, seeking rebel points of light. To walk on the wild side meant the Club A'Go-Go, the Downbeat, the New Orleans. Beyond those, the only game in town was the all-night waiting room at Central Station.

Even so, I loved it here. There was a hardness, a strength, that shot me up with pure adrenaline. I was a mamma's boy when I arrived here, trained to tremble at the unknown. It was Newcastle that taught me to embrace the dark.

My memories of my years here, fifteen through seventeen, are now split cleanly in two. On one side sits the formal remembrance, factual but without resonance. There was a house, a park, a school around the corner, a blazer with a badge on it. The school song had a Latin title, "Fortiter Defendit." My English teacher, who was nicknamed Birdman, called James Joyce a distempered Gael. I wrote a short story for the school mag, but it was turned down. My balls ached a lot.

And then there was the night. I was in love with Elvis, and also with John Coltrane. Rock & Roll brought me to the Mecca on Friday nights, and to a girl called Tonya, who had bright orange lipstick, slathered on thick as cream. When "Blue Velvet" played, the Mecca lights turned blue to match, and Tonya whispered, "Swoon me." One night, we were fumbling each other out by the toilets when a Rocker in full leathers came out of the Gents and, without breaking stride or saying a word, nutted me square between the eyes. I went down as though shot and assumed the foetal position, waiting to be nursed. But Tonya was long gone. Took off with the leather boy, and left me to bleed.

Coltrane, by those standards, was civilisation. There was an evening class in jazz history, taught by first one and then another local trumpeter, and I became their nemesis, forever comparing Thelonious Monk solos to haikus. Instead of strangling me, however, the trumpeters took me drinking. Smuggled me in underage to the Percy Arms and got me rat-arsed on Vaux. Left me free passes to their gigs, and sometimes sloppy seconds. Rather than orange lipstick, the girls round them had long blonde hair and high cheekbones, and liked to see themselves as Tyneside Jeanne Moreaus. One of them, letting me down gently, said she slept only with musicians, so I bought a tenor sax and shut myself up in a basement. After four months, I could manage the theme of "Goodbye Pork Pie Hat," but Jeanne Moreau was not impressed.

I roamed the night city, trying to connect up the dots of light—a leather pub in Gateshead, a boxers' pub in Byker, a tarts' pub off the Scotswood Road—into a coherent cosmology. Self-conscious myself, I worshipped abandon in others. And Newcastle, against all probabilities, turned out to be full of the stuff. The city's bleak surfaces hid all manner of chameleons and inspired excessives: Eric Burdon transforming himself into a Mississippi sharecropper; a lady named Gala who swallowed flames in the nude; and the raddled old queen, met late one boozy night at Central Station, who claimed to have been raped by Winston Churchill.

"Winnie the Poof," the old queen called him, and showed me, wrapped up in a white lace handkerchief, the tarnished half-crown he claimed had been his hush money.

For me, this was a secret city. There were the public streets, four-square and massive, aggressively masculine. And then there was the hidden: the jigsaw of chares and alleys and precipice drops that cobwebbed the docks and the hillside above them, with half a dozen bridges flung across the top like a steel comb-over. There was a derelict eighteenth-century church with an overgrown graveyard, where I used to lurk on gale-force winter Sundays and stare down at the morning market alongside the Tyne. Shipyards and tankers and cranes thronged the river upstream; the clothing stalls in the market far below were like so many splashes of paint, red and sky blue and gold. When I rolled on to my back, the Tyne Bridge soared above me, with the great vault of its girders, a pure leap into space.

Clubs seemed like bunkers then. The Downbeat was a stark room at the top of an abandoned warehouse, the A'Go-Go stuck down a cul-de-sac, the New Orleans a rotting tooth in a razed street. Jazz and the blues were a code, and nightlife an underworld—not criminal, exactly, but seductively outlaw. A girl I knew started writing a satirical gothic-dreadful, set around the Downbeat. I still recall the last sentence of the opening chapter: "Of the godless scenes that prevailed," it read, "the terrified burghers dared speak only in whispers . . ."

No USE to whisper now. It would take a sonic boom to cause a ripple along the docks, never mind in Bigg Market. The noise level inside the pubs is industrial strength, a relentless clubland pounding, so heavy on the bass that you can feel the shock waves in your shins. The bodies move in tidal waves, surging from one bar to the next, five minutes per drink, then on. The girls are decked out in Wonderbras, and skirts the size of pocket handkerchiefs. One sports a long blond hairpiece hung with plastic cocks.

Overdressed, Mary and I take shelter down a side-alley, in the George. The drinkers here are an older set, ripe and raucous by any normal standards, but mere mumblers in this context. The music machine is playing Mariah Carey, not Prodigy, and the men at the next table beg Mary's pardon each time a four-letter word escapes. "You'll have to excuse us," says one, who seems to dominate. "We're filthy swine."

He's monumental, this man. Nineteen stone, at a guess: swag-bellied in middle age but still a mighty machine, barrel-chested and bull-necked, thighs so massive he has to sit spread-legged, an arse that swallows up his whole chair.

Beyond simple heft, he also exudes star presence. Everything about him has gusto—his deep laugh, his big-jawed grin, his head of jet-black hair and the juicy way that words roll on his tongue, deeply savoured. "Nae worries," he keeps saying, rocking back on his seat. At every move, the seams strain under his armpits, across those prodigious thighs.

When the man goes to take a leak, I ask his companions who he is. "Why, that's Billy Wright, man," one answers, incredulous that I'd need to be told. "Best centre-forward Whitley Bay ever had."

"Hardest, too," another adds. "A one-man wrecking crew. Rocket shot, a granite head and lethal-weapon elbows."

"He was a legend on Tyneside, Billy Wright."

"Still is, man. Still is."

When Wright returns, we get into conversation. In spite of his size and lurid repute, the legend appears affable. "You're not a goalkeeper," he explains. Besides, his skull-crushing years are long over. He's fifty-four, his knees are shot, and he is almost six stone over his playing weight. These days he drives a taxi.

I tell him about the economic Newcastle I knew, and how greatly changed it seems. "Changed? It's a different city," he says. "You might as well have dropped down in Timbuktu."

I ask about the economic boom. "What boom?" he says. "They tore down half the town. If I drove you through the old working areas like Byker, round where I was born, you'd hardly find a street standing. All the ter-raced housing, gone; the little pubs, the corner shops, the local businesses, gone as well. And the industry with them, mind." The shipyards are finished. No more Swan Hunter, no more Parsons. Vickers Armstrong is still keep-ing going, just barely, on government support. "But look at the Tyne, man. Where's the smoke today? The cranes, and the dry docks, and the ships getting built? There's hardly a trace."

Even so, the Toon is jumping. One survey has placed it tenth among the planet's top entertainment centres, right up there with Amsterdam and New Orleans. How come? "Search me," says Wright. "There's no work to be found here; not a hope. I have two grown sons, both of them bright lads, but they couldn't raise a ripple, so they had to emigrate. One of them's in Australia now, the other in Japan. When they come back to visit, all they can do is shake their heads."

Newcastle, from where he sits, is two towns in one: the old working-class city, now on its deathbed; and the new party model, unrooted, wild to spend. In place of heavy industry, Tyneside has become a Mecca for the service trades: German microchips, Korean clothing, Japanese cars, American fast-food restaurants. The new workforce—university-educated, computer-literate—is an alien breed. "The nights when I'm driving my taxi, making pickups from the flash clubs and casinos, I hardly hear a Geordie voice."

A mass madness has hit the city. It's as though the

words Boom Toon have crept into the communal psyche and driven out all sanity. Not only among the feckless young, but in every age group, at every social level. The Metro-Centre, the mammoth shopping complex across the river in Durham, is thronged with rampaging house-wives, running up their credit cards. "I see them coming home, man. The pavements are piled high with junk, stuff they'll never use in a hundred years. And meantime their old man's out of work, permanent, and the car's repossessed, and the kids are living on frozen chips. The world's coming down round their ears, and they buy themselves a wine basket."

Walk up Bigg Market, and the money is literally thrown about. Fat, sodden wads of banknotes, fives and tens and even twenties, flying back and forth above the bars. They can't all derive from thieving, and the dole wouldn't last two nights at this pace. Unemployment on Tyneside is running at twenty per cent, and that's just the official figure; the true number is probably double that. "But every bugger keeps spending, just the same," says Wright. Fetching in a fresh round, he sups, and puzzles, and sups some more. "Where do they find the readies?" A baffled silence settles about the table; Wright scratches at his massive thighs. "Who holds the key to the golden door?" somebody demands, quoting an old line from a quiz show. But no one has an answer.

THE FOLLOWING morning, Wright takes me riding in his cab. We circuit the East End, his old stomping ground. His father was a driller in the shipyards, and he himself worked on the 180-foot cranes at Swan Hunter. When he started playing serious football, he'd clock into work at seven each morning, work through till four-forty, then run home without a shower, grab up his playing gear, dash down to Wallsend Station and jump on the five o'clock train to practice.

There were no showers at Swan's in the early sixties,

and only one toilet for a hundred men. "If you didn't like it, out you went." But there was always another job to be found. "Any lad that was able-bodied, he had nae worries then."

For most of his football career, he was semi-pro, paid by the match. He was almost signed by Wolves once, but his knees were bad, even then, and he failed the fitness test. So he played 330 games for Whitley Bay, five pounds a match, and then moved on to Ashington, where they paid him eight pounds, and on Sunday mornings he turned out for Bird's Nest Social Club. By the time he was done, he'd scored over five hundred goals. Within his own world, he was king. He could walk into any pub or working men's club on Tyneside, any dance hall or drinking party, and everything stopped. "Local hero," one of his mates had said last night at the George. "That phrase was invented for Billy Wright."

His pomp was less than thirty years ago, but it belongs to a vanished world. He talks of railroading on the back of trams, delivering the morning papers down to the Quays. Or, in his earliest remembrance, slicing off his fingertips, aged three, having caught them in sharp metal grating, and then sitting in the kitchen, with his hand bandaged and a blanket round him, warming at the steel fire in the centre of the room, waiting for his mother to come in from work. "The neighbours took care of us, like. 'Course, people still had neighbours then."

Not any more. The areas we drive through—Wallsend, North Shields, Tynemouth—have all been laid waste. We scour the streets he grew up in, searching for relics, but none survive. Then we stand on a disused wharf, looking up and down the river. A few cranes, standing idle, are the only traces left of the dense steel skyline I knew, and hardly a boat moves on the water. "Memory's a mug's game," Wright says. There is not false sentiment in him, just a recognition of things past. "It's all water under the crapper, anyhow," he says. So we head back towards Bigg Market, and EVERY NIGHT A RIOT!

Yes We Have No

. . .

THE LONGER we stay in Newcastle, the worse we're flum-
moxed by its contradictions. We stroll the city centre,
handsome as ever. The smooth façades of Granger and
Grey streets, sand-blasted, are the colour of clotted cream
on sunlit mornings, a faint rosy pink at dusk. Their
glassed arcades are full of high-priced boutiques and
designer kitsch. Then we cruise the Scotswood Road, a
mile away. The side streets are rubbish dumps, piled with
scrap metal and rotting floorboards. Those terraced
houses that aren't bricked up have parts of their roofs
missing, collapsing walls and steel cages round the letter
boxes, to guard against explosives.

In North Shields, I take a walk round Meadowell Estate
with a sixteen-year-old called Lee. There were riots here, a
few years back. I ask Lee what caused them. "Shite life,"
he says.

I've met him in the offices of a community magazine
called *NE29,* which runs features on the United Kingdom
of Punk and how to use drugs safely. It shares premises
with the local police station in a steel-doored, red-brick
building like an army fort in a western, stuck on a patch
of scrubland, with stray litter and tumbleweeds flapping
idly at its walls.

Pasty and round-faced, with remnants of puppy fat,
Lee does drawings for the mag and uses its offices as a second home. His father lost an arm in a work accident, took
the compensation money and ran. His mother's new
boyfriend beat him up. There was a quarrel and the
boyfriend bombed the house. His five-year-old sister was
abused. A baby brother perished of cot-death syndrome.
After the bombing, Lee went to live with his granny and
two aunts. One of the aunts was getting such bad beatings, she almost died. When Lee told his mother, the aunt
threw him out. At ten, he was in foster homes. With two
other lads, he stole a car. *Confiscated a motor vehicle,* he
calls it. The foster home threw him out. He was put into
care. There was a fight with the man in the house. He was

punched and kicked in the throat, the guts and the groin. The woman in the house threw him out. He was dispatched to special school. He committed an assault, and then he threatened to burn the school down. The school threw him out. So he was put into another home. The woman in the house was an alcoholic. She got so drunk, she kept injuring herself. Lee informed the authorities. The authorities threw him out.

His voice is dispassionate. It's as though he's speaking of someone else. "This was acceptable," he says of one foster-parental beating that landed him in hospital. "I was a cheeky little fuck."

Walking me round Meadowell, he points out the landmarks from the riot in a tour guide's flat singsong: the stoning, the burning, the cars overturned. The houses are standard grey semi-detacheds, some abandoned, many more half-empty. I ask about unemployment. "That's all there is," Lee says. Yet almost half the boys playing in the streets are wearing Newcastle United shirts, black-and-white magpie stripes, at £40 a time. A sign on a wall reads WE HAVE LICENSE TO FART.

As we finish the tour, we see Mary waiting by Teal Wheels. "Is she your girlfriend?" Lee asks, then answers his own question. "Nae way," he says. "She's more important than that."

He wants to develop his drawing skills, work in computer graphics. There are good people at NE29; they help keep him straight, out of trouble. He's been on an Outward Bound course, and on sponsored trips to Germany, Finland, Russia. "I've got a bit of anger in me," he says, still blank-voiced. "I get depressed, and I need a boost. But I still have a prayer." In the long run, he hopes to end up in the army, on a fighting line. Combat will help channel his aggression, he feels. "In the army, when you kill someone, it's legal," he says. "That's your job."

WE TALK TO laid-off shipyard workers, to construction workers, to social workers, we even talk to an ex–Tory councillor, and all of them paint a similar picture. No jobs, no money, no future. Yet the nightly carnival never slackens, and it's all paid for in hard cash.

The workers in the German microchip factories and Japanese computer firms do their spending down the great plunging Georgian sweep of Grey Street, in the upscale restaurants and supper clubs of the Quayside. This is the land of Dolce & Gabbana. BMWs and Mercedes sit double-parked outside cocktail bars, and flighty young things in little black dresses go teetering along the cobblestones under the Tyne Bridge. Across the river, on a converted cruiser, the lights of a disco make dazzles and starbursts in the night.

I walk the docksides and chares, once the heart of my secret city, in a daze. I knew a woman who rented a room down here, a few yards up the street from the candlelit bistro that now features Pacific-rim cuisine and rocket salads. She introduced me to Jack Kerouac and marijuana, and we'd sprawl across the mattress by her window, looking out at the empty streets and the tramp steamers passing on the river. There was one rough-trade sailor's pub round the corner, and a restaurant that specialised in gammon with pineapple slices, and a few forlorn tarts in doorways. Otherwise, the area was so deserted, you could hear a footfall at fifty paces.

The tarts are now courtesans in Manolo Blahnik stilettos, and the doorways blare Eurotrash dance hits. Dario G rules, and there are no more secrets, only rumours.

ON THE DAY we're leaving Tyneside, I take a final walk. The Toon was always glorious to my eyes, and its visual magic has not been lost. The city planners have done away with many of its old bastions, the new motorways and one-way systems are an abomination, but there are plenty of brave sights left, not least the statue of Jackie Milburn in Northumberland Street. Forget Alan Shearer or Gazza—Wor Jackie will always be the Tyne's prime footballing god, and the bronze sculpture shows him in full splendour, shooting for goal. *Footballer and gentleman,* the humble inscription reads.

Sixteen again, I roam through Dobson's great Central Station, the Age of Steam incarnate, past the Grecian porticos and under the vaulted glass ceilings, into the waiting-room. The drunks and tarts and raddled queens have gone, and so has the ghost of Winnie the Poof, but not the smells: wet clothes, diesel oil, yesterday's meat pasties, and the faintest fishy whiff of Whitley Bay, borne down the Tyne on the North Sea winds.

High above the Quayside, I find the derelict churchyard again and look up to see the high bridges and the jigsaw jumble of the buildings, piled layer upon layer, century on century, monastery and gatehouse, castle keep and almshouse, cathedral and court and office block. Seagulls wheel above the water. A train rumbles past above my head. I go and get a haircut.

I pick a place in Gallowgate, upstairs above a bookie's. It's a plain and greasy barbershop with spotty mirrors, razor-strops and red leather chairs—the kind of clippy that used to provide dog-eared copies of *Titbits* and *Men Only* while you waited your turn. Now the offered reading is a Toon Army fanzine and last Tuesday's *Sun.*

Next to me in line sits a buzzcut youth with an INTERNATIONAL SEX MASTER tattoo, lime-green boots and Viking cheekbones. He gives his name as Keith, and says he lives in Heaton. He works, when he works, on building sites.

None of those sites are local. When he needs a cash boost, he goes abroad to Germany or Holland, where there's ready demand for top-class brickies and he can work off the books, cash in hand, no worries. A couple of months over there, and he can be up a good few thousand quid. "I spend nothing. Just save myself up, like a monk," he says. Then he comes back to Bigg Market and blows the lot. "It's all about the merries," he says.

Being broke never bothers him. He can always put in another stint on the Continent. "Initiative, that's all it takes. The way people whinge, it's just pathetic. *No jobs, no readies;* no bottle, if you ask me. Anyone that's willing to use his nut and has a bit of nerve, they can write their own ticket round here."

He isn't just talking about bricklaying. "That's specialised. Not everyone is fitted." Besides, there are so many other ways to get ahead. Moonlighting; resales; the black market. Drug dealing, of course, is always a staple. Or dole fraud. Or selling jewellery round the estates. There are housewives so bored, so desperate for action, they'll buy any glitz you show them, and throw in a blow job for luck.

"My philosophy's simple in life: when one dog craps out, buy another," Keith says, riffling his buzzcut for scurf. "The old ways have had it. Forget the shipyards, the munitions factories, steady work, security, all that hearth and home shite—none of it's ever coming back. You have to learn a new tune." His girlfriend's an aromatherapist, his best friend a pastry chef. "It's not so much *you take what you can get,* more *you get what you can take.*"

His turn in the barber's chair comes up. Checking himself in the mirror, he shoots me a look of vague irritation, sick of all these dumb questions. Where does the money come from?

"Other people's pockets," says Keith.

W E'VE BEEN ON the road so long, it seems our natural habitat. The Little Chef has become our patron saint, his sign on a deserted night motorway our sanctuary. We're in Huddersfield, we're in Dorchester, we're in Jarrow. We're in Mansfield, and the Tom Jones wannabe in the karaoke pub at the top of the market is belting out "Delilah," and the trains are roaring over the viaduct a hundred feet above our heads, and a woman well past fifty, with platinum blonde hair in a Marilyn Monroe bubble-cut and a chest like a child's dirty drawing, is unbuttoning her blouse to get some air, and crying, and singing along, *forgive me, forgive me, I just couldn't take any more,* and a man comes to her across the bar, half her size, and tries to grapple her in his arms, soothing her, giving her wet kisses, and her run mascara comes off on his lips, his whole mouth is smeared black, and the woman, seeing him, grabs him by his ears and draws him down into her bosom, smothering him against her heart, and still she's singing, *forgive me, forgive me,* sobbing to the beat, and when the number ends, the would-be Tom Jones comes down off the stage, washed in sweat, and hands her a plastic tulip.

We're in Gawthorpe, we're in Ossett. A sign reads, IF YOU FEED GREED, YOU STARVE COMPASSION. And we're in Dewsbury, ambling through an outdoor market that's three-quarters Asian, a souk full of spices and cheap silks. A man with an Ayatollah Khomeini beard is telling ancient jokes—"Do you like kids?" "Yeah, but I couldn't manage a whole 'un"—and the groans of his audience don't faze him a bit. "I've got a million knee-slappers," he crows, unabashed. "They call me the Knut from Kashmir."

We're in Gulliver's Kingdom, we're on the Heights of Abraham. We're in the Rock Island Diner at Tamworth, a forties-style American palace of Eats, scoffing BLTs and cheeseburgers and chocolate fudge sundaes, drinking strawberry milkshakes, and the Everly Brothers are on the jukebox, singing "Bye Bye Love," and our waitress is a bobby sox teen dream, there's chrome everywhere, gleaming, glinting, the sun is shining, and Eisenhower is president, and all the world is peachy keen.

But then we're in Grimsby, where great fishing fleets used to mass, and we're walking the now deserted wharves in an evil rain, and I duck into a pub to ask directions. A man at the bar, spotting an alien voice, asks me what I think of his town so far. "Wet," I answer diplomatically. "Aye," he says. "If you haven't seen Grimsby, you haven't died."

On the north side of Sheffield, amid the ruins of the steel industry, I stand in Brendan Ingle's boxing gym at Wincobank, the spawning ground of Prince Naseem Hamed and Herol "Bomber" Graham, and I listen to the rhythmic pounding of umpteen pairs of fists, whaling away at padded gloves and punching bags, and the runaway train-rattle of the speed balls. The gym occupies St. Thomas' disused church hall. You pass through a massive wooden door, and inside it's a fight factory. The labourers range from nightclub bouncers, sixteen stone of flaunting muscle, down to small boys of nine or ten, but all of them—Yemenis, Africans, West Indians, Saxons, Irish, Serbs—are joined in a single rhythm, and in a single goal: escape. For three minutes straight, relentless, they follow their drills. Then a corner bell rings, and there's sixty seconds' rest. The bell rings again, and the drills restart. Three minutes, and rest, three minutes, and rest, for hour after grinding hour. The posters on the walls are faded, the floor weights rusty, the stale air choked with sweat and raw breath. The hardwood floor is layered with ingrained dust and marked with a cabalistic pattern of circles and lines, symbolic of stances, foot positions, jabs, hooks, feints. "The stations of the cross," an onlooker calls them. And the corner bell rings, and everyone stops. And the bell rings, and everyone starts. And the rhythm—shuffling, hammering, echoing through the old church hall—sinks through my flesh and into my bones until it becomes my own beat, the only sound on earth.

Across the city, meanwhile, on Sheffield's south side, a group of Chileans are gathered in another church hall, making masks for 18 September, their Independence Day, when they stage fiestas and carnivals all over the city. Most of them arrived in England as refugees. They were socialists, supporters of Allende. Then Allende fell and was murdered, and the military dictatorship took over. The national football stadium became a concentration camp, ruled by Pinochet's thugs, and the men in the church hall, many of them children or teenagers then, were housed in cages. Victor Jara, the great folk singer and activist, had his hands cut off before being shot, while the caged were made to watch. Some of their fathers were tortured. Beatings and burnings, electrodes to the testicles. And others, of course, were slaughtered. Then came the deportations. Amnesty and other groups campaigned to get them out, and Sheffield took them in. This was in the middle seventies, in the prime of the People's Republic of South Yorkshire. Two hundred Chileans were billeted in Sheffield and Rotherham. The men went down the mines or worked in the steel factories. "We were all working-class people together," I'm told, "one beneath the skin. And Sheffield was rich with life. The spirit, the heart, was so great." But it isn't as easy now. The collapse of coal and steel has hit them like everyone else. One man complains that he no longer feels welcome here, wishes he could be home in Chile again, but he's shouted down as an ingrate. "Where would we be without Sheffield? All dead in one mass grave, perhaps." Here they're safe to gather and play *rayuela* and drink a few beers, and remember other places, other times. They can play their music, bang their drums on Independence Day, stick pictures of Allende on their kitchen walls, and nobody says boo. "I want to tell you the most beautiful word. The best word in all the world," an old man says, clutching at my wrist. He has a large wart in the centre of his forehead; it gleams like a third eye. *"Citizens,"* he says.

And in the streets outside, and all over the south side, in Hunter's Bar and Nether Edge, the republic rolls on, unstoppable. The sober-sided Victorian houses, built for civic worthies, are riddled with squatters, anarchists, dreadlocked whities, skinhead blacks, erotic bakers, Buddhists, the odd voodoo priestess, and bands, an army of bands. In the middle of the road, as we drive by, a youth with a blonde wig stands shouting in his underpants, crying out, with a voice of terminal outrage, "That bitch! That dirty bitch! She's burned my grass skirt . . ."

And we're in Todmorden, Chickenley, Skenk. And Halifax, off Gibbet Lane, just up the road from Talk of the Gibbet Amusements, watching Asian children play hopscotch outside a row of Victorian cottages, and a teenage girl, veiled, is reading Cindy Crawford's beauty tips in a glossy magazine, oblivious to the chalked message on the wall behind her back: SOON IT WILL HAPPEN TO YOU 'COS YOURE JUST FUCKED YOU EAT FROM YOUR NEIGHBOURS PLATE THEN YOU SHIT IN IT CALL YOURSELF GOOD MUSLIMS THE ONLY DECENT THING ABOUT YOU IS YOURE MUSLIM YOU ARE ALL JUST SCUM.

But the Little Chef is very kind. In the dread reaches of the night, when the motorways start turning to quicksand, it takes us in and comforts us, and feeds us grease, and feeds us slime. It slathers us in egg, sausage, bacon, mushrooms, fried tomatoes and chips, all sculpted out of India rubber, and then it tumbles us downstairs, bloated but beatific, into the amusement arcade, where Mary conquers Silverstone, shoots down the bad guys, destroys the bug-eyed monsters from Mars, and I shoot lazy pin-ball, and the dead air swallows our belches. Insomniac salesmen and lorry drivers roam the hallways, red-eyed, speed-crazed. We are home.

And the local papers never run dry. A gang of mini-yobs, aged seven to ten, are accused of satanic practices in Prestwich, and a mother of three in Worksop sues a hormone doctor for growing her a glossy black beard that makes her look like Captain Hook, she says. A man in Carshalton breeds tarantulas in his greenhouse, a man in Milton Keynes is arrested for sexually molesting a Child of Prague, a man in Leighton Buzzard claims he can communicate with ETs by banging out a secret code on his satellite dish, and a Peterborough grandmother, out walking her Lhasa apso of a night, sees the Virgin Mary, nestled among the pork chops and lamb kidneys, in the window of her family butcher.

And we're in Cromer, we're in March. We're in Fakenham, where the car park is under TV surveillance, on the hunt for muggers, thieves and, above all, illicit urinators, and a man, looking up at the evil eye, says bitterly, "At this rate, they'll have all our foreskins on file."

And then we're in King's Lynn, and the press officer for the town council is telling us that car parks are beginners' stuff. In King's Lynn, he says, closed-circuit TV scans almost everything—the shopping precinct, the industrial zone, residential streets and the whole of the Hillington Square estate, which has been judged a trouble spot. So I take a walk over there, and the place is hushed, there is hardly a soul out of doors, and the little black eyes perch halfway up the walls, missing nothing. Through an open window, I see that John Wayne is riding the range on the afternoon telly. "Fill your hand, you sonofabitch," Duke drawls. Then a man walks up behind me, carrying a four-pack of Special Brews. We watch the gunfight through the window till the woman indoors catches us and draws her curtains. Shame-faced, we shuffle off, as the closed-circuit cameras look down, and suddenly I realise that the whole scene has been captured, live. Some android thought-policeman in his windowless office has got me carded and coded: peeping tom; gun fetishist; Special Brew sympathiser. And a red mist sweeps over me. "Nice talking to you," the man with the four-pack mumbles, scurrying away, as I put my hand to my crotch, and I give my tackle a shake, good, hard and dirty, right in the camera's eye.

In Lowestoft, at a seafarers' union club, a man says he has an infallible cure for crabs, requiring nothing but faith, Tetley's tea bags and a fresh razor blade. In Hunstanton-on-Sea a funfair ride promises to take you to Hell & Back for a quid. And in Great Yarmouth, as a vicious nor'easter sweeps the piers, Mary smashes me at füssball. She plays in foul-mouthed frenzy, twisting herself off the ground at every swipe of the puck, roaring damnation on my head every time I sneak a consolation goal. We eat soggy hot dogs at the speedway track, marvelling at the skill of Michelle, a blonde teenage wonder-girl, who whips her battered racer inside and outside all rivals, knifing through like an electric eel. And afterwards in the pits, when I ask her secret, she smiles through a mask of muck and oil, schoolgirl-shy, and will only say, "My dad doesn't like me to lose." The wind is howling across the track, a wild swirling dust-storm, and the drivers' jumpsuits are billowing like sails, and one lad, trying to tune up his motor, throws down his tools. "I'm off up to King Street and visit Raquel, I need my spark plugs cleaned," he says, and Michelle blushes, and the roar of revving cars above the gale feels like the world's end. And Mary clutches my elbow, grappling tight, shouting shrill as a curlew above the din. "Don't let this ever end," she cries. "Never, ever end."

And we're in Ipswich. And we're in Newmarket.

And we're in Cambridge, in the Champion of the Thames, and I get talking to a man called Bernard, who's reading the *Racing Post,* and he tells me about last Saturday night.

It was meant to be a quiet celebration. Nadine had wanted to throw him a party, celebrate his birthday in style, but he didn't care for a lot of fuss. Just a meal at the Curry Queen, perhaps a few pints, then home to bed.

To tell the truth, he says, he had been feeling a bit below par. He'd got into a hassle with Mal Platt, who lived two streets away. Threats and menaces, loads of verbals all around, and it had rattled him. The unfairness of it, too. Because the whole thing was bollocks. If he'd wanted Platt's wife, he'd have had her, simple as that. Only she wasn't his type. Bleached blonde and a voice like a boiling kettle, he wouldn't have lowered himself.

Of course, he couldn't explain that to her husband as such. In Mal Platt's case, he couldn't explain anything. Just stand there and take the abuse, and try not to lose his head. If you hit him, you'd be descending to his level. Besides, the man was built like a brick shithouse.

It was an embarrassment, stuff like that. Bernard was not from Cambridge originally, but he had lived here for eighteen years, and he'd come to feel it was his town. The area around Mill Road, in particular. He'd worked there and drunk there, made a home there, while Mal Platt was a Johnny-come-lately. A fen boy, less than two years off the farm, and here he was causing all this upset. Calling Bernard a sex rat, and a whole lot worse, things you couldn't even repeat, they made you sick to think about.

Thank God for small mercies, at least Nadine was still in his corner. After fourteen years of marriage, she wasn't going to let a loose cannon like Mal Platt drag them down. "Take no notice. I don't," she kept telling Bernard. Of course, it was easier for her: she wasn't a man.

Anyway, that was why he'd wanted his birthday spent quiet. Keep out of harm's way, and wait for everything to blow over. But even that didn't work out the way he'd planned. When they got to the Curry Queen, his food wouldn't go down right. A lump of bhuna gosht stuck in his throat, he started to choke. Nerves acting up, that was all. People didn't think he was sensitive, but that's because they didn't know him. As a child, his goldfish had been his life, he'd cried for days every time one died, and he was no different now, he just put up a front. So there he was choking. It ruined the meal.

Some bloody birthday. And then, the capper. When they got back to the house, the motor was gone.

A blue Fiesta, only five years on it. Of course, he knew right away who'd taken it. Nadine tried to tell him it might be some kids out joyriding, but his gut told him different. He could almost see the words *Mal Platt* spelled out in acid indigestion, and those kinds of feelings don't lie.

Something snapped in him then. All his nerves went away, and he was left fighting mad. It was past closing time, but there was a drinking club nearby that stayed open after hours. Better not to mention its name, let's just say it was a right pisspot, therefore Mal Platt's favourite hangout. Bernard went charging in, fists up. Mal Platt took one look at him, hardly seemed to move. Then Bernard was on the floor.

By the time he got up, Platt had left. Done a runner, more or less. Someone said he'd gone on to a techno rave, whatever that might be. A place out beyond Cherry Hinton. It cost an arm and a leg for the cab, with Nadine whingeing the whole bloody way. Bernard could have thumped her. But no, he was saving the thumps for Platt.

When he got to the rave, all he found was a dirty great barn of a place, looked like a disused aircraft hangar, and loads of sweaty kids milling round aimlessly in near-darkness. And the noise, the beat, he'd never heard a din like it. Never mind; he wasn't quitting now. He kept working his way through the crowds until he found Mal Platt dancing by himself in a corner. Next thing he knew, he was back on the floor again and Platt had done another runner.

This time he'd been hit in the eye. Nadine flashed a bit of leg, got someone to give them a lift back to Mill Road. They were penniless, and Bernard's eye was swollen up shut. The throbbing made him want to throw up, but he wouldn't let himself, not till this thing was settled. Nadine, of course, thought he'd lost his mind. That was because she had no conception of manhood. No idea of honour, if you like. He was tired and hurt, and he didn't even feel angry any more, he'd gone past that. But he couldn't give up.

When they passed the Platts' house and saw that the lights were on upstairs, he didn't hesitate. Blind eye and all, he went straight to the back door, put his boot through a kitchen window.

After that, things got a bit out of hand.

Someone took a header down the stairs and ripped a great gash in the front door. Nadine's scalp was cut by flying glass, one side of her face was all blood. Then somehow the people next door got involved. Later on, he heard that an old woman had been tipped out of her wheelchair, and Bernard felt really bad. For the moment, though, he kept striking out, until someone got him in a sleeper hold, and that calmed him down in a hurry.

It was a uniformed cop, and suddenly Bernard was finished. "What's all this then?" the copper asked.

"That bastard stole my car," Bernard began, then he stopped. Something had clicked in his mind. The car wasn't parked outside his house tonight, after all. Never had been. He'd stuck it round the corner, in a neighbour's yard. To save it from being stolen.

"Which just goes to show," Bernard says.

And then we're in Walberswick. It's an old Suffolk fishing village, which I first visited at the age of sixteen, hitchhiking round East Anglia. I spent a night on top of the bluffs at Southwold, a few miles away, buffeted by a wild April storm, and at dawn, sleepless and sopping, stiff as a frozen cod fillet, I walked along the coast path to Walberswick, where the girl I believed I loved was staying. As watery sunlight pierced the storm clouds, a ferry bore me across the river and I served myself up, a drowned offering, at my true love's doorstep. "Oh," said Isabel. "It's you."

The memory still rankles. At some level, I still harbour hopes that if I knock on that door again, I'll be greeted not with dirty looks and bad cess but with a bleary-eyed waking smile, soft fuzzy kisses, a whispered "At last."

Dream on. The house, stilt-raised above the estuary mud, has long since changed hands. Some kids are playing wannabe Oasis in the sludge, air-guitaring to "Wonderwall." "I'll be Noel, and you can be the wanker," one says.

And that's not the only change. Where are the fishermen? Their smacks and nets? The village green is lined with tour buses, the pubs swarmed by day-trippers. But at least the setting's the same. The ferry still crosses the narrow river, and the marsh birds still wheel and cry overhead, waiting for the kill, and the Suffolk sky above the dunes is as immense as ever. And Margaret Thompson still sits inside her hut, out by the dunes, supervising her camping site.

I remember her as a gracefully made woman with a proud walk and a glint of challenge in her eyes. She had a past reputation for rakishness. There were tales of high passions, of fast cars and moonlit nights and American GIs. Now we find her, in her eighties, surrounded by clutter, every inch of her tiny hut filled with old clothes and discarded magazines and bits of broken bric-a-brac, and she's sitting in the doorway with her face turned to the sun. She has a wispy white beard, and she's wearing her blonde wig at a cockeyed angle, tilted down above one eye. Her lipstick is a smeared crimson hoop around her mouth, and her bright clothes are worn in layers, silks and satins, cottons and wools, like a crazy quilt.

When I introduce myself, she claims to recall me, and she takes my hand and holds it, and her long nails burrow into my palm. "They want to kick me out," she says, her high voice quavering. "They're trying to make me install Portakabins. They say it isn't sanitary, just going off in the dunes, and I've got to conform to regulations, or they're going to close down the site. But I don't want any loos—

dirty, smelly things!—and I don't want to conform. I just want to stay where I am. Within the sound of the sea. Oh, I'd die without the sea."

Children play lethargically around the tents, and dope-heads loll beside guttered fires, and lovers giggle in the long grass. A yellow mongrel keeps burying a stone in the sand, then digging it up again, faking amazement each time he finds it intact, while the breakers rolling in, unseen beyond the dunes, make muffled shushing sounds like skates slithering on ice. "An inspector came the other day. He said it's a hole," says Margaret, and she looks out over her kingdom, at the mess and mud, the litter, the sun-dazed bodies, the sky. "Perhaps he's right; I don't know. Perhaps it is a hole," she says. Her bearded chin quivers, and her nails dig harder into the soft pads of my palm. Her feet in their ancient tennis shoes, with stockings rolled down to the knee, give a little reflex kick, and she rocks in her chair, and the smeared lipstick around her mouth makes her look like a small girl dolled up. "But, oh," says Margaret. "It's so lovely to have a hole to fall in."

And we're in Lincoln; we're in Leicester.

We're on a road south out of Birmingham, and then we're in Stratford-upon-Avon, or Shakespeare's Stratford as the signposts call it now. It's raining, and the tourists in their plastic macs with plastic hoods are disconsolate, and all ye olde eating houses on Bridge Street are packed to the fake timber beams. So we walk along the sodden streets, past the Shakespeare Centre and the Shakespeare Trust, Shakespeare's School, the World of Shakespeare & Heritage Centre, the Royal Shakespeare Theatre, and the Birthplace Trust Coach Terminal, and then we start along by the river, under dripping trees. The rain starts drumming harder, and we're forced to take shelter at the Brass Rubbing Centre. The two Ss in brass have been scratched out, and about a dozen teenagers are hanging out in the old stone hallway, drinking cider and smoking bongs. Hunkered down on the pitted flagstones, they regard us warily, but Mary soon has them sweet. The bong circulates, and I enquire what life is like here, and one boy tries to tell me. "Shakespeare's from here, you know," he explains earnestly. The town's a museum, all tourists, and nothing left over for people. "What can I tell you?" The boy draws deep, and passes the bong. "It's just a small, shit town."

But we're off to the Bulldog Bash.

A few miles south of Stratford, forty thousand bikers have set up camp around a disused airfield for three days and nights of non-stop blasting. A demon cavalry, barrelling through the suburbs and byroads of the Midlands with throttles wide open.

We're sitting outside a roadside pub in a quiet village with one of everything—butcher, baker, bookie—when the first rumble reaches us. A distant disturbance to begin with, like thunder deep in the earth, and then a gathering howl, a doomsday shuddering and roiling that sends all the other traffic hurtling for shelter and makes our glasses dance on the table-top. And suddenly the road blows apart, and here they are, hundreds upon hundreds of black-leather horsemen, all ages and sizes, eighteen to seventy, shrimps to man-monsters, their torsos bared to the wind, weather-burned and tattooed, long hair streaming or crop-skulled, hard-bellied or beer-tubbed, with their righteous old ladies hanging on their backs, as they fly past the licensed chemist and the quality confectioner, the turf accountant, the tanning salon, and off away to the ends of the world, or Netherhasset Airfield, whichever comes first.

And Mary races hot behind them. Her fantasy life has always teemed with hard men, desperadoes, dodgy propositions in general. "A little bit whee and a little bit woah," is how she describes her ideal. And here she has her pick. "Please, mister, could I have a ride?" she asks the first Bulldog who meets her eye. Then she's gone, careening down the airfield slip road in a blaze of exhaust fumes and glory. And I'm left behind, to sort through her dust.

It's only mid-afternoon, but the Bash is already percolating nicely. Despite its title, it has no political purpose, beyond a vague allegiance to country and flag. If there are any neo-Nazis around, they keep their swastikas under wraps. To be a Bulldog in good standing, all you need is wheels, a strong head for drink, and a rebel heart.

The airfield is blanketed by a sea of tents, each with its own hog. Countless thousands of Yamahas, Hondas and Harleys, gleaming in the sun. Low-slung, wide-handled godkissers. Bodywork spray-painted with space travellers, or Arnold Schwarzenegger barbarians, or bazunga-breasted amazons. Luminescent purples and atomic reds, midnight blues, Day-Glo golds. Wild horses of the Apocalypse.

There are white-bearded grandads with hair to their waists popping wheelies up and down the aisles, their grandsons perched on their shoulders. And old ladies who are truly old ladies, card-carrying pensioners, in halter-tops and cut-offs, their big bellies displayed with pride and their shoulders like hod carriers. And apprentice sweet mamas, barely past puberty, dressed to make the Spice Girls look prudish. And weekend wheelers in denim, clean-shaven and trim. And Hell's Angels in full colours, biker pirates with death's head belt-buckles.

The revving and roaring never stop. Long lines of racers queue up for the drag strip, two by two, like supplicants at Noah's Ark, waiting to burn up that quarter mile. The air hangs heavy with the smells of scorched rubber, and grease, and hash, and frying foods. Onstage in the main tent, leather girls sing dirty about their bodies, and leather boys sing dirty about their bikes. The beer goes down in quarts and gallons, and sometimes comes up again. There's yelling and cursing and carrying on. But no violence. Amazingly, in all this heat and din, there isn't a single fight.

At midnight, the big tent is packed, and the last heavy-metal band has finished its set. Most of the Bulldogs are lying sprawled, drunk, stoned, completely wasted.

And then the strippers come on and suddenly the whole zapped multitude is back on its feet, miraculously cured. The strippers do nuns, and pinstriped business-men, and naughty schoolgirls, and they're full of zip, legs kicking, breasts flashing, big raunchy grins. They're con-spirators, egging the bikers on, and every time another nipple is exposed, another bare buttock rolled, the howl-ing and stomping jump to a new level, till the tent threat-ens to lift off and blow us all away.

An eighteen-stone Angel keeps hammering on my back, and a sweet mama wants to spit beer in my mouth, and the strippers turn their backs on the crowd, bend over to touch their toes, and they shake that thing, shake it till it hurts. And Mary's back. Oddly flushed, a little bug-eyed, but in one piece. A leather belt flies through the air, its buckle flashing in the stage lights. The strippers do policemen.

And we're back in Yorkshire.

Hebden Bridge is a former textile town in Calderdale, on the Yorkshire side of the Pennines, midway along the old pack-horse route between Burnley and Halifax. Not much more than a village, really, centred round a canal and a string of hump-backed bridges. But the place is an amazement. It stands in the pit of a deep bowl, with streets that rise in steep layered stacks like cardboard cut-outs, black stone houses set into sheer black rock, zigzag-ging to the clifftops. Hairpin roads climb seeming precipices; mill chimneys loom stark against the sky; and many of the dwellings are up-and-unders, with the top halves facing one way and the lower halves reversed, so that the whole town bears the mark of Janus, two-faced.

Who lives here? "Lotus eaters," we're told. The mills began to run down in the late sixties, and the town seemed due to die. A lot of younger workers moved out. At the same time, city dropouts started moving in; hip-pies, craftworkers, Zen Buddhists. As late as the mid-seventies, a terraced house could still be bought for £1,300. Gas lighting and no indoor toilet, admittedly, but still a solid structure; a home. Whole streets were turned into virtual communes. Colonies of leatherworkers and woodcarvers sprang up, glassblowers and ethnic weavers. And gradually they evolved into the new bourgeoisie. As house prices began to rise again, social workers and media types jumped on board, and Hebden Bridge, back from the brink of oblivion, acquired a whole new life cycle. Instead of a mill town, it became an all-purpose boho paradise. Funky, but not dangerous. Free, but not too free.

It seems in permanent fiesta. The central streets and squares are full of revellers in ponchos and sandals, plunking at guitars or tootling on penny whistles. In Broughton Street, rugs and fabrics and clothes are strung on lines between the houses, bright streams of colour above our heads, and flowers are sprouting everywhere, in boxes, along the back alleys, between pavement cracks. There are painted chairs in the doors, and a sofa, of course, the inevitable weatherlogged sofa, draped in a Peruvian blanket and trailing Madras cottons.

For the first time in weeks, we stop racing. Outside a pub in the main square, Mary lays her head on a table and sleeps like a small child, impervious to jolts or slopped beer. Drinkers settle around us. A Barbadian alto-sax player, a drug dealer in from Leeds, and a cider-swilling Belfast man named Sean, with ruined teeth and drink-shiny eyes. He works as a bailiff and dreams of Bournemouth. It's the Garden of Eden, he says. Hebden Bridge, by comparison, is too soft on New Age travellers. They set up their sites outside town, stink up the streets and spread disease. Bournemouth wouldn't let them stop a day.

Hearing him rant, the other drinkers just smile. Confrontation is not in vogue here. Even Sean, when Mary wakes, goes soft. "Wee gurrel," he calls her, with a flash of his graveyard teeth. In the square, a girl is braiding her friend's black hair with corkscrew blonde dreadlocks, and a troubadour is mangling "Mellow Yellow."

In the morning, I take a walk across the moors from our B&B and down a steep rocky path to a mountain stream. At the water's edge, I come to a flat slab of rock and two sun worshippers—a bearded anorak in his socks and underpants, and a nubile blonde, stretched out topless on her back, with her limbs arrayed as spokes on a wheel.

They seem unstartled to see me. The blonde's name is Rachel, and she says she is a white witch, running the two words together, so that they melt into one and come out sounding like a surname: Whitewitch. She's here to fight bad vibes.

Her home is in Huddersfield. During the week, she works as a dental hygienist, but witchcraft is her true calling. "All for the good, of course," she makes clear. No orgies or satanic rituals, no sacrifices. "Absolutely not."

Everything about her speaks of shining resolution. Her pale, goose-pimpled flesh looks freshly scrubbed, and her blue eyes dare me to mock. "My job is invocation," she says, chin determinedly jutting, little pink nipples rigid. "Malignant powers are at work. I'm summoning up spirits to head them off."

A chill breeze comes up. Reluctantly, as if forced to hide her true colours, she puts her breasts away and lights up a Silk Cut. The anorak, meanwhile, says not a word; simply stares into space, and looks moth-eaten. "What malignant powers?" I enquire.

Rachel beams. "I'm happy you asked me that," she says. Hebden Bridge is an ancient and empowered site. The whole area is chock-full of secret forces, most of them benign, and its recent regrowth has been an expression of this. "Healing currents. Magical awakenings." But now all the good is threatened. Certain evil spirits—Satanists and black witches—have targeted the town. They can't bear to see such harmony, so much spiritual freedom. "It drives them out of their trees," Rachel says. Heavy spells and curses have been called up. Her job is to repel them.

How's she doing so far? "It's hard work," she admits.

She's outnumbered, and she lacks full knowledge. Alec, her partner in the anorak, is a much more advanced adept, but he's reluctant to clue her in. "He thinks I'm a groupie," she says loudly, clearly hoping to raise a response. But Alec doesn't turn his head, gives no sign of hearing. "I'm a little out of my depth here," Rachel says, not ashamed to plead. Just the same, she won't be defeated. The moment the sun reappears, she strips off and assumes the position again. A thrush, perched above her on a bough, flies off in a splatter of feathers, and I prepare to follow. "Nice talking to you," Rachel Whitewitch says, and gives me a phone number. If I get the chance, she says, could I call her mam in Huddersfield, and tell her not to bother with tea.

And we head south for the last time.

The evenings are drawing in, the nights turning chilly; we can feel the season closing in. So we race through seaside resorts, in search of residual heat. We're in Margate, we're in Hastings, we're in Eastbourne. We're in Poole, and then in Bournemouth, Sean the bailiff's Garden of Eden, shivering in the Pleasure Gardens and sucking on ice lollies.

A combo is playing swing on the bandstand, and a sturdy blonde who might once have been a Forces' favourite is singing the good old good ones, and holidaymakers are dozing in deckchairs, lapping up the thin sunlight, and there are banks of flowers everywhere. Then it's night, and the clubbing starts. All the surfer boys and surfer girls come out to play. So we make a midnight run. Out into the country, down narrow lanes and over wooded hilltops, driving blind, abjectly lost, till we give up all thought of direction and let Teal Wheels lead us on at random. And we find ourselves at the Manor.

It's a converted country mansion, a cut-rate Manderley, with a great hall and vaulted ceilings, a sweeping staircase and a labyrinth of side rooms, swept by fluorescent lights that turn all materials a ghostly white. The DJ is playing cheesy house, but we drift on to the dance floor and let our bodies be moved. The dancers are almost all girls, their long blonde limbs cut by tiny strips of blanched cloth. They move in groups, swarm around us like shoals of white sharks. And one of the girls bears down on me. Golden hair, and cancelled eyes. She looks too zonked to see, yet she finds me even so. Other girls are behind her, egging her on. She puts her hand to my face, and she kisses me. On a dare, I suppose. And she slips me tongue. Drives her tongue deep into my throat. And then she stops. She pulls away with a startled jerk and starts to wipe her mouth. The other girls are laughing and jeering, but she looks shocked. "I thought you were my dad," she says.

THE WHEEL stops in Brighton.

Late one fog-bound evening, Teal Wheels rolls us gently along the front, and we smell the brine through the open windows, feel the salt spray lash our faces, and it's like sailing safely into port; dropping anchor.

This is the only town where the republic feels like the ruling party. Instead of a rebel uprising, ducking and diving to survive, it is its own Establishment here, free to flaunt itself openly, the more riotously the better. Eco warriors and techno anarchists have state-of-the-art studios and renovated warehouses to play in, and there's an endless round of parades and demos, free parties, fetish balls.

Mary has a friend I'll call Jess, a fetish model who used to keep a slave. We arrange to meet in a music pub, and she enters like a whirlwind, striding across the floor in full costume—a black leather jacket of many zippers, a matching minidress, and heavy black boots she's designed herself, replete with straps and buckles. Her uniform is dazzling; her laughter, husky and warm, unfiltered, sweeps me away.

She leads me through the backstreets at twilight, down the hill to the Blue Parrot, across the street from the Pavilion. Jess sits on the balcony, glugging Beck's from the bottle while she tells me why she acquired her slave. "I wanted to test myself," she explains. "I wanted to explore the boundaries of my strength and power, instead of being the usual sad old bag that men leave behind. So I put an ad in *Fetish Times* and this young black guy responded. Soft-spoken, with very nice manners. He used to do the housework nude in a pinny, but my dog, Emma, God love her, found that too tempting to pass up, so I let him wear cycling shorts and a dog collar instead. I have to say, he did nice work. He scrubbed my boots and painted my toenails, cleaned the toilet, grovelled at my feet, all that good stuff."

For a time they got on fine. "It was the first time either of us had been involved in a mistress/slave situation, but he didn't know that, so I had to fake experience. That made the whole act nerve-racking at first, but then it got exciting. In a way, it felt like watching a film. Basically, I was just playing a role, trying on different scenes for size, to see if they suited me." And did they? "Yes, and no. Exploring different needs, that was stimulating. Not sexually, nothing like that. But mentally, yes, it turned me on at times. That sense of breaking new ground. Of going beyond."

She never fully trusted him, though. On the surface, he was totally obedient, everything the well-trained slave should be, but behind her back he got up to games. He slept with one of her best friends, then lied about it, and she couldn't be having that. Lying is the one thing she can't stomach. So she had to boot him out.

"I fell into a trap," Jess says. "Because he was honest about his sexuality, I thought he'd be honest with everything else. But why should that follow? People are so full of contradictions. When you get below the surface, slaves will tell porky-pies like anyone else. They can be bitchy, and backstabbing, and full of shit. So many games, you wouldn't believe—it drove me up the wall."

The slave didn't take his dismissal lightly. He kept writing her letters, begging for another chance, but too late, he'd blown it. "Besides, the whole idea was beginning to turn me off. I didn't enjoy the obsession with control. I've never stood still for being controlled myself, and I found I couldn't do it to others, either. I don't get off on people being belittled, even with their consent."

The domes and minarets of the Pavilion loom dimly through the dark. "Weird shit," says Jess, and shakes her head in bafflement. She has had a bullwhip tattooed on one arm, she has pierced nipples and a pierced clitoris, and she looks radiant. But vulnerable, too; one prick away from a burst paper bag.

Her great beauty is in her eyes. Framed by a fringe of dyed black hair, they are immense, and full of shifting currents. "I've seen a lot," she says.

As a child, the oldest of three, she was kept constantly on the move. Her father was sick in the head, a paranoid manic-depressive, who never could settle. The first year or so in each new place, he'd seem to be doing better. Then the rages would start again. He thought that Jess and her mother were plotting against him, conspiring to drive him crazy; he thought that Jess's mother had a lover. He beat the shit out of her, then he tried suicide; it was just horrible.

They ended up in Norfolk. They were living in a farmhouse, a lovely old place but a shambles. There was no proper heat in the winters and rain poured in through the leaks in the roof. Still, there were compensations. They kept sheep and goats, and ate from their vegetable garden, and sold lettuces and onions. Jess used to shear the sheep with kitchen scissors and bring in the harvest in the back of a Morris Minor.

She shows me old photographs: a weathered stone house; flat Norfolk landscape; children grinning with their eyes screwed up against the sunlight; and a woman smiling shyly, looking worn but lovely, in a plain room. "My mother held all of us together. She had a hideous fucking life, almost non-stop abuse, but she shielded us totally. She was always giggling and cuddling us; and she was so young. She had me when she was twenty, so she seemed like an older sister, our friend, not an authority figure."

Boxing Day, the year that Jess was sixteen and her mother thirty-six, they went out to Mass together. When they got home, the walls inside the farmhouse were covered with notes from her father, accusing them of every crime under the sun. Then her father started screaming, out of his head, calling them whores and bitches. So Jess went to stay with neighbours. Next day, her mother was found strangled.

The father did only two years in jail. The law let him plead diminished responsibility and he himself seemed to have no sense of having done wrong. When Jess went to visit him, he kept talking about her mother being in a better place and how she was looking down on them, smiling.

She didn't fancy sticking around when her father got out, so she took off to Australia. For a year she lived in the outback with her mother's father. He was a magical man, there was a sense of peace around him, and Jess could feel free. But when she returned to England, bad times came again: "Wrong men, wrong scenes. I got involved with this blind guy. Not being able to see me, I thought he might sense who I was inside and not get distracted by the trappings." But when he said he loved her, all he really meant was control, and she couldn't breathe that air. Control and lies, they kill you.

Her wide mouth, postbox-red, drains another Beck's, yet she shows not the smallest effect. She drinks too much, she says; does too much of everything: "A born extremist." Her favourite word is *outrageous*. But often, when telling a story, her voice trails off at the end of a phrase, and she murmurs "Hmmm," as if baffled, as if she's lost the thread.

When she first arrived in Brighton, she started working with the mentally ill. For two and a half years, she was in a shared house full of chronic cases. Her special project there was a woman named Mariella. "Four foot eleven, just over six stone, one tooth in her head, and she had the deepest brown eyes, incredibly intense. One look in those eyes and you could see all her suffering, it was far beyond words."

At times Mariella could be murderous. She'd cover herself in her own excrement, eat it if she got the chance, then come flying at you when your guard was down, trying to smear you, too. Pulling your hair, or digging at your arms with her nails; she had a genius for pain. She never spoke, just stared and waited to pounce. But Jess loved her. "There was so much soul in her, it was like buried treasure. No way could I walk away." And with time Mariella calmed. She learned to be still, she could even show affection. Sometimes, not often, she smiled.

For Jess, that was true fulfilment; a far deeper satisfaction than slaves could ever be. But the job in the shared house ended and she moved on again. She sang in a punk band, then she worked as a bricklayer, restoring old houses. And now she does a bit of everything. She tends bar, she models, she is a personage about town. Her image in leather catsuit and elbow-length leather gloves adorns a flyer for The Pleasure Principle, a night of "orgazmic techno and banging house" presented by Get Down on Your Knees and Beg for It.

Her involvement in the fetish scene came almost by accident. She was skint, as usual, and feeling trapped, and she heard about a French photographer who needed a new model. She had already been through her period as a slave-keeper, and emerged more or less unscathed, so why not? She did the photo session in metal underwear; no damage was done. Soon afterwards, she found herself on a bus to Munich with thirty strangers, the cream of British fetishists, driving to a rave in a disused airport. For the first time, Jess donned the leathers and chains. And she liked the way they felt. "They gave me a licence to strut," she says. "In my private sex life, I'd always been at the other extreme—a big pair of eyes hiding under the covers. When I started performing, though, I was a totally different person. There were no sexual demands on me; I wasn't put up for judgement. I was free to explore fantasies and there wasn't any payback."

These days most of her income comes from S&M. She does a lot of modelling—"dom and submissive, dyke scenarios, gadgets, masks, whatever comes along." She's worked with Trevor Watson, the David Bailey of S&M, and she also does live performances, which take her all over Europe. Collar-and-leash shows are her speciality, but she likes variety: "The wilder the better, really." Though she isn't into pain, she likes role-playing; the idea of crossing boundaries. "I just want to find out, I suppose."

Her personal life is a tangle, though. You might think that all this self-discovery and stretching would help her resolve her problems; so far it hasn't worked out that way. She keeps falling in love, then finding she's picked another wrong 'un. One week she'll be flying, certain she has found her dream love; the next, her dream man has turned into a boot-faced zombie who spends half his waking life in front of the telly, picking his nose and sneering.

"None of this is simple," Jess muses, scabbing idly at the label of her Beck's. Just because she sports black leather and a bullwhip tattoo, it doesn't mean she can't be hurt. Sometimes, on the contrary, her image seems like an open invitation; a challenge to destroy. Men look at her, and they're attracted by the life in her, the passion. That's what brings them buzzing around her. But that's also what they end up running from, or trying to crush.

How will she end up? She can't guess. Some days she feels she'd like to try music again, other days she feels more tempted by films. And she still hopes to find one person she could be with. A total relation, with no fear or compromise: "That has to exist some place," she suggests, then shakes her head in doubt. Strong women, free women—perhaps these are fated to be alone. "Goddesses don't exactly crowd the pavements," says Jess, and she flexes her arm. The bullwhip flicks like a snake's tongue.

IDOLATRY

O N A DULL and grizzling night, when the breeze is chill enough to make me turn up my jacket collar, I come home again to King's Cross.

The Hotel Montana has a NO VACANCIES sign on the door, so I settle for the Alhambra down the street, but it is no substitute. There's a proper mattress on the bed and the door locks; there's even a shower stall. "We're upping the world," the woman on the front desk says, and that seems true of the whole Cross. When I take a stroll round my old manor, I find myself surrounded by the Jesus Army, Jews for Jesus and Hare Krishnas. Three West Indian women are singing a Christian pop song about walking up a mountain to warm by the sacred fire, and when they fail to put enough verve into it, their overseer, a waspish little white man, orders them to pep it up. "God isn't a dirty secret," he reminds them.

Indeed He isn't. On the contrary, He's being shouted and sold from every corner of the republic. All through our odyssey, He has been a constant companion, as ubiquitous as Elvis.

This is a radical turnabout. In England as I first knew it, faith was rarely discussed. If anything, it was actively avoided. Too much belief, too freely expressed, was seen as anti-social. God had His place, but that place was tightly bordered. He had a cameo role in the Queen's job description, and He got a weekly plug on *Songs of Praise*. For the rest, He was lucky if He got the odd hymn or two for Christmas, a passing nod at Easter.

Spiritual yearning, at least in terms of public display, was mostly restricted to Speakers' Corner and occasional tours by Billy Graham, and even Graham's appearances were strangely insubstantial. Curious to see what had brought him worldwide fame, I attended one of his Earls Court crusades in the middle sixties. The crowd was impressive in size, not far short of a sell-out, but it hardly made a sound. No shouting and stomping, and no hallelujahs. Instead, the atmosphere reminded me of school assembly, with Graham himself as headmaster. He seemed to think that the kids had been slacking off, letting the devil muck us about, and if we expected to pass our finals, we'd need to pull our socks up.

New Age movements, in those days, were completely beyond the pale. When L. Ron Hubbard launched his Church of Scientology here and his minions put on some live shows in Croydon, I went down to the Fairfield Halls to see what the fuss was about. The audience, fifty at most, seemed split between curiosity-seekers like myself and afternoon drunks in out of the rain. Onstage, the choir kept prancing in step and chanting "Free, Free, Thanks to Scien-tol-o-gee!," and exhorting us to join them on The Quest. Not one soul responded.

Sneaking home early, I asked my parish priest what he himself thought of questing, by and large. "Very poor taste," he said, and quickly changed the subject.

He's dead now, Father Thomas, and maybe it's just as well. As the age of certainty has passed and England has fallen into the threshing machine, quests have become a boom industry. Their ads are plastered outside every church and chapel, every storefront ministry. Even London Transport has got into the act. THE EVENT THAT WILL CHANGE YOUR LIFE FOR EVER, blares a slogan on passing buses. *Seek, and ye shall find.*

Some of the new messiahs have proved to be Elmer Gantrys. There was the case of Chris Brain, whose Nine O'Clock Service flourished briefly but spectacularly in Sheffield, only to collapse in sexual scandal. His use of film loops, evangelical techno and dancers in black lycra bikinis to pump out messages on the environment started a national trend. Unfortunately, so did his taste for seducing his acolytes. As a result, the Sunday papers have found themselves gifted with a rich seam of philandering prophets and orgiastic hanky-panky under God's disco ball.

Behind the lurid headlines, though, spiritual hungers run deep. It's easy for liberal agnostics to sneer. The language of the new movements—holistic Christians and charismatics, Men Alive for God, the holy Joes, and many others—tends to make them easy targets. Nonetheless, they express real needs.

"EVERYONE ALIVE wants answers," Gilles told me, back in Fraggle Rock. Wanting answers myself, I start my explorations at the centre, with the Church of England. I'm aware that its former bland passivity has been disturbed by an upsurge of charismatics, in thrall to the miraculous and supernatural, but I don't quite grasp how deeply these have penetrated the mainstream till I read a story in the *Evening Standard* about Reverend Banner of Tunbridge Wells, a former TV evangelist, who doubles as an exorcist.

Satanic possession in Tunbridge Wells? If that last bastion of retired Indian colonels and pink gin isn't safe, nowhere is.

John Banner turns out to be a brisk and blunt-spoken man from Birkenhead. Fighting fit in his sixties, he has thick white hair swept up in an Elvis-style quiff, a clipped moustache and an oddly unblinking stare, and he doesn't speak so much as testify.

He tells me that Tunbridge Wells, far from a sanctuary, is a microcosm of a world gone sick. "Every Friday night, all hell is let loose. Three hundred kids run amok, drinking themselves stupid, vomiting and breaking windows. Or flirting with Satanism and the occult. Four teenagers in the town have caused a quarter million pounds' damage to various churches and graveyards, claiming they've been built on pagan sites. Oh, the Evil One is everywhere."

The Reverend can't be lightly dismissed. Recently elected to the General Synod, he is regarded as a radical force—dynamic, populist, youth-orientated. Before Tunbridge Wells, he ministered in the slums of Bootle and Wigan, in mental asylums, in Australia, and when I ask him how he describes himself, he says he's a born warrior. "I'm constantly up in arms. On the battlefront." Grappling with bureaucracy; preaching discipline, commitment, respect; above all, defying decadence. "The powers of darkness don't terrorise me," he proclaims. "I fight them back, inch by inch."

Such talk seems wildly exotic to me. The Anglican vicars I've met in the past have been mostly bleaters, men of sticky cakes and potted pieties, not action. But the Reverend Banner says he's always been tough. "At sixteen, I was a wild one; the ringleader of my gang. What you might call an SNL—Strong Natural Leader. Also a BDH—Big Dame Hunter."

His conversion was sudden and dramatic. "I used to hang around the local youth club, and one night this evangelist gave us a talk. He asked us to imagine Christ looking into the well of our lives. What would He see? Well, I was horrified. I knew He'd see thievery, blasphemy and heavy petting. 'Cor,' I thought to myself, 'I am one guilty teenager.'"

That same night, as he was leaving the youth club, a blinding flash of light appeared through an open door. His first thought was that a lorry was making a three-point turn. But no, it was the moon: "A radiance bright as day," he says, fixing me with his blinkless stare. "I had brand-new eyes. For the first time in my life, I could truly see."

The charged language, the comic-strip revelations, the dated slang—they're all typical of the Church's new approach. "We can't afford to be passive," the Reverend says, justifying the influx of pop theatrics. "Satan packs a wicked wallop, so we have to beat him to the punch."

That's why he took up exorcism. "I couldn't stand by idly and see such atrocities go unchallenged, I had to take up the cudgels." He takes a hard glug of tea and chomps his muscular jaws. "You'd hardly credit the mischief I've seen." One time, he had to deal with a woman possessed by demons. Although a rich and beautiful blonde and a director in a thriving metal-screw company, she kept mucking about with tarot cards and Ouija boards. Her husband took her to Majorca for a rest-cure and they went to see a bullfight. Halfway through, the wife suddenly stood up and departed. She walked for miles through the town, till she reached a wood, where she stopped. As if she was saying, "This is where I belong." And this wood was home to a witches' coven.

What good were the woman's wealth and beauty to her now, or all the metal screws in creation? Back in England, her husband begged John Banner for help. For four hours solid, the Reverend prayed over her in an empty chapel, while five men held her down. The blonde kept writhing like Linda Blair, as if in an epileptic fit. The screams and howls that came from her, and the language, you wouldn't believe your ears. But Banner would not be gainsaid. By midnight, he had driven out nine demonic spirits. Then she vomited a stream of green and khaki bile. The smell was horrendous, but at least she could sit up and have a cup of tea. It was over; she was cleansed.

Tunbridge Wells as Sin City, the General Synod as a spiritual SAS—these are images so startling, I can't quite adjust. The only churches that still offer a simple prayer and sermon, it seems, are the empty ones. "If you want to survive in this business, you've got to give it some juice," a female helper at the Elim Pentecostal Temple tells me, sounding like an agent for Raymond's Revuebar.

And in a sense, of course, that's exactly what she is. In these new approaches to faith, the one constant is an emphasis on display. The act of worship has become exactly that—an act—and the altars are beseiged by sacramental strip-o-grams.

From the C of E, I venture outwards. I sample a male-bonding session in Streatham, held in a disused cinema, where a mixed body of seekers call on God to bless their masculinity. Some are fat and bald in Sunday-best suits, others crop-skulled in leathers and boots. Many sport combat gear, emblazoned with *Jesus Army: Fighting for You.* They sing "The Lord Is a Warrior" and shout "I'm a Man, I'm a Man, I'm a Holy Spirit Man." Then they fall into each other's arms, embracing and singing, offering up praise. As men, they are the chosen of God; His only beloveds. And women? They are the chosen of men.

Undeterred, I press on, and drag Mary with me. Devout Catholic that she is, she's none too thrilled. Still, research is research; she forces herself to endure. We sing out at a Pentecostal service in the Tottenham Green Leisure Centre, and at a Rivers of Faith rally in the Valley, Charlton Athletic's football ground. Both times, we are the only white faces, surrounded by black jubilators, mostly big-boned women in flowing white dresses and picture hats, gospel-chanting and stomping. When the spirit comes on them and their bodies start to move of their own volition, we're swept away to Alabama, Kingston, Lagos. The London skies are leaden grey; the chill in the air tightens daily. Down on these praying floors, though, we're seared by sacred heat.

Other sorties are less triumphal. Once, while Mary is at Mass, I venture alone to a Creation Spirituality event in the East End. An Edwardian parish church, its air still redolent of rising damp and pious spinsters with permanent chest colds, has been made over as a nightclub. Though Chris Brain of the Nine O'Clock Service may stand discredited, the influence of his Planetary Mass clearly survives. I find myself in semi-darkness, listening to a disembodied voice telling me to beg forgiveness for destroying the planet.

There are sounds of running water and birdsong, and projected images of an eclipse, the Berlin Wall coming down, starving children. Ambient music drifts in and out. A long-haired preacher, described as a shaman, intones a chanted prose-poem about pollution. He's dressed all in black, as are his handmaidens. After a brief segment of body prayer, which looks like Yoga for Beginners, and a lot of formless wailing, the music machine goes on the blink. A moment's confusion is resolved by the shaman telling us that the dysfunction is symbolic. "We are all in meltdown," he explains. The projector flashes images of cattle in a slaughterhouse, blanket bombing in Vietnam. "Creator God, we confess our sin," the shaman chants. As my eyes adjust to the gloom, I realise that his long hair is, in fact, a wig. "Release us, and deliver us," he prays. A picture of a glowing pink sunrise, as drawn by a child, appears. Then the projector breaks down.

Shuffling out into Poplar High Street, the congregation seems well satisfied. Youngish and exclusively white, the men neat in pressed jeans and leisure shirts, the women in skirts and sensible shoes, they look like social workers on the razzle, discreetly festive. I spot the occasional piercing, a few bindhis. Otherwise, the nearest to a defining symbol seems to be the Nike swoosh.

One hungry-looking young woman, spotting an outsider, invites me to join her group over coffee. So we pile into a greasy spoon, five strong, and slake our thirsts with tepid dishwater.

The young woman's name is Sandra; she's wearing a Minnie Mouse watch. A schoolteacher working with challenged children, as she calls them, she has heavy black eyebrows that meet in the middle, and says she's been lost. Ever since her teens, she has been searching for a faith to fill her emptiness. She has tried evangelical, charismatic, Pentecostal; even had a walkabout with the Moonies.

She used to be eight stone overweight. She kept eating all day long, sweets and sticky buns and chocolate éclairs, anything with sugar, yet nothing could satisfy her craving. "I was on a mission to blow myself up," she says, fastidiously crumbling a tea biscuit. She tried all kinds of cures—diets, hypnosis, pills—to make herself stop. Then her best friend, Gloria, who is a Methodist, told her it was God, not a sugar-rush, she sought.

The others in her group nod sagely. They are clearly itching to uncork their own tales, but they force themselves to be patient. I'm Sandra's catch, after all; it's only right that she should get first dibs. They murmur supportively when she speaks of her pain and a Nordic amazon named Klara, with beefy forearms and rhinestone glasses, rubs her shoulders. "Share the burden," Klara tells her, "pass the weight."

"You are so good," Sandra says.

As soon as she realised the truth, she began to shed. Not just pounds, but her abusive boyfriend, her faithless friends, her unsympathetic family. Even Gloria, the Methodist, has been stripped away. There is no space in her life for anyone who isn't travelling the same road as herself. "It wouldn't be fair," she says. The tea biscuit has been ground to crumbs, but not one grain has passed her lips. "I've got twelve pounds left to lose," she tells me ardently, though she already looks stick-thin. "I'm almost there." Sometimes, she confesses, she wonders if the two quests—slimness and sanctity—might not be somehow connected. Maybe, when the last flab has been burned off and she's down to her bare bones, God will be able to see her more clearly; and she, in turn, will see Him.

"I will lift up my nakedness to His sight," she offers. But the others don't like the sound of that. There are shufflings and anxious sighs, and Norman, a man with a ginger goatee, coughs into his hand. "Are you holistic?" he asks me.

"Not exactly."

"Unchurched?"

"Let's just say I'm resting."

The man leans forward across the table, avid to question me further, but Sandra isn't having it, she hasn't finished her turn. "I'm sorry," she says stubbornly. "I'm making a point here." She waggles her Minnie Mouse watch and her black eyebrows contract. "I will lift up my nakedness," she repeats through clenched teeth. "I will travel His cyberspace."

"Have another tea biscuit," Norman says.

THE WRITING is on the wall. WE ARE LED BY FOOLS WHO WASTE OUR LIVES. BE YOUR OWN LEADER, YOU FEEBLE BURKE, it reads. But that's easier daubed than done. The people shambling into the Rainbow in Finsbury Park look rudderless. "God love them," Mary says. "They couldn't lead themselves to the bog." So they've come to see the faith healers.

The supplicants seem raw with expectation. As they toil up the sweeping stairways to the upper rooms where the Holy Spirit awaits, some wheeze, some walk on sticks and some leave trails of wadded Handy Andies. Their eyes are big and starving.

The overall numbers this Sunday aren't large enough to fill the main auditorium, which I knew as a seventies Rock venue, so we're split into groups, maybe thirty per platoon. Mary and I are consigned to the care of a preacher from Cape Verde—*café au lait*, smoothly handsome and slicker than rice on ice. Dazzling in a shot-silk cream suit and Gucci loafers, black hair glossy with rose water, gold rings clustered on his elegant, long-fingered hands, he cries out for his own TV show.

His flock, as befits the Rainbow, is multicoloured: Africans; Jamaicans; an Indian family from Trinidad; a dreadlocked Rasta; two old Sikhs with white beards and turbans; a young couple from Croatia, and the husband's wheelchair-bound mother; a gaggle of Bangladeshis; Irish. Every brand in fact, but Anglo-Saxon.

The preacher begins his address in a low-pitched murmur like running water, then gradually stokes up the volume. He speaks of God's grace and power, His infinite bounty. But this seems largely incidental. Heat and urgency enter the preacher's voice only when he starts to talk about money. We are sick, we are troubled, he tells us. Our problems are eating us up. We can't sleep and we can't function. We can't win advancement in our work, can't buy the fine homes that fill our dreams. Our children abandon us. They are martyrs to drugs, to crime, and we are powerless to help. And why? Because we won't reach in our pockets. Won't give up one small part of our worldly goods for the Lord. If only we keep faith, all the earth's good fruits can be ours. But first we must set the ball rolling. Dig deep in our souls, and bring up some cash.

As his diatribe gathers pace, the preacher becomes agitated; begins to run from side to side along the rows of his flock, touching us and staring into our eyes. "Do you suffer?" he asks one immense black woman, and she clutches at her groin, as if unable to hold her water. "Do you have a sickness? A demon in your insides?" The woman moans and starts to shake. "Cast it out!" the preacher cries, and he puts his hand to her head. An aide, also resplendent in a silk suit, looms up behind him and starts shouting, "Cast it out! Let it go!" The preacher's voice keeps rising. He shrieks, he roars. He races among us, ranting, touching, exhorting. His smooth hand descends on my scalp and his long fingers squeeze my temples, drawing out my troubles like toothpaste from a tube. "Out! Out!" he screams and flings the detritus from him. The demons, powerless now, are hurled to the floor, dashed against the temple walls. "You're free! You are whole!" the preacher announces, and moves on to Mary. I see his hand dropping, and Mary biting her bottom lip. "Not a penny," she hisses. "Not one cent."

AND SO TO Earls Court. That's where I witnessed Billy Graham, thirty years ago, when the crowd made hardly a sound. Now the crusader-in-chief is Morris Cerullo, and the crowd is baying as if it's the World Cup Final.

Cerullo's mission is booked for a week, with near sell-outs on every night. Over a quarter-million of the faithful are expected in all. Showing up on spec, we can only get tickets for the nose-bleed seats, so remote from the stage that the preachers look like stick figures and their performances, borne across space, are robbed of all physical impact. We can see them stomping and flinging their arms about; and the afflicted being led up on stage, on their crutches, in wheelchairs, doubled over with pain; and the healers making sacramental passes over their bowed skulls and slapping them on the foreheads; and the bodies bowled over like skittles, limbs rigid, fainting dead away; and the multitudes on their feet, shouting Hallelujah! But it's all just a puppet show.

Our neighbours are a mixed crowd, about evenly split between blacks and whites. The Anglo-Saxons absent from the Rainbow are here in strength, most of them in couples and small families. Bright and scrubbed and beaming, happy-clapping, they seem undismayed by their seating. "Can't you feel the power?" the man next to me keeps asking. Every few seconds, he throws up his hands. Down below us, meanwhile, the stricken keep coming in unending lines, crippled and cancered, sick at heart. The stage is strewn with white lilies, and the massed choir is exulting, and Morris Cerullo, a portly party, is bellowing out exhortations. "God is in me! In you!" my neighbour cries, and he throws up his hands again. I can't feel a thing.

At one point, I duck out to the toilet. Only one other man is in there, combing his hair in the mirror. Seeing me, he flashes a smile in the glass. "Praise the Lord," he says.

He's polished to a high gloss; tanned and coiffed and powdered. With his blue suit and snow-blind white shirt, his mouth full of capped teeth, he looks like a fifties pop singer, a direct descendant of Dickie Valentine or Ronnie Hilton; and simply to say he's combing his hair is to do him a rank injustice. He's styling it, petting it, loving it up. Shaping its frontal wave to a crest and slicking back the sides. Tucking in a few stray wisps behind his ears, just so. Then lacing the whole confection with gel.

For me, it's the performance of the evening. Here is all the immediacy and passion that the stage acts have lacked. What's more, I'm catching it in close-up. "Are you with the crusade?" I ask.

"I wish," the man replies.

His name is Terry Hutcher—"Call me Tel"—and he's been here every night of the week. As often as not, he's the first one in through the doors, the last one out. "I can't get enough," he tells me. "The atmosphere; the glow. This feeling of boundless faith. And I'm part of it."

When I tell him I'm disappointed, he can't believe his ears. "This is the wonder zone," he insists. Lost souls are being found every minute. Hundreds and thousands are seeking shelter in God, are being raised up and given new life. "And the lame shall walk, and the blind shall see," Tel says, patting down a loose lock. "Do you know what we call that, my friend?" He gives me a hard stare, straight out of John Banner's textbook. "We call it hope."

If only Mary were here. In her absence, I mumble about being seated too far away, but Hutcher is having none of it. "The only thing that's out of range is your heart," he points out, then softens a bit. "Just give yourself a chance. One shot at goal is all that God ever needs."

He offers to give me instruction. If I'd care to pop round to his place some night, he knows I won't regret it. "Let yourself be led," he says. Then he goes back to his hair.

His home is in Shepherd's Bush, on an estate near White City. These names, in the context, take on a missionary ring, but the council flats where he and his wife, Deanna, live prove less than blessed. Used condoms litter the walkways; "Smack My Bitch Up" snarls from an unseen ghetto-blaster. "Welcome to the wilderness," Tel says wryly, and ushers me indoors. A series of bolts and chains are shot home behind me. "Deanna has baked a sponge," I'm told.

I've been expecting a religious shrine, but God is confined to one bookshelf full of sacred texts. The other shelves and the mantelpiece, meanwhile, are consecrated with an array of trophies. Gilded, silvered, ornate, discreet, they turn out to be for ballroom dancing.

"That's the second arrow to my bow," Tel says, elaborately offhand. Away from the public eye, his blue suit has been swapped for a casual look—Hush Puppies, knife-creased polyester trousers and a V-necked Lacoste pullover—but his hair is as picture-perfect as ever.

We sit facing each other across his hearth, wallowing in the depths of twin naugahyde armchairs, while he tells me of his sins, when he was growing up wild and aimless round Loftus Road. "I used to be a right hooligan," he confides, his voice thick with the preening relish that afflicts so many of the saved when they talk about their past transgressions. But he had quickly learned his lesson. "Violence, to coin a phrase, is ignorance by any other name. As soon as I started going out with Deanna, I spruced up my act." The capped teeth give another flash; he gives his armchair a swivel. "The love of a good woman."

Spark on cue, Deanna emerges from the kitchen, bearing tea and sponge cake. Like her husband, she has a retro look: pencil skirt, fluffy crimson slippers and big hair piled high. Tawny-blonde, she has a lissome body, long-legged and sway-backed, and the style of cuteness that used to be called winsome. Her only visible flaw is her ankles, which look oddly puffy.

According to Tel, she's not only good, but house-proud, too. "A true home is a temple," he says. There's a waft of metal polish from the dance trophies and the plastic plate I'm handed comes fresh from the packet. "I'm a fortunate man," says Tel, and Deanna hops in his lap. Her feet in their fluffy slippers extend towards the glowing fake logs of the electric fire and her skirt rides up above her knees. "Delicious," says Tel, presumably meaning the sponge, and starts to massage her swollen ankles.

They've been married eighteen years. At the time they met, Tel had just gotten out of Borstal and Deanna, who came from a good family and was planning to be an air hostess, was none too sure that she could handle him. "I suppose, to start with, I saw him as a challenge. A reclamation project." Besides, he was a fantastic dancer.

They met in a club on the Uxbridge Road. Deanna wasn't really into modern dance, had always felt more at home with ballroom, but the moment she saw Tel's moves, she knew he was something special. "He was total John Travolta." The white suit, the platform heels, the hair—every detail was spot on. "He looked like a movie star come to life." And he took her hand. Led her out on the floor, swept her into "Le Freak." They were married ten months later.

Her family went bananas. To tell the truth, they still haven't come around fully. "There's a touch of frisson, to coin a phrase," Tel agrees. "But you know what they say? Love conquers all."

For the first few years of marriage, everything went smoothly. Both of them worked in boutiques, and most nights they went out dancing. When disco went out of style, they started concentrating on ballroom and quickly reached competition standard. "Tango, rumba; the paso doble was our speciality," Deanna says. She gives a little reflexive kick, almost dislodging her fluffy mules. "We were on *Come Dancing.* We didn't win or get placed or anything, but that's just the system. The judges make you prove yourself; you have to work your way up the ladder. You could be world-beaters, but you still wouldn't win."

It seemed that their way was set clear then. They had total faith in their dancing; they were certain they would prevail. Costumes and rehearsal, grooming, new routines and the labyrinths of ballroom politics—this was their whole life. Then Deanna's ankles went south.

They blew up overnight. "I looked down my legs in the morning and they were grotesque. These massive elephant swellings." And no one could tell them why. They went to endless specialists and clinics; tried every kind of miracle cure. The bloating became so chronic that Deanna could barely walk across the room, let alone do the paso doble. "I was worse than suicidal," she says, unfurling from her husband's lap. She fetches a photo album from the bedroom, and hands me a polaroid of her darkest day—her thirty-fifth birthday party, three years ago now. She's at an Italian restaurant, propped up on crutches. Her face and body are essentially the same, but her lower legs are monstrous: vast shapeless hams, pitted and mottled and raw, the texture of papier-mâché.

Where could she go from here? "Where I should have gone all along," she says. She dusted off her Bible and remembered how to pray. Learned how to prostrate herself, shorn of false pride and worldly ambition. "I started travelling God's road. Not trying to run or even walk. Just happy to be crawling, inch by inch."

Tel wasn't thrilled at first. Not that he was anti-religion; merely unschooled. "I'd never been exposed as such." When he saw the comfort God brought Deanna, however, he couldn't help but be curious. "This woman had taught me so much. To be honest, and keep myself decent, and turn my back on viciousness. Why not let her teach me faith?"

He proved to be a quick study. In no time, he was attending prayer meetings, leading Bible studies, quoting scriptures from memory. Then he found out he was a healer. One of their neighbours, an anti-drug campaigner, had been beaten up by dealers. They took a metal pipe to him, smashed his ribs and both his legs, and left him dying. By the time Tel found him, he had gone into convulsions. But Tel knelt down and laid his hands on the neighbour's head and started stroking his hair, soothing him, the way you would an injured animal. And he prayed; he prayed as he never had in his life. And the neighbour grew calm.

That was the start of a journey. Tel didn't care to blow his own horn; self-promotion was never his style. He just tried to help where he was wanted. Among relatives and close friends, mostly, and a few people around the estate. And Deanna's ankles, of course; he made it his mission to heal his wife.

The journey brought them at last to Earls Court. Two years ago, Deanna was carried up on stage at Morris Cerullo's crusade. One of Cerullo's disciples touched the swellings, then passed his hand across her brow. "I felt a jolt like lightning; it knocked me flying. It was as if I was falling through space and there was nothing to stop me. I had no weight, no will. I just *was*." Then she fainted, and the attendants hauled her away, and she was back in her seat. Tel was holding her and crying, and everyone was shouting "Hallelujah!" And she just lay there, wrapped up in Tel's arms, but also nestled in God's hand. She couldn't feel her body and she'd lost all sense of time and her head was filled with a slow, deep pulsation. "It felt like the earth breathing."

Her ankles started healing within a month, and they've been improving ever since. She isn't quite back to *Come Dancing* form, she says, but that's her only limitation. "If you saw me some days, you'd think I was mad. I'll be working in the kitchen, baking or doing the chores, and suddenly I'll be lifted up. It's as if I have no force of gravity. My legs, my rotten ankles, just disappear, and I start whirling round in circles like a little kid, ring-a-ring-a-rosie, all fall down."

On other days, not so good, she gives herself over to Tel. He might not be a trained healer, not yet, but when he massages her trouble spots, she feels God flow through his fingertips. And it's not just her; he's helped many others. "Talk to my cousin Maeve," Deanna says with a slight edge, as if I've been disputing her. "She was a martyr to gas all her life and now she never even burps."

"It's all God's power, not mine," says Tel modestly. Still, he can't help thinking that he has a calling. "More than what I've got now, anyhow." Because of Deanna's ankles, she hasn't been able to hold down a steady job, so he's been the only wage-earner. He works at the same Oxford Street boutique as when they got married, at virtually the same wage level, with no real hope of promotion. "I'm totally dead-ended," he says. And it's driving him up the wall. To know he possesses a God-blessed gift, yet to be trapped like this, constantly struggling to keep afloat. "Everything tries to pull us down," he says. "This estate. The drugs and crime, the gangs. The whole shooting match." Only Christ's love buoys him up.

Deanna, listening, bites her lip. "His will be done," she says. And Tel recovers himself. After all, he has his health and strength, he has Deanna, he has his friend in God, he has his hair. And faith. He has his faith.

Rising from his armchair, he takes the Bible from its shelf. "John 13:35," he announces. *"Walk while ye have the light, lest darkness come upon you."* And Deanna, nodding, says Amen. The electric logs glow red in the hearth, and the ballroom trophies glisten. "To coin a phrase," says Tel. "The last shall be first."

ONE GOD LEADS to another. Some days, travelling the city, it seems there's a different version of the Almighty on every street corner. Familiar favourites like the Jehovah's Witnesses and the Plymouth Brethren compete for space with Rastafarians, Odinists, Wiccans, Zoroastrians. By the year 2002, the number of practising Muslims in England will outstrip the Anglicans. There are also, I read, a quarter-million pagans, and fifty thousand Satanists. The republic is a babel. It speaks in tongues.

WE'RE TOOLING through Transpontium again, past Wandsworth Station, when we pass a figure of stunning elegance: a Rasta, tall and lean and commanding, with hands that carve and scythe as he speaks. His clothes are immaculate and his dreadlocks gathered up beneath an outsize knitted cap, striped red, gold and green. His carriage is kingly.

He's delivering a sermon about Ethiopia. Something to do with a stolen manuscript, and the Fall of Magdala, and the Covenant of Mercy. Documents and photocopied letters surround his patch on the pavement and he discourses in measured tones, far from the usual street-preacher rant. His lack of shrillness, combined with traffic noise, makes his exact message elusive. So I make an appointment to visit him at his headquarters in Kennington.

His home base is a West Indian community centre in a row of tumbledown terraced houses. A young woman in long white robes opens the door to me, but doesn't ask me in. Clearly, she doesn't care for my looks. "Do you have a written invitation?" she demands. Two young bloods hanging out across the street, meanwhile, are eyeing me speculatively. *Kosher beef,* they seem to be thinking. Then the street preacher appears, mutters a few words and all problems vanish.

His name is Seymour Mclean, and today he is dressed still more stylishly, the knitted cap offset by a naval-style blazer with brass buttons and the Lion of Judah embossed on the breast pocket, a silver Star of Victory medallion and a long white silken scarf, which matches his polo-necked sweater.

For all the exoticism, there is a sense of suavity about him. He has the soothing tones and deceptive ease of a born diplomat, and a habit of lacing his long fingers, beautifully kept, in a bridge beneath his chin. Every word he utters is considered; a formal statement. Small wonder in that, he says. Before he took up the cause of Ethiopia, he was a rising power in the Conservative Party. He wore pinstripe suits and cuff links, dealt in unit trusts, and hobnobbed with Michael Heseltine and Cecil Parkinson.

Originally from Clarendon in Jamaica, his childhood followed a pattern I've grown familiar with. Much like Laurence in King's Cross, and Caf in Hackney, he was raised out in the country, with a moral code far stricter than anything he was to find in England. "Discipline and honesty, total respect. Education was everything; you had to improve yourself. There were no lights in the village and we grew our own food. Yams and potatoes, beans, salad. I learned to rely on myself, no one else."

When his mother brought him to England, aged ten, he was shocked by the backwardness. "It was all so uncivilised here. No concept of responsibility, no honour. The whole idea behind school seemed not to expand the brain, more contract it. Channel it into sloppy, third-rate thinking. I have to admit, I fell into that trap myself. For years, I was seduced by the lure of riches. I thought that being Someone in the World was the ultimate goal. And all this time, of course, I was denying my heritage."

In those years, he made a model Thatcherite Tory—raised in council housing, schooled at a secondary modern and trained as an electrician, but with limitless ambition. "I had fire in the belly, I could picture the top of the mountain." So he taught himself high finance. "I conceptualised the institutions." Lloyds of London, the Bank of England. Around Smith Square, he built up a reputation as a problem solver. By 1984, he was a candidate to address the Tory Party conference.

Then he switched on his TV. "I saw footage of the Ethiopian famine and the suffering hit me so deep, it shattered my brain. So I went up to Smith Square, I said, 'We've got to do something.' But the big boys just looked at me sideways. 'You're the problem solver; now go away and solve,' they said. With that smirky little laugh those people have. Like 'You handle Ethiopia, we're busy.' Well, what else could I do? I walked out."

Seeing Ethiopia on TV, those terrible scenes of starvation and pestilence, showed him his own falsehood. Spurned in Smith Square, he went home and started reading, set about remaking himself. In the past, when somebody like Hezza asked him about Rastafarians, he'd disavowed them. "People of no consequence. Street riff-raff," he called them. Blinded to his own roots. But now his vision was cleared.

He learned about Haile Selassie—Ras Tafari, King of Kings, the Lion of Judah. Threw away his pinstripes and took to pristine white robes; started listening to Bob Marley. And he discovered the Fall of Magdala.

Thirteenth of April, 1868. The Emperor Theodore, trapped inside his citadel, realises that he can't defeat the British Army, so he sends General Napier a peace offering. Fifteen thousand cattle, which are accepted. The Emperor relaxes, believing he won't be attacked. But the

British strike anyhow. Breech-loading Snyder repeating rifles against spears—it's the original massacre. The Emperor and all his nobles are murdered. Then the British rape the tomb of the Abuna, head of the Ethiopian Church. Ten thousand sacred manuscripts are stolen, along with gold bars and jewellery, priceless treasures, and carried back to England. The loot is scattered in different places, Oxford and Cambridge, Windsor Castle and the V&A, three hundred and fifty manuscripts in the Blackfriars Road, and others dispersed around Europe as diplomatic gifts. Russia and Australia, Paris, Vienna, Dublin. "And not one is ever returned. Restored to its rightful owners. Not one, to this day."

All his life, in his heart of hearts, Mclean had believed that he possessed a great destiny. Now he'd found it. To recover the looted manuscripts and take them home to Ethiopia.

"It came on me as a thunderbolt. Like a fiery river of truth, it took over my whole being." To aid him in his crusade, he taught himself Amharic and the written language of Ge'ez, in which the manuscripts were written. He wrote letters to MPs and religious leaders, Secretaries of State, European Commissioners, even Buckingham Palace. "I don't give up. Never. If I lose my courage for the fight, I can't live with my face in the mirror," he says. Then he took the battle to the streets.

That was ten years ago. Now Mclean teaches Ethiopian history all over south London, on pavements and in underground stations, illustrating his lectures with photocopies of the Covenant of Mercy, the most sacred document in Ethiopian Christianity, and of the mealy-mouthed, stone-walling letters he has received from officialdom: "A thankless task, you say? My duty, I reply."

His erudition is as spotless as his laundry. "The body of my knowledge is derived directly from the Emperor Haile Selassie's autobiography, *My Life and Ethiopia's Progress, 1892–1937*," he informs me. "It sits on my bedside table, along with the Bible in Ge'ez. A volume no man could ever exhaust." He gazes at me levelly across the sprung vault of his fingertips. "Do you know Amharic?" he asks, and smiles condescendingly when I answer no. "A most high language—it raises the mentality to a mountain top, from which all other languages can be seen in their own places, far below."

Every morning, he says, he teaches Amharic and Ge'ez to his four children. He also instructs twenty local children, entertaining them in song and rhyme. Then there is Ras Tafari Consultants, his company: "A cultural campaign," he says, "to promulgate the Ethiopian way. Its history and ethos. Thereby, of course, strengthening our cause. Our quest for justice."

How is the cause going? "A little slowly, as of now," Mclean confesses. He isn't discouraged, however; losing faith is not the Ethiopian way. "Those manuscripts will be returned. They must," he insists. "The Queen of England is sitting on stolen property, she's breaking her Bible-sworn oath."

Raising a tapered forefinger, he asks me to share in a vision. "Imagine an angel visiting the House of Windsor, or the V&A, where the Abuna's looted crown, rings and chalice are kept. Now picture the angel in judgement, weighing the Queen in the balance, and finding her wanting." He's laughing now, the Star of Victory flashing at his throat. "Can you just imagine?" he says. "The Queen of England is a criminal. A common thief." He slaps his open palm on the table-top, and he furls his silk scarf about his throat, and he throws back his dreads in their Rasta cap, red, gold and green. "Can't you see this?" he demands. And his laughter stops dead. "I can."

A QUEST FOR Odinists had first led me to Mary. Now at last she delivers, and takes me to Colin Patterson, one-time enforcer with the British National Party.

He lives past Ascot, in the far reaches of Surrey. It is an anodyne world, mostly theme parks and new towns, but his own home is a semi-detached on a council estate, with an outsize Union Jack draped over the front door.

He receives me in the nude. Or almost. Apart from rubber cycling shorts and battered running shoes, the rest of him is fully exposed. His body, rock-hard, is covered with tattoos—Rudolf Hess, Thor, a rose, a sunwheel, a rising phoenix, a Celtic knot.

A Staffordshire bull terrier sniffs at my feet. Its brow is furrowed, its whole demeanour puzzled, as if debating whether to take off my ankle at a single snap or favour it with a prolonged mastication. "Cohn," says Colin Patterson. "Would that be a Jewish name?"

"It would."

"I thought so." His manner is soft-spoken, most scrupulously polite. "Well, I have to tell you, I don't believe you belong here. In England, I mean. Nothing personal, but it's my belief you should go back where you came from."

"Derry?"

"*Londonderry.*" He corrects me with scant patience. "To be honest, I was thinking a little farther afield."

This doesn't mean that I'm under threat from him. "Those days are well behind me," Colin says. So long as England is stuck with me, he'll behave like a gentleman. "I'll speak to you, let you in my house, I'll even shake your hand." But I shouldn't get ideas, even so. "Jews, Catholics, Asians, homosexuals—at the end of the day, I see no call for any of them."

If not for Odinism, he would be even less tolerant. Until the last few years, he was committed to violence. He thought it solved everything. Now he isn't so sure. "In a way, I've weakened," he confesses. "But then, in another way, I've grown."

He was brought up by his grandparents. They adopted him when he was seven and he went to school in Kilburn. Eighty per cent of his classmates were West Indians or Asians; his best friend was Jamaican. Then they had a fist fight. "Nothing heavy, just a lot of racial slagging on both sides. But I was the only one punished. The white one. That started my mind working."

His grandparents managed a small hotel in Bayswater. On retirement, they applied for council housing. "But they were told to forget it. There were no vacancies for them, only ethnics need apply. This was the seventies— Arabs and Asians swarming all over the shop, but whites had no place. No rights in our own country; we'd been abandoned."

Colin's family ended up in Milton Keynes—"an ideal town for an ideal world; unfortunately, this world's not ideal." The urban planners had laid the whole place out on a geometric grid, hoping to create a model city, perfect in order and logic. Unfortunately, they'd overlooked the humans. "Sod all to do, wasn't there? Take nice walks, watch TV." Or join the BNP.

Right-wing groups at least offered action. "At the start, the BNP was mostly a giggle. Then I started to assimilate the ideology. *Britain for Britons*, it made a lot of sense. I was going to rallies and marches, Blood and Honour gigs, and the violence just naturally followed. Asians, yes, but it was the ANL I hated worst, the Anti-Nazi League. Traitors to their own blood. To Britain's history."

Someone like myself could never understand. "All I did wrong was love my country. This great heritage, which generations fought to build, and suddenly I'm told No, it isn't yours, your time's up, there's nothing here for you any more."

He soon built a reputation in the party as a dependable hardman. There were prison terms for assault, and for dogfighting. In between, he made pilgrimages to Nuremburg for Nazi anniversaries, went to Belfast to support the Loyalists. He railed against the Jewish State, the hydraheaded conspiracy he believed controlled, and was destroying, British culture. While he was at it, he beat people up.

Most of it he classes as self-defence. "You might not believe this, you probably won't, but I never set out to attack anyone. All I did was feed them the bait. Provoke them past the snapping point, so they'd make the first move, then the rest was automatic. Riots or beatings or whatever. But no one could say I started it."

Those were strong years. The Party was full of spunk, not yet split by internal wars. "We had great pride in ourselves. That's what the media couldn't stand. They wanted us to be riff-raff. How dare we believe in ourselves?"

Framed pictures of BNP rallies still hang on his living room walls; an Aryan magazine lies on the floor. Children of various ages wander in from the kitchen, and Karla, Colin's partner, brings us mugs of tea. She doesn't look a woman to be trifled with. Darkly exotic, with multiple gold earrings and a golden nose ring, she exudes willpower; inner strength.

She's changed his life, Colin says. If not for Karla, he might still be on the battlefront, breaking heads. But she has shown him a different way. When they first met, she was divorced, with three children. At twenty-one, she'd given birth to a dead baby. Since then, she has been on a search.

Like Colin, she believes she's been robbed of her birthright. "British heritage, the old white culture, handed down since Viking times, that's nothing now. It's us that are the outsiders," she says. If Asians ask for an all-Asian social club, they get it, but just try asking for an all-white club, and the media call you a Nazi. "We've been dispossessed."

Still, she has no taste for violence. It gets you nowhere, only plays into your enemies' hands. The only hope is through reason; the power of the mind. That's where Odinism comes in.

This isn't a religion I know much about. I have a vague image of Odin, war god and protector of heroes, who manifests himself as a one-eyed wanderer, and I know he was a big favourite with the Third Reich. Heinrich Himmler was a Nordic pagan. The swastika itself was once a runic symbol. But what else does the faith involve? "Honesty and loyalty," Karla says. "Strength in the family and friends. Not backing down from your principles, that's all."

She has steeped herself in Odinic studies. Mastered the art of writing in runes, learned to write runic poems and now she has started teaching other women on the estate. "Bit by bit, I'm spreading the word," she says, but it's hard work. "Some people have closed minds, and some are just thick."

She wishes she and Colin could meet and talk to other believers, but most tend to snub them. The majority are pacifists, who regard the BNP with horror. "We're not your average Odinists," Karla says.

"It gets a bit lonely at times. Isolated," Colin adds. Yet his basic belief is strong. "Eating, drinking and fighting in Valhalla—it's the business. Definitely more exciting than Christianity, sitting in some old geezer's lap and polishing stars. All Christian ritual has been stolen and perverted from Odinism, anyhow."

How many British Odinists are there? "Hard to say." While paganism as a whole is a major growth industry and Odin a key player, numbers can never be trusted. "Twenty thousand, fifty, it's all just guesswork," Karla says. Whatever his following, the war god still gets scant respect. His cult is not a recognised religion here; Colin and Karla had to go to Iceland to get married in him.

They were the first British couple to be united by Odinic rite. The *gothi*, or priest, conducted the ceremony before an image of Freya, the fertility goddess, and they toasted their betrothal with a horn full of Viking beer, followed by a goblet of wine—"which the *gothi* paid for himself, bless him," Karla says.

Now they have a Freya of their own, a year-old daughter. Mary plays with her on the shag carpet, overlooked by a photograph of Blackshirts on parade, and Colin stretches, tattoos flexing. "I haven't changed my views, I just have a wider perspective. More depth to my thinking. I'm rising thirty-three, and you can't go on punching walls for ever. But if it came to civil war, of course, I'd pick up a gun to defend my country and my family, it would be my duty." He yawns hugely. "I'm not a Nazi, just a Briton," Colin says. "Make of that what you will."

The sofa on which he sits is backed by a large plate-glass window. Now something massive and indeterminate begins to stir behind it. At first, I think it might be another hound. Then I realise it's a snake. Not just any snake, either, but a Burmese python, almost twenty feet long, with black and gold coils as thick as a man's waist, and its great head slowly nodding, as if drugged.

"Some baby," I mumble.

"Sweet as a nut," says Colin with pride, moving towards the snakepit. "If you'd care to sit tight, I can let her out."

MEANWHILE, in Tufnell Park, in the basement of her rambling Victorian home, Freya Aswynn rolls a smoke. "Odin," she murmurs, drawing out the O in a long, train-whistle moan. She smiles to herself, as if at a private joke, then claps her hands. "Yesss, Odin!" she cries out, exulting. "Oh, he is the bollocks of a god."

She is sitting in a tiny windowless temple, a subterranean cell lit by candles. Images of one-eyed Odin surround her, in posters and carvings, and so do the war god's symbolic props: a wolf's skin, a staff, a drinking horn, a hangman's noose. The effect is unearthly, yet oddly playful. "Odin loves a good party," Freya explains. "Plenty of mead, lots of feasting. He's got no time for weaklings. Sanctimonious bastards give him a pain."

I've heard about her from other pagans. Among the more straight-laced, she is regarded as shocking, a dangerous renegade, whose whiplash tongue is mentioned with genteel shudders. But no one denies her power. When she speaks at Pagan Federation meetings, the house is always packed. "Freya Aswynn means bums on seats," she says herself, and blows a perfect smoke ring.

Tall and willowy, her limbs swathed in diaphanous

flimsies, she gives a first impression of fragility, even fey-
ness, an illusion that shatters the moment she speaks. Her
voice, a husky rasp, comes from deep in her diaphragm,
and a heavy Dutch accent adds colour. Every sentence is
spiced with *fookers, vankers* and *conts:* "No point in beating about the bush—Odin kicks ass. He speaks through
me sometimes, and the old bastard has a dirty mouth. If I
started to talk all mealy-mouthed, he'd flay me alive."

When I first knocked at her door, she was wary. Many
people had come to her of late, some in search of genuine
enlightenment, others to play silly buggers, and she was
tired of being used. "If you're vanking, do it somewhere
else," she said, plonking me down at her kitchen table
and fixing me with a look that would strip paint.
Acolytes, both male and female, joined the scrutiny. So
did a massive white cat. Dragging deep on her roll-up,
Freya seemed to slip into a trance, then snapped awake.
"Odin says okay, I can trust you," she informed me, and
led the way downstairs to the temple. "Sit," she said, indicating an overstuffed beanbag on the floor. A bottle of
mead stood at hand. "Odin says drink. So let's fucking
drink."

Among her detractors, this style of talk is supposed to
prove her lack of gravitas, but Freya is unrepentant.
"Just because I'm not a hypocrite, why does that make
me superficial? These armchair pagans, they have no
passion."

Passion is her great strength; always has been. "I've
needed it to survive. In Holland, until I was nineteen, I
was kept locked up in cells. Children's homes, beatings,
abuse. Guard dogs and barbed-wire fences, isolation cells,
forced drugs—by the time I got out finally, I had such a
rage in me, I could have ended up a terrorist, chucking
bombs with the Baader-Meinhof gang. If not for Odin, I
could have gone to killing, easy. The occult was in me
always, though. Even as a small child, I used to run down
the street with my cape wide open to catch the wind, trying to fly." From infancy up, she felt convinced that she

had once possessed another body, had been gifted with powers of flight. "So my family, of course, they thought I must be mental. They kept dragging me to different shrinks; that's why I was locked away. Maladjusted, they said I was. Fuck that! I had instinctive knowledge, that's all."

Once freed, she started evolving that knowledge. For years, she embraced a succession of occult disciplines—spiritualism, Rosicrucianism, astrology, the cabala and, finally, witchcraft. In the early eighties, moving to England, she formed a witches' coven. Yet something seemed missing. The Craft was based on Greco-Roman and Celtic gods, and these left her unfulfilled. She herself was Nordic, after all. So why not turn to the old Norse gods? In her confusion, she called out Odin's name, and he answered her. She's been in his service ever since.

In this decaying house, which is her world headquarters, she dedicates her life to runic divination, and to Asatru, the truths of the Aesirs. Freya isn't her born name, but it sounds right. Under its banner, she travels all over Europe, lecturing and teaching. Her book, *Leaves of Yggdrasil*—for the sacred ash tree, whose branches contain the nine worlds—is regarded by her followers as an Odinic classic.

At home, her life revolves around those followers, who form her extended family. Freya calls them the Kindred and they meet frequently for rituals and feastings.

Her attitude to them is both protective and autocratic. She counsels them in their travails and rejoices in their spiritual breakthroughs. At the same time, she is not slow to chastise them when they err. "What kind of pagan are you?" she berates one woman who has neglected to record *The X-Files* on the VCR. "Odin will be rightly pissed."

Efficiency is essential, she claims; the war god can't abide sloppiness. "He's a hard bastard, yes, but that's why we love him. He insists on honour and he won't take less. When he sees an abuse, like the way we treat our old people, he gets fucking raging. The same with lying or whining or living by excuses—alibis drive him nuts. Then again, he's realistic. He asks nothing that any strong person of faith can't give. And he never bullshits. He's a warrior, and he lives by a warrior's rules. Like the time when the Vikings slaughtered two legions of Romans. Some people call that human sacrifice. Well, of course it was; all religions kill. The only thing different is that Odinists don't deny the fact." She takes a swift swig of mead. "We celebrate it, don't we?"

Leaping up, she takes three paces through the room and gives a mighty roar: "No remorse!"

Squatting on my beanbag, I'm starting to cramp up; the airless, smoke-choked heat stings my eyes. I picture Colin Patterson in his living room, busy with his snakes and his Aryan magazines. What does Freya think of BNP Odinists? "We have nothing to do with Fascist scum," she snaps. "Or chaos magicians, neither. Any bugger that tries that Nazi shit with me, I'll hand him his balls on a platter."

As for her relationship with Odin, it's literally a marriage. After the death of her partner Lionel, two years ago, Freya took a vow of celibacy. Since then, the war god has been her only lover. "I don't have time for messing about." There's too much work to be done. In the next hundred years, she believes, Asatru will become the dominant religion. "It has to come. It must. Because it's not some New Age airy-fairy crap or happy-clappy mindlessness—it's the truth. With a smashing set of gods, and the bollocks of rituals."

Elegant, fierce, mysterious, she smiles her secret smile. The Kindred are filling the temple, about a dozen of them, gathering about her. It's Saturday night. Time to feast and toast their ancestors.

They are a motley crowd, impossible to stereotype. A number of Freya-adoring young women, one or two older men, some couples. Baggy sweaters are prevalent.

Apart from Freya herself, three figures stand out: a lean

and earnest youth, avid to display his occult expertise; an emaciated young woman, raw with nerves, who keeps fiddling with her long black hair; and a robed and hooded attendant. At different moments, they try to assert themselves, making suggestions for the ritual or arguing fine points in Odinic lore. Freya hears their disputations with indulgence, then with a rising testiness. "Too much fucking talk, it's making my head hurt," she says at last. Instantly, all debate is dead. The ceremony begins.

A fresh bottle of mead is opened, its contents poured into a well-worn drinking horn. Sickly honey-sweet, I find it hard to stomach, though the others seem to relish it. There is a general slurping and smacking of lips. Then the overhead light is killed, leaving only candles, and the Kindred form a circle, standing with eyes shut, while Freya makes an invocation before each in turn. After that, the robed attendant invokes Odin himself. And a new presence enters the temple.

In the half-light, I see Freya stagger, almost fall. Some magnetic force seems to draw her forward, blindly groping, her movements those of an old woman. Her speech has turned rhythmic, its guttural rasp changed to a high-pitched keening. As she fights for balance, one of her sleeves brushes against my wrist. Her eyes are rolled up in her head, only the whites left visible, and her lips have pulled back from her teeth. For a moment, she seems on the verge of collapse. Then the presence passes, and she is returned to herself.

Afterwards, she is exhausted but exultant. "He was here," she says, her voice still shaking. "The old bastard was in the room." And she lets loose a wild war-whoop. "What a god!" she cries out. "What a fucking master!"

ON A RAW, drizzly day with autumn in its bones, Mary and I make a pit stop in Kentish Town and discover that we've received a letter. "Twickenham Conservative Association have finally succeeded in expelling me from the organisation. I suspect their methods bordered on the unconstitutional, but no matter," it says, and continues: "I AM THE ANTICHRIST. Some explanation will be necessary . . ."

The writer answers to the name of David Griffiths and lives in Isleworth. His intention is to stand as the Antichrist in the next general election, but he's having trouble reaching the voters. "I intend to hold a public meeting soon," he writes. "The problem is no one will allow me to hire a room or a hall. The Cabbage Patch pub, near Twickenham Station, chickened out. The land-lady took my deposit of a hundred pounds but returned it by post a week later. The Clifden Centre refused to allow me to hold a meeting, as did the St. Mathias Church Hall."

His brazenness intrigues me. Traditionally, the Antichrist has always worked in disguise. He appears as a smiling smooth man, the Great Seducer, who fools the unwary by faking great benevolence. On the surface, he seems to work for universal peace and harmony. Only when he has achieved domination does he whip off the mask.

Through the ages, the candidates for this role have ranged from Nero to Napoleon, Lenin to Pope John, all the way down to Bill Clinton and Mikhail Gorbachev, even Tony Blair. But none of these has ever had the brass to come right out and declare himself. In that, to my knowledge, David Griffiths is a first.

The address he gives is Haweswater House, Summer-wood Road. I picture an eighteenth-century mansion, possibly Palladian, with sunken rose gardens, a maze and billiard-table lawns. Instead, I find a cluster of tower blocks, stuck behind a row of derelict shops.

David Griffiths' own flat is austere, embellished only by a pentagram, a blown-up photo of a nuclear ex-plosion, a couple of candles stuck in wine bottles. Philosophic tomes and The World's Classics line the book-shelves, along with CDs of Gregorian Chants and

Frank Sinatra. Above a doorway, painted in ornate script, is a quotation from Chateaubriand: "What do I care if it be the King or the Law that drags me to the guillotine?"

The Antichrist himself proves to be a strapping figure in his mid-thirties, tall and heavy-shouldered, with a Mussolini head, knife-creased jeans and gleaming boots, a wet-lipped grin. His skull has been shaved to hide its baldness, but no ruse can disguise the buck teeth, the absence of chin. The overall effect is one part *Übermensch*, one part Yogi Bear.

Normal interview techniques seem inadequate here. But the matter is taken out of my hands. Griffiths has his story all wrapped and ready, and he reels it off unprompted. "I must have been about five. One night I was lying in bed when a silvery-white disc appeared at the window. A huge hand descended, either from the ceiling or from inside the disc itself, and touched my forehead. Then, many years later, in the Book of Revelation, I came upon that passage— 'And there appeared a great wonder in heaven; a woman clothed in the sun, and the moon under her feet, and upon her head a crown of twelve stars . . . and behold a great red dragon'—and the penny just sort of dropped. The flag of the European Union has twelve stars, you see, and the dragon is a Welsh emblem, and Griffiths is a Welsh name, meaning Red Lord. So it all hung together. I thought to myself, *I am not God, no. Well, then, I must be the Antichrist.*"

The question of why he was thinking in such terms to begin with is brushed aside as irrelevant. No fripperies are allowed to disturb the appointed order of his tale. At the time of his great revelation, he continues, he was fascinated by sci-fi, but now he started exploring the occult, and then came Aristotle. When his parents died, they left him £37,000, which allowed him to continue his studies undisturbed. He wrote a book; described himself as a businessman and a member of MENSA, with an IQ of 161; stood as a Democratic Liberal Conservative in the 1992 election, scoring 103 votes; was given a suspended sentence for assault; and offered to father babies by artificial insemination, at £1,000 a shot, to "help both this country and humanity in general by injecting more people of high intelligence into the population."

All of this, of course, was small potatoes, the sort of stuff that an Antichrist on his way up tosses off in passing. "I was just biding my time. Waiting for my moment to strike. The right moment to spread my true message."

And that is? "The degenerate scum are oozing up through the cracks in the pavement," Griffiths beams, wet grin unwavering. "Kill them all. Or allow them to starve to death. Mass suicide would come in handy. Anything to counteract the absurd, useless pity that 'decent' people waste on the world's filth." He sucks his teeth, groping for an aphorism. "Compassion is the deadly sin," he says. *"Blessed are the first, for they shall eat the last."*

The problem is, nobody seems to hear him. Some Sundays he performs at Speakers' Corner, in an anorak and a sensible woolly, even on the hottest days. But the people only laugh or shout him down, and he's driven back to Haweswater House. "Inside these walls I feel safe, therefore calm," he says. "I rise at six and I have a breakfast of bread, eggs, milk and spices. Then I write. Poetry, letters, speeches. Then I ride my bike. I may cycle to Richmond Library or I take the air. Then I come home. Have another meal, listen to my music. Then I go to bed."

All this information is conveyed in the same dead monotone, as if by rote. Even when his words are full of slaughter and hate, his delivery remains dispassionate. He might as well be reciting football scores.

Looking round his living room, I try to picture him at play. Leafing through his copy of Plato's *Republic*, say, or listening to Sinatra, late at night, with the lighting down low and "One for My Baby" on deck. It is an image not of evil but of a vast loneliness.

What about his sex life? Does he ever go out with girls? "Not as often as I'd like. I tend to socialise in bars, have a drink on a weekend. Real Ale is my tipple, and when I've sunk a few pints, I start talking to females. I'm not averse to telling them who I am; they're usually quite intrigued. But I feel no need for close human contact. I did have a hunger for sexual entanglement between the ages of thirteen and twenty-eight, but not anymore. Dependency is weakness, and weakness is fatal."

So I leave him. "I am the smiling face that lures people to the devil's work," he tells me in parting. Out of doors, a fitful wind gusts among the tower blocks. When I look up, trying to make out Griffiths' windows, they look like all the rest. No trace of the pentagram, or 666, or that awful void that would cause a man, any man, to sit down and write to the world: "I AM THE ANTICHRIST. Some explanation will be necessary . . ."

COMES THE LAST day: the end of our road. Teal Wheels goes back to the rental yard on the Finchley Road, and Mary jams her woollen hat hard down over her eyes, and we hit the West End for one final onslaught. It's just after dawn on a Saturday morning, and we have twenty-four hours to live.

When I left my hotel, the lad on the night desk cast a withering look on my suit, worn shapeless and stained from its travels. "Off to join the homeless, are we?" he commented chirpily.

Now I stand shivering in the early-morning chill, the damp of coming autumn in my lungs, watching as the bodies in the doorways begin to stir. The mounds of cardboard boxes and wadded newspapers and old clothes break apart, as arms and legs emerge. A young Scot with caked blood on his face reaches for his black dog and takes it into his arms. The dog has a scabby bald patch on its rear. "I call him Mo Mowlam," the Scot says, and feeds it the last mouthful of a Bounty bar.

When the park gates open, the long night's survivors gather on benches, exchange war stories and pool their liquid assets. One man has suffered a major kicking. He thinks some ribs might be broken, but refuses to go to a hospital. "A brew will see me right," he says, and a can of McEwan's is handed to him. "And a snout," he adds hastily, and a roll-up is conjured up, too. An Irish woman binds his ribs with her headscarf. She has long bright-coloured braids in her grey hair, orange and white and green for the Irish flag, but only three teeth. "I'm a registered nurse," she says, as she ministers.

"Show us your papers," the Scot demands, tickling Mo Mowlam behind the ears. And the woman, not missing a beat, flips up her long dress to show her arse.

THE MORNING is slow to warm up. To keep our blood alive, we make a tour of the waking streets, and fall across an early seller of the *Big Issue*. His name is Richie, he tells us. When he was nineteen, his parents died and he inherited £180,000. For two years he travelled; blew the lot. Now he's twenty-two, and selling papers on Charing Cross Road.

He's a handsome boy and gently spoken, with fine cheekbones, unreliable eyes. When he was growing up in Dublin, in the affluent suburb of Clontarf, his father was a successful sales rep and he lived in a big house with every status symbol. If you looked at his life, you'd say he had an open goal. But he couldn't make his mind up to shoot. University didn't attract him, nor any line of work. "I had no focus. Never have had. It's as if I was born with a part missing."

His father died of lupus and, a few months later, his mother overdosed on pills. "How did that make me feel? I'm not exactly sure, it's all a bit of a blur." Then came the money, and he wasn't sure what he felt about that, either. The rest of his family, all his aunts and uncles, had certain expectations. He was supposed to spread his good fortune around, look after his younger sister, but he just couldn't face it. "So I told them to stick it up their arse sideways. They weren't too well pleased, actually."

It wasn't malice that drove him, just the need to get away. "I had some distant idea of sorting myself out; very distant. And I thought that going places might be my answer."

He travelled in high style. Nice hotels, fancy restaurants, the best of everything, all paid for in cash, great thick wads of the stuff. And what he had, he shared. "I started to buy people up." Stood them air flights across the world, paid their bills: "I was a bottomless pit." Until the day, early this year, when he woke up in an Earls Court hotel, down to his last £6,000. Then that got stolen, leaving him destitute.

Calling on an old friend of his family, he let himself be fed and comforted, then borrowed fifty pounds. That night, he checked into one last hotel room, ordered up a good bottle of wine. Crawled between the crisp white sheets and slept. Then, refreshed, he cast himself on the streets.

His first day of penury, he wandered the West End at random, feeling like The Man Who Fell to Earth. The only thing he knew for certain was that he had to eat. He met a girl on the street who sold the *Big Issue,* and she showed him the ropes. You buy a stack of papers for 40p each, then sell them at £1, and you live off the difference, hoping in time to build up a small stash and rejoin the upwardly mobile. "But that never happens; never will," Richie says, dispassionate. "Not in my case, at least."

The way things are, he can see no way out. If he stands at his pitch all day, he might clear £20, sometimes £30. Out of that, he has to pay £3.20 for his Travel Card, plus food money and his keep at the housing co-op in New Cross where he's hung his hat for now. Then there are the incidentals—beer, fruit machines, the odd blow-out. A masochist or a born ascetic might thrive on the sacrifice. Scrimp and save, somehow haul himself clear. But austerity has never been Richie's strong point: "I wouldn't say I place a great value on surviving. Basically, I have no will to live, no will to die."

Telling us this, standing in an office doorway, he makes no attempt to push his merchandise. "What good would it do?" he asks, gazing bleakly at the passers-by. Nobody who hasn't been on the streets can know how vicious the kindness of strangers really is: the verbals, the swearing and spitting, the drunken rants.

One evening in high summer, things got so bad that Richie did a runner. He'd sold three papers all day and everyone that passed him, in the heat and West End stink, seemed bent on smashing him. So off he went to London Bridge and tried his luck outside the station, though that wasn't his pitch. Around eight-thirty, five youths passed by. *"Big Issue,"* Richie said.

"What's so fucking big about it? Doesn't look so big to me," one of the youths taunted him. Then he was encircled, shoved up against a wall. "Get lost. Just get the fuck away from me," he told them, too sick and tired to feel fear. Even when a machete appeared out of someone's shirt, he couldn't make himself react. He saw the blade flash, felt it catch the back of his skull. Then a woman came screaming out of the station and the youths scattered. Blood was everywhere. "You all right?" the woman asked. "Don't know," Richie told her. But the truth was, he didn't care. He simply couldn't be bothered.

Most of the time, he still can't. "Don't point a gun at me, I might just help you pull the trigger," he says. "I never counted on a pension anyhow."

By now the pubs are open and we're sitting in a saloon bar round the corner from Richie's pitch. The fruit machine is luring him; he stacks his morning's meagre take in neat piles. Of course, the machines are a rip-off; he knows that. "Economic hari-kari," he calls them. But what the fuck?

The only good thing about falling off the edge, as far as he can see, is the class of people he's met on his way down. To say that the destitute, the homeless, the totally fucked, are the most generous and honest people he's ever known might sound sentimental tosh, but it is plain fact. Like Big Ron, who sold the *Big Issue* across the street. An alcoholic, a hopeless case, but Jesus, the heart of him. Whatever he had, bread or booze, he shared it. No strings, no judgements, no questions asked. Then he made up his mind to get sober. Detox, rehab, the lot. Only someone gave him a hit of smack, which normally he never touched. And now he's down in Brighton, stuck in the morgue, with nobody to claim him.

How do you live with something like that? Richie's only

crutch is the thought of a room all his own. "A TV, a couch, a kettle." But that hardly seems in the cards; and what makes it worse, there's no one to blame. "I'm fully aware I have no gripe. I did it to myself, every last little bit."

Rising from his seat, he gives the fruit machine a few offhand spins. On the third pass, £30 comes barrelling out. A nice little earner, you might think. But Richie only shrugs. "Cast a cold eye on life, on death," he remarks. "Arsehole, pass by."

THE DAY TAKES shape sloppily, in random swirls and blobs. We don't try to steer for ourselves, just follow the rear views most likely. A beautiful boy in a tight pink dress leads us to Covent Garden, where a couple of gypsy fortune tellers, camped up with shawls and sprigs of lucky heather, refuse to let us be till we dip into our pockets, after which they fade away, and we see a flame-swallower juggling three flambeaux on the open space outside the Inigo Jones church and keeping up a non-stop stream of patter, which falters only at the sight of a long blonde ice maiden with a backpack and minuscule white shorts, who blows him a kiss, then disappears into a cellar bar, where she buys a lid of hash from a youth in a *Mr. Nice* T-shirt, who carries the loot to Old Compton Street, where he buys a gin and tonic for a man who works in the porn store across the street, where we browse through racks of rubber dildos, among them a lifesize replica of Jeff Stryker's endowment, said to measure fifteen inches, and I think of my friend Astrid, who used to design custom-made willie-warmers for a select clientele and hang the plaster moulds from the ceiling of her basement flat, cocks of all shapes and sizes, like ranks of pink stalactites.

FOOTBALL'S BACK. One of the first major matches is slated for tomorrow afternoon, Arsenal and Newcastle United, and the advance guard of the Toon Army starts trickling down by early afternoon. They set up camp in Trafalgar Square, at the base of Nelson's Column, on the very same spot where the English fans massed that first night of riot.

Ploughing through the crush, with her ratty woollen hat and her boy's pants, Mary looks more than ever like the Artful Dodger. Even she is beginning to wear down at the edges, though. Her purple boots are splitting along the uppers and the gap in her back teeth has started to ache, the way an amputated limb is said to do.

It's mid-afternoon. In Piccadilly Circus, the steps round Eros are crowded with global tourists. Germans and Scandinavians, Russians and Japanese and Americans; backpackers and druggies and sexual salespersons. A boy named Quinn, who looks about fourteen, asks me if I want a shag. When I tell him I don't, he passes me on to his girlfriend, a Sikh who calls herself Sam. She's a runaway from Rochdale, only a few weeks in London, and the going seems to be wearing on her. Wild eyes and wild mouth and wild black hair, she crouches on the bottom step like a cornered feral cat. The first thing she says is that she's clean; no drugs. The second is that she needs ten quid.

In compromise, I buy her an ice cream and she tells me about her home town. "A hole," she says. They still think that women are slaves there; that girls are only born to be found a husband and breed. Her father runs a pub and he's up drinking every night. Half his customers are whores and pimps and dealers, and he doesn't give a toss. "His friends get up to all sorts and he thinks it's a big laugh." But if his little daughter dares to look at a white boy or doesn't get home before curfew, suddenly he's the righteous Sikh patriarch. He never wears a turban or goes to the *gudwara,* but that's doesn't stop him from spouting off about his reputation, his precious *izzat,* and how her carryings-on have brought the family to shame. Just because she has a mind of her own and her mother found a condom in her room, and a little powder too. Well, that's what you get for snooping. "I told them straight, the shame is on you," Sam says. "If they kept their noses out of my knickers, they wouldn't be bothered by the stink." That's when her father raised his hand and she started running.

Living rough on the London streets has so far proved a mixed bag. "It's dead exciting at times, and also dead hard," Sam says, fussing with the wild black tangle of her hair. Smearage from her Magnum has left a chocolate ring above her upper lip and she keeps trying to lick it clean. I hand her a tissue, but she disdains it, keeps on straining with her tongue. "Don't let anyone fool you that London's a piece of cake. There's some right buggers about; they'd kill you for laughs," she says. But good things happen, too. "This boy I hardly knew gave me a twenty last night. For nothing. Just my eyes, he said. He wanted to see the look in my eyes."

TEATIME, and we take a stroll through Regent's Park. It's like falling back into the fifties. Space, and ease, and time on your hands. Around the bandstand by the lake, old-age pensioners lie back in striped deck chairs, luxuriating in the summer's last warmth. The women wear floral dresses, the men cardigans and grey flannels. The Carlton Main Frickley Colliery Band plays an oompah arrangement of Ravel's *Bolero,* replacing lust with a soft pulsing regret, and the music drifts over the water, past the lovers in rowing boats and the tourists feeding the ducks. For this moment, nothing has changed; England's world is still secure. Then we come to the London Central Mosque, its golden dome glinting in the dying sun. A pack of youths in phat pants and Nike tops gathers round a boom box blasting Puff Daddy's "No Way Out." The house-wrecking bass and hardcore lyrics—"Can you feel me, baby? Can I love you, baby? Climb up in it slow"— mingle with the final chords of *Bolero* from across the lake, and put them to the sword.

The evening's long burn is beginning. When we roll

back into Leicester Square, it's a solid wall of flesh, so densely packed we can hardly move. Every tongue and dialect on the planet seems gathered here, joined together in a single uproar. A universal hunger, beyond language or specific meaning, to speed and sweat, and go bang in the night.

The sexual charge is overwhelming. It's as though there are no limits, and virtually no categories. In Soho, on Windmill Street and Brewer Street, the heart of striptease country, the prostitutes are dressed like techno girls, the clubbers dressed as whores and nobody seems bothered either way.

Outside the London Palladium, another flame-swallower is at work. Not the one we glimpsed earlier in Covent Garden, but a girl with chipped teeth, who reeks of lighter fluid and is dressed like a chic street urchin in loose-fitting drawstring pants and a layered top, a fancy jerkin and a wide-necked blouse that slips open when she leans forward to light another flambeau, revealing her small breasts.

Her act is based on incompetence. Each time she ventures a new trick, she tells the crowd she's unlikely to pull it off, and often enough she's right. Flambeaux refuse to light or go tumbling in the street; her clothes are singed; her mouth gets scorched. But none of this seems to faze her. "Oh, well," her body language says, impervious to reverses. The flames are beaten out, the fallen props picked up. Then she starts again, with infinite airy grace.

There's a lightness to her, a perfect street-corner elegance in the long easy sweep of her arms as she tosses the torches above her head, in the twists and twirls of her filthy bare feet, and the quick inward flicker of her eyes each time a move goes wrong.

Lisa, her name is, and her big black dog is Boo. They've been busking together for almost five years, living together in squats, in a disused railway shed, in a derelict Brighton church. She has no great ambitions, she says, and no illusions. Boo snuffles at her hand and she tosses him a milkbone. What does she want of life? "A new set of torches would be nice."

On the corner of Great Marlborough Street, she turns one way and we go another. It's the heart of the evening and Soho is so overstuffed it can't contain the influx. Alleys and pavements overflow and the crowds take over the roadways. They swirl in and out of traffic, reducing the trapped cars to the level of fixed objects; markers in a point-to-point.

We bob along on the tide, resistless as floated corks. The current drags us in circles and loops, over rocks, down rapids. We're caught up in a whirlpool of In'its, Asian gang kids out to conquer the West. Spat out in Leicester Square with the Egyptian kebab sellers and Tunisian touts. Dragged on to Piccadilly Circus by a troupe of papier-mâché masquers from Amsterdam, done up as pink elephants. Foundered on Old Compton Street with an albino Ghanaian, who offers to sell me a mechanical porno-doll. Swept on again by a backwash from the Toon Army, caterwauling "The Blaydon Races." And washed up, finally, in Cambridge Circus, where we clutch hold of a passing lamp-post and hang on tight, waiting for the pounding to stop.

When it does, we're faced by a smiling man in rubber.

His name is Rubber Ron and he's famous in Camden Town, from where he masterminds a periodic club night called Submission, one of the biggest fetish balls in Europe. In between, he walks around in rubber chaps and a skintight rubber T-shirt, and surveys the world through outsize spectacles, like a benevolent, if kinky, brown owl.

He's been hooked on erotica since he was ten, when he got his hands on some copies of *Search* and *Relate,* bondage magazines of the day, and found himself riveted by their pictures of women in tight corsets and fishnet stockings. "It wasn't just the sexiness; they had a special aura. A high, stark look, almost like priestesses." He beams, he sighs. "Allure," he says softly, as though speaking the magic word.

MIDNIGHT PASSES, and one o'clock, and the carnival has still not reached its peak. With each hour, the pace grows more frenetic, the charge more intense, till the whole West End appears to me like a dance floor swept by swirling spotlights, a hallucinated jumble of faces and voices, random gestures that flash up from the darkness, catch my eye for a beat, and are lost again. The turn of a neck; a cigarette's spiral. A woman with blue lips drops to her knees. A white skinhead in African tribal robes sells books on Malcolm X and Martin Luther King, and an Arabic chant rises out of a basement in Frith Street. The young Scot with the blood-caked face, now spotted with scabs, is feeding Mo Mowlam a Mars bar. A red fez is flung in the air on Gerrard Street, then punched from hand to hand like a party balloon, tassel flying, and a blue-eyed Aryan boy with a fuzz crewcut races past, one frame of his wire-rimmed glasses shattered in a starburst. A man keeps shouting about Babylon. An Asian woman clutches my arm as if drowning. Mary's mouth is open wide, shouting words I can't catch. Spandex and lycra, a PVC bustier, a lost faux-pearl earring. *Beneath the weeping willow lies a weeping wino.* A mongrel howls in Soho Square.

And then, quite suddenly, we collapse.

One moment we're still speeding; the next, our battery has gone dead. It's as if the weight of our whole journey has come crashing down at once, and we fall down, spent, in a doorway of the Cambridge Theatre.

It's starting to rain; a thin, misty drizzle. A fat Turk is selling doner kebabs a few yards away. We lean back against a poster for *Les Misérables* and drift into an uneasy doze, wrapped in the smell of frying onions.

A police siren jerks me awake.

It's past four o'clock. A man in a dark blue coat is saying that it's dossers like us, pathetic alky misfits, who are ruining the West End for tourists and taxpayers. Police vans are streaming down the Charing Cross Road and a megaphoned voice is blaring. We hoist ourselves to our feet; turn our faces to the south. The man in the blue coat has gone. So has the fat Turk. We head for Trafalgar Square.

This is the vision that awaits us:

The Toon Army, unwearied, still massed at the foot of Nelson's Column, chanting, swaying, waving their striped shirts.

Three black skateboarders, all stripped to the waist, flying around the stone lions and off across the concourse, spinning and doing back-flips, cartwheeling through space.

Two girls in evening-dresses, their tongues down each other's throats.

A boom-box blasting hip-hop.

Five Arabs, seated in a circle, playing cards.

Men and boys sleeping under the steps, washed by the rain.

A cordon of riot police.

And the night sky above, bruised purple.

Wearied too deep in bone and blood to walk another step, we slide down a parapet and drop to the damp stones. The Toon Army is chanting Eng-a-land, Eng-a-land; the square is filled with moving bodies. And they sing, and they dance, at the heart of the great republic.

Teac̓ Néilí, July 31st, 1998

A NOTE ON THE TYPE

This book was set in Garamond, a type named for the Parisian typecutter Claude Garamond (ca. 1480–1561). Garamond, a pupil of Geoffroy Tory, based his letter on the types of the Aldine Press in Venice, but he introduced a number of important differences, and it is to him that we owe the letter now known as "old style."

Composed by NK Graphics,
Keene, New Hampshire
Printed and bound by R. R. Donnelley & Sons,
Crawfordsville, Indiana
Designed by Anthea Lingeman

DATE DUE